DEATH AND DISORDER

DEATH AND DISORDER

A HISTORY OF EARLY MODERN ENGLAND, 1485–1690

Ken MacMillan

UNIVERSITY OF TORONTO PRESS
Toronto Buffalo London

© University of Toronto Press 2020
Toronto Buffalo London
utorontopress.com
Printed in Canada

ISBN 978-1-4875-8849-6 (cloth)   ISBN 978-1-4875-8850-2 (EPUB)
ISBN 978-1-4875-8848-9 (paper)   ISBN 978-1-4875-8851-9 (PDF)

Library and Archives Canada Cataloguing in Publication

Title: Death and disorder : a history of early modern England, 1485–1690 / Ken MacMillan.
Names: MacMillan, Ken, author.
Description: Includes bibliographical references and index.
Identifiers: Canadiana (print) 20200207474 | Canadiana (ebook) 20200207490 | ISBN 9781487588496 (cloth) | ISBN 9781487588489 (softcover) | ISBN 9781487588502 (EPUB) | ISBN 9781487588519 (PDF)
Subjects: LCSH: Great Britain – History – Tudors, 1485–1603. | LCSH: Great Britain – History – Stuarts, 1603–1714.
Classification: LCC DA315 .M33 2020 | DDC 942.05 – dc23

We welcome comments and suggestions regarding any aspect of our publications – please feel free to contact us at news@utorontopress.com or visit us at utorontopress.com.

Every effort has been made to contact copyright holders; in the event of an error or omission, please notify the publisher.

University of Toronto Press acknowledges the financial assistance to its publishing program of the Canada Council for the Arts and the Ontario Arts Council, an agency of the Government of Ontario.

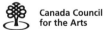 

For Owen and Lewis

CONTENTS

ILLUSTRATIONS

ACKNOWLEDGMENTS

Death and Disorder: A History of Early Modern England is the result of my teaching at the University of Calgary over two decades, which has involved, over several different courses, both the history of crime and criminal justice in England and the political, constitutional, imperial, and social history of early modern England. I have devoted a great deal of my efforts to developing classroom activities and methods of assessment that allow the history to come alive, and I have discovered that focusing on death is a surprisingly effective way to accomplish this goal. A draft of this book was used in a pilot course attended by its target audience: early stage undergraduate students new to English history, who may or may not be pursuing history degrees. My thanks to the emerging scholars in that course for offering advice and feedback, and for modeling how the book could be used in a classroom setting. Thanks also to Jon Rozhon for undertaking some early research.

At the University of Toronto Press, Natalie Fingerhut invited me to write the book, and she and Alexandra Grieve provided considerable guidance and support along the way. Janice Evans managed the book's production, and Tania Therien provided expert copyediting. Several outside reviewers offered valuable suggestions and helped to correct some errors. All errors that remain are my own. Finally, I must express my gratitude to the many scholars who have written about the subjects discussed in this book. Although some of the works used in this book's preparation are mentioned in footnotes and the list of further resources, these do not adequately reflect the debt I owe to other historians.

As always, Luna has been a constant source of love and support. This book is dedicated to our sons, Owen and Lewis.

CONVENTIONS

Spelling and Punctuation

In early modern England, place and personal names were spelled differently in various sources, largely because their spelling was based on how the word sounded to the reporter. For consistency and clarity, in this book all names and places are spelled using the modern or most consistent usage. In all quotations from early modern sources, spelling and punctuation are modernized. To ease further research, book and treatise titles given in the text and notes retain their original spelling.

Dates

Before 1752, the new year in England began on Lady Day, March 25. Thus, for example, March 24, 1602, was followed by March 25, 1603. To avoid confusion and conform to modern conventions, all dates are given as if the year began on January 1.

Currency

The main unit of currency was the English pound (£), whose denominations were different than the modern pound sterling. The primary units were the following:

Pound (£ – from the Latin *libra*)   £1 or 20s
Shilling (s)   1s or 12d
Pence (d – from the Latin *denarius*)   1d

TIMELINE OF KEY EVENTS

Bold denotes events discussed in *Death and Disorder* or *Voices of the Past* sections.

1485 **Death of Richard III at Bosworth Field**; Henry VII establishes Tudor dynasty

1486 Birth of Prince Arthur

1487 Pretender Lambert Simnel claims right to throne

1491 Birth of Prince Henry [VIII]

1495 **Perkin Warbeck claims right to throne (to 1497, executed 1499)**

1502 Death of Prince Arthur, making Henry heir to the throne

1509 Accession of Henry VIII

1512 Beginning of Anglo-French War (to 1514)

1515 Thomas Wolsey becomes lord chancellor

1516 Birth of Princess Mary [I]

1517 **Evil May Day Riot**

1529 Wolsey stripped of offices (dies 1530); Thomas More becomes chancellor; beginning of Reformation Parliament (to 1536)

1532 Installation of Thomas Cranmer as archbishop of Canterbury

1533 Henry marries Anne Boleyn; birth of Princess Elizabeth [I]; Act in Restraint of Appeals

1535 Execution of More; Thomas Cromwell becomes chief minister and vicegerent

1536 Dissolution of the monasteries begins; Pilgrimage of Grace; execution of Anne Boleyn; Henry marries Jane Seymour

1537 Birth of Prince Edward [VI]

1540 Execution of Cromwell

1541 Henry becomes king of Ireland; beginnings of "Tudor conquest of Ireland"

1543 Beginning of "Rough Wooing" in Scotland

1546 **Execution of Anne Askew**

1547 Accession of Edward VI; duke of Somerset becomes lord protector; beginnings of Protestant Reformation

1548 Publication of *Hall's Chronicle*, a major source for Shakespeare

1607   Settlement of Jamestown, Virginia, as first permanent colony

1609   Beginning of Ulster Plantation in Ireland

1611   Completion of *King James Bible*

1612   Death of Prince Henry, making Charles heir to the throne

1614   Arrival of George Villiers, later duke of Buckingham, to court

1616   Death of Shakespeare; dismissal of Edward Coke as chief justice

1618   Francis Bacon becomes lord chancellor (to 1621)

1620   Bacon publishes *Novum organum*; voyage of the *Mayflower* to America

1622   **Jamestown Massacre**

1623   Publication of first collected plays of Shakespeare

1625   Accession of Charles I; marriage to French princess Henrietta Maria; beginning of Anglo-Spanish War (to 1629) as part of Thirty Years' War

1627   Anglo-French War (to 1629); start of settlement in Caribbean

1628   **Assassination of Buckingham**; parliament issues Petition of Right; first part of Coke's *Institutes of the Lawes of England* (to 1644)

1629   Charles begins personal rule (to 1640); Massachusetts Bay Company established

1630   Birth of Prince Charles [II]

1632   Settlement of Maryland as Catholic colony

1633   Birth of Prince James [II]; William Laud becomes archbishop of Canterbury

1639   Bishops' Wars in Scotland (to 1640)

1640   Short and Long Parliaments called

1641   Parliament issues Grand Remonstrance; Irish Rebellion; execution of Thomas Wentworth, earl of Strafford

1642   Beginning of Civil War with **Battle of Edgehill** (to 1648)

1643   Solemn League and Covenant

1644   Battle of Marston Moor

1645   Execution of Laud; creation of New Model Army; Battle of Naseby

1646   Charles surrenders to the Scots

1647   Preparation of Heads of Proposals and Agreement of the People; Putney Debates

1649   Trial and **execution of Charles I**; accession of Charles II; England becomes commonwealth; conquest of Ireland (to 1652)

1651   Navigation Act; publication of Thomas Hobbes's *Leviathan*

1652   Beginning of Anglo-Dutch Wars (intermittently to 1674)

1653   Oliver Cromwell dissolves parliament; John Lambert writes Instrument of Government; Cromwell becomes lord protector

1655   Beginning of Anglo-Spanish War (to 1660); conquest of Jamaica

1658   Death of Oliver Cromwell and accession of Richard Cromwell (resigned 1659)

1660   Charles II issues Declaration of Breda; founding of Royal Society of London

1661   Cavalier Parliament enacts Clarendon Code (to 1665)

1662   Birth of Princess Mary [II]

1664   Passage of Triennial Act

1666   **Great Fire of London**; last plague in London

1667   Publication of John Milton's *Paradise Lost*; England acquires New York by treaty

1668   Rise of ministerial Cabal

1670   Treaty of Dover with France

1673   Passage of Test Act; the duke of York marries Mary of Modena

1677   Marriage of Princess Mary [II] to William [III] of Orange

1678   Beginning of **Titus Oates's Popish Plot**

1679   Beginning of Exclusion Parliaments (to 1681); rise of Whig and Tory parties

1681   Founding of Pennsylvania

1683   Rye House Plot

1685   Accession of James II; **Monmouth Rebellion and "Bloody Assizes"**

1687   Declaration of Indulgence suspends Clarendon Code; publication of Isaac Newton's *Principia Mathematica*

1688   Birth of Prince James (the Old Pretender); Revolution of 1688

1689   Accession of William III and Mary II; passage of Bill of Rights

1690   Publication of John Locke's *Two Treatises on Government*

GENEALOGIES

Note: Charts are simplified. They do not include issue not material to the line of succession or spouses, except as shown. CAPITAL LETTERS denote monarchs, while **BOLD CAPITAL LETTERS** denote recognized English monarchs.

1. The Lancastrians and Yorkists

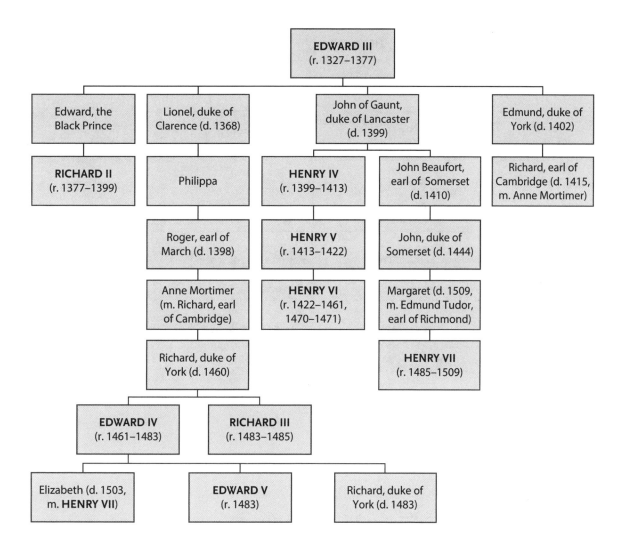

2. The Tudors

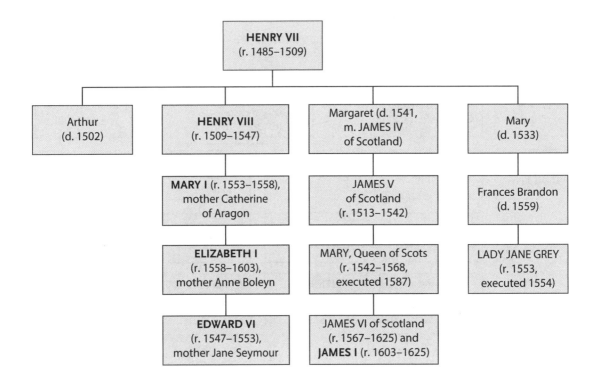

HENRY VII
(r. 1485–1509)

Arthur
(d. 1502)

HENRY VIII
(r. 1509–1547)

Margaret (d. 1541,
m. JAMES IV
of Scotland)

Mary
(d. 1533)

MARY I (r. 1553–1558),
mother Catherine
of Aragon

JAMES V
of Scotland
(r. 1513–1542)

Frances Brandon
(d. 1559)

ELIZABETH I
(r. 1558–1603),
mother Anne Boleyn

MARY, Queen of Scots
(r. 1542–1568,
executed 1587)

LADY JANE GREY
(r. 1553,
executed 1554)

EDWARD VI
(r. 1547–1553),
mother Jane Seymour

JAMES VI of Scotland
(r. 1567–1625) and
JAMES I (r. 1603–1625)

3. The Stuarts

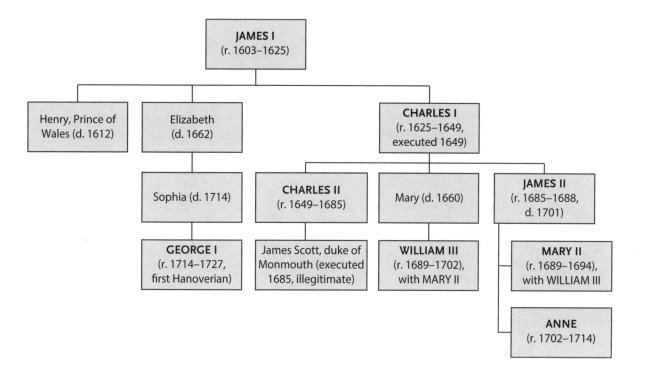

INTRODUCTION

From the accession of the Tudor dynasty in 1485 to the immediate aftermath of the Revolution of 1688, England experienced significant political, religious, intellectual, legal, economic, and social developments that continue to have relevance in many countries around the world today. This period saw the beginnings of the Westminster system of government and the creation of an enduring Church of England; extraordinary literary achievements, such as the plays of William Shakespeare; the development of modern scientific methods, as exemplified in the work of Sir Isaac Newton; and the beginnings of the British Empire. By the end of the seventeenth century, these and other developments made England a key figure in global affairs, well on its way to becoming a modern "great power." If England in 1485 was a minor and backward nation with insular and xenophobic tendencies, the same certainly cannot be said of England in 1690.

While seeking to offer readers an introduction to this important historical period, this book focuses the narrative somewhat by looking in greater depth at two of the most overarching themes in early modern England, namely death from causes other than old age, and the disorder that often accompanied it. During this period, various political and dynastic crises saw the assassination of great officers of state and several kings and queens, an event known as regicide. Securing loyalty and heirs encouraged monarchs to charge their nobles and gentlemen with treason, which usually resulted in swift execution. Wars and rebellions saw the death of many thousands of English subjects, either on the field of battle or as retribution in the aftermath. Changes in England's religion also resulted in many deaths, both of Catholics who refused to convert to Protestantism or capitulate to the demands of the state, and Protestants who were unwilling to return to Catholicism when monarchs so demanded.

These two centuries were also the peak period of execution in English history, far more so than the medieval period that preceded it and the modern period that followed. All serious crimes upset the social order and, therefore, were felonies punishable by hanging at the gallows, burning at the stake, drawing and quartering, or beheading. Most of these forms of death were carried out in the presence of large crowds to act as a deterrent and to show the authority of the state over English subjects. This period also saw the publication of hundreds of pamphlets and trial accounts that described heinous acts of killing perpetrated by disorderly subjects against their parents, spouses, children, masters, servants, and neighbors. Using murder and execution as their primary theme, these sources reinforced the power of the monarch, state, and church, and the importance of order in English society.

There were many other causes of death and disorder, too, such as an extremely high rate of infant mortality, the frequency of plague in the crowded cities, attempts to conquer New World inhabitants through violence, and the limited ability of early modern medicine to deal with serious illness. Whatever its cause, whether mercifully swift or agonizingly slow, death was recognized in this society as inevitable, universal, and – because many believed that eternal bliss awaited in the afterlife – even desirable. The culture of death was so pervasive that themes of *carpe diem* (seize the day), *memento mori* (remember you will die), *danse macabre* (dance of death), and *ars moriendi* (art of dying) infused the period's literature, artwork, religion, and thought. In short, early modern England suffered from, to quote historian J.A. Sharpe, a "crisis of mortality."[1]

I must emphasize from the outset that early modern England was not a draconian bloodbath of death and disorder. This was not a society out of control, nor, to use Christopher Hill's phrase, a "world turned upside down."[2] It was not, despite depictions in television, movies, and historical novels, one in which people constantly feared for their lives from despotic kings, tyrannical nobles, abusive husbands, evil witches, or bands of marauders murdering their way through the countryside. On the contrary, many people carried out perfectly orderly and ordinary lives, although everybody who lived during this period experienced a great deal more exposure to death than most of us do today. England was a nation obsessed with order, and it is often through death that order was restored to a society that otherwise had few mechanisms to do so.

I must also emphasize that this book is not a chronicle of death in early modern England, nor a study of the beliefs and practices surrounding it, both of which have been expertly examined by others.[3] Explored in and of itself, death through murder, execution, assassination, war, plague, and other means is not a particularly valuable way to learn about the complexities of early modern English history. Nor do I seek to glorify or romanticize death or criticize those who caused it, all of which are beyond the purview of the historian. Rather, this book uses vignettes of death and disorder as, I hope, an interesting and provocative way to introduce readers to some of the key events of English history during this time.

---

1 J.A. Sharpe, *Early Modern England: A Social History, 1550–1760* (London: Arnold, 1997), 49–55.

2 Christopher Hill, *The World Turned Upside Down: Radical Ideas during the English Revolution* (London: Penguin, 1972).

3 For examples, see "Death and Disorder" in the Further Resources section.

My choice to focus on death and disorder serves to enhance the core skills that students of history must develop: understanding cause-and-effect relationships, assessing continuity and change over time, enhancing critical thinking, showing empathy for those who lived and died in the past, and undertaking deeper scholarly inquiry into topics of personal interest. However, while death and disorder serve as entry points into the broader themes of early modern English history, it is not my purpose to undermine or ignore the traditional narrative, which offers important, foundational knowledge for readers new to the subject and is necessary background for students who wish to advance into more specialized areas of English, British, imperial, political, religious, and social history. The overarching themes of death and disorder are meant to exist alongside and enliven, but are not meant to displace or subvert, other historical developments in early modern England.

Organization

This book is organized into three parts: "The Tudors, 1485–1603," "The Stuarts, 1603–1690," and "Empire and Society."[4] Parts One and Two employ traditional chapter structures, following the reigns of successive monarchs in a manner that is common in many textbooks on the subject. These parts are designed to facilitate the delivery of material consistent with how many courses on early modern England are taught.[5] Part Three is more wide ranging, covering a variety of subjects that require examination beyond chronological periodization, such as the rise of empire, elite and popular culture, and lifecycles. To an extent, the final few chapters are designed to introduce readers to the ordinary people of early modern England, rather than focusing on monarchs, politics, and religion, which tend to dominate the first two parts.

Adhering to the overarching themes of this book, each chapter begins with a "Death and Disorder" vignette, an introduction of sorts that describes the death of one or more people and the disorder with which it was closely related. These tales are instructive in themselves but also shed some light on the topics covered in the chapter. Each chapter ends with a "Voices of the Past" section, which includes an extract from a primary source, such as a historical treatise,

---

4   It is worth mentioning that the Stuart period did not end until 1714, with the death of Queen Anne. However, the year 1690 reflects both the end of a series of constitutional struggles between English monarchs and their people, and a significant decline in the number of premature deaths because of changes to the criminal justice system and advancements in other areas of society.
5   Although no discussion of England during these two centuries can exclude Ireland, Scotland, and Wales, this book focuses on England and reflects on the remainder of the British Isles only as they impacted English history.

pamphlet, or other description drawn from contemporary printed documents. These sources reflect some of the themes discussed in the chapters and introduce readers to the type of materials historians use to understand and contextualize the past. These narratives show the descriptions of death and disorder that early modern readers were exposed to, which framed their understanding of various causes and consequences associated with certain unwanted behavior. Like all historical sources, these documents also reveal biases based on factors such as authorship, intended readership, and contemporary political, religious, and social concerns that the authors wittingly or unwittingly passed on to their audiences. Learning how to interrogate documents of this nature for their arguments, biases, and value both to early modern readers and modern historians is yet another core skill for students of history to develop. Each chapter also has a series of five discussion questions interspersed throughout the narrative, the answers to which might require knowledge gained in earlier chapters or additional inquiry.

It is my hope that teachers and students will use these various components of the book, in combination with the main narrative in each chapter, to engage more deeply with and to critically investigate the history of early modern England during collaborative in-class activities, such as "buzz group" and "think-pair-share" sessions, and in course assignments that promote research and inquiry into topics that pique individual interests. I should end by reiterating that although this book is designed to offer readers an introduction to the history of early modern England, it is not intended to be comprehensive. Many topics are discussed only briefly and are worthy of further investigation. The Further Resources section at the end of the book can be used as a means of starting this research.

PART ONE
THE TUDORS, 1485–1603

Historians often consider the arrival of the Tudors to the English throne in 1485 (see **Genealogy 2**) to signal the end of medieval and the start of early modern England. This process did not, of course, occur overnight, and although some scholars have claimed that the Tudor age represented a significant amount of change from its medieval past, particularly in areas such as religion and intellectual ideas, others have argued that there was also a great deal of continuity, particularly in areas such as government and social organization.

The five Tudor monarchs – Henry VII, Henry VIII, Edward VI, Mary I, and Elizabeth I – together make up perhaps the best-known royal dynasty in English history, if not all of Western Europe. Once the Tudors forged their dynasty through conquest, they fought hard to gain loyalty from their subjects and recognition from other European rulers. Efforts to strengthen the power of the central government and change religion to a form consistent with Protestant worship caused dissension among nobles and commoners alike, which led to numerous rebellions that were violently suppressed throughout the sixteenth century. The accession to the monarchy of a young boy and two women led to infighting among senior advisors and the upper nobility, and various attempts to restore order resulted in much taking of life.

CHAPTER ONE

ESTABLISHING THE TUDOR DYNASTY, 1485–1509

DEATH AND DISORDER: THE BATTLE OF BOSWORTH FIELD

The Battle of Bosworth Field began the Tudor dynasty and brought an end to the Wars of the Roses, a series of disorderly events that pitted the Yorkist and Lancastrian lines of the English royal family against one another (see **Genealogy 1**). By 1485, the king was Richard III, head of the Yorkist line, who is best known for orchestrating the deaths of his nephews, twelve-year-old Edward V, king from April to July 1483, and his nine-year-old brother, Richard, duke of York. Young Edward had become king upon the death of his father, Edward IV, but as a minor he needed adult supervision in the form of lord protector. The job was taken up by Edward's uncle Richard, duke of Gloucester, who had been a faithful servant to his brother and was a natural and experienced choice for the council's leadership.

Rather than rally in support of his nephew, however, Richard met the young king en route to London and escorted him to lodgings in the Tower of London, where he was soon joined by his younger brother. While the princes resided in the Tower, Richard declared his brother's secret marriage to Elizabeth Woodville invalid on slim legal grounds,

which made their children bastards and, thus, ineligible to claim the throne. With the support of parliament, the throne therefore passed to Richard, who became Richard III (r. 1483–5). The two boys were never seen again, and Richard quickly became English history's most legendary villain, in part because of William Shakespeare's famous portrayal of him as an amoral and deformed murderer of children. Nearly two centuries later, workmen at the Tower unearthed a wooden box under a staircase containing two human skeletons the size of pre-teen children.

Richard's usurpation of the crown and probable murder of his nephews quickly led to uprisings throughout southern and western England and the resumption of the Wars of the Roses. His opponent was Henry Tudor, earl of Richmond, nominal head of the Lancastrian line through his mother, Margaret Beaufort, great-granddaughter of John of Gaunt, duke of Lancaster. Henry's bloodline, however, was tainted; his mother descended from Kathryn Swinford, Gaunt's mistress, which prevented Henry from a natural succession to the throne and made him an unlikely Lancastrian challenger. If Henry was to claim the throne and secure his dynasty, therefore, it would have to be by right of conquest on the field of battle.

After several months of planning and gathering troops and supporters, Henry and Richard clashed at Bosworth Field, in Leicestershire, on August 22, 1485. Henry arrived on the field of battle with several thousand mercenary troops from Scotland and Normandy, accompanied by defecting Yorkists and Woodville supporters. The king's army was larger, estimated at around 10,000 men. Despite Henry's numerical inferiority, his army proved better at close combat and held its ground, and one of Richard's battle groups seems to have slowed its attack, either out of rebellion against Richard or because the landscape made forward movement difficult. Meanwhile, Richard decided to take the battle directly to Henry by moving several mounted men toward the rear, where armed guards protected Henry. Richard seemed poised for success; he needed only take out Henry's guard and kill his rival.

The turning point in the battle came from Sir William Stanley, the brother of Henry Tudor's stepfather, Lord Thomas Stanley. When the king was separated from the main battle and Henry's bodyguards were becoming overwhelmed, Stanley sent his troops into battle against Richard. As Stanley's forces pushed Richard several hundred yards from Henry, the king's horse stumbled and he lost his helmet, upon which also rested a coronet (a small open crown). It is doubtful that Richard III uttered Shakespeare's famous line "A horse! A horse! My kingdom for a horse!" but his unhorsing led to his death by the single blow of a halberd. According to one sixteenth-century historian, Lord Thomas officially ended the battle by retrieving the fallen coronet from under a bush and placing it on Henry's head, symbolically beginning the Tudor dynasty.

The Battle of Bosworth Field brought an end of the thirty-year conflict known as the Wars of the Roses, which saw the death of many thousands of English subjects and the killing of three kings, including Edward V and Richard III, an act known as regicide. There can be no question that the Tudor dynasty began in bloodshed.

* * *

Discussion Question 1.1: Why was it important for Henry Tudor to be crowned with Richard III's coronet on the field of battle after Bosworth?

England in 1485

At the end of the fifteenth century, the English nation was, literally and figuratively, insular. Together with Scotland in the north and Wales in the west, England is one of three nations on the island of Albion, a term used by classical geographers and poets to describe what is today better known as Great Britain. It was also, at 130,000 square kilometers, the largest of the three nations, although England was much smaller (by land size and by population) than France, Spain, and what was then known as the Holy Roman Empire. England is physically separated from Continental Europe by the English Channel, which historically provided both natural protection against military invasion (though this did occur, especially in 1066 and 1688) and a sense of distinction from other European nations. England had, for example, its own common law, which developed very differently from the brands of law used on the Continent, a fact that many English people rarely tired of repeating.

These differences, however, should not be exaggerated. During the early modern period, England involved itself in numerous Continental wars and English subjects traveled to Europe and traded for goods that England, by virtue of its climate, could not produce itself, such as olive oil and wine. English gentlemen attended European universities and returned with new ideas about art, religion, learning, science, and politics, the impact of which was clearly seen in English society. Moreover, England developed the same feudal structure that most European countries possessed and, partly as a result, also used similar systems of government, rank structures, and economies. Thus, although early modern England certainly had its own history, there were many parallels between what was going on in England and the affairs of Continental Europe. Although its nation and people were more insular than many Europeans, it is a mistake to accept blindly early modern English subjects' claims to the uniqueness of their society.

In 1485, England's population was about 2 million people, much smaller than the modern figure exceeding 50 million. The population had been higher in the fourteenth century, perhaps approaching 4 million before the black death (1348–9) wiped out a third to half of England's population. It would take until nearly 1700 for the population to return to its pre-plague level, a doubling of the population during the sixteenth and seventeenth centuries that caused numerous problems, including food shortages, inflation, unemployment, and the significant increase in poverty. By comparison, France and the Holy Roman Empire each had about 15 million people, Italy 10 million, and the Iberian countries of Spain and Portugal 7 million. This demography helps to explain why France, Italy, and the Empire tended to dominate the politics of early modern Europe (see Figure 1.1).

For administrative purposes, England was divided into several dozen counties, or shires, each of different size according to its location and population. Most of the population lived in the south and east parts of England from about Herefordshire in the west across to Essex in the east, and all parts south, including Cornwall, Devon, and the Home Counties, in which lies London. This region was more populated because its landscape was flatter, its soil more fertile, and its weather milder, allowing for a longer growing season for crops. The north and west parts of England were mountainous and rocky, with thin soil and a shorter growing season. The south also boasted Westminster, England's administrative capital, immediately adjacent to which was London, England's most populous city and its largest port. Bisecting London was the Thames River, which allowed for the movement of goods and access to the English Channel and Europe via the Port of Dover in nearby Kent. This population distribution remained largely static until the onset of the Industrial Revolution toward the end of the eighteenth century.

Figure 1.1 *Map of Tudor England.*

Credit: Antiqua Print Gallery/Alamy Stock Photo.

About 10 per cent of English people lived in urban environments, or cities exceeding 5,000 inhabitants. London was by far the largest, having a population of around 50,000 in 1500, 200,000 by 1600, and more than half a million by 1700. Other large cities included business centers such as Bristol, Coventry, Exeter, and Newcastle; the cathedral cities of Canterbury, Lincoln, Salisbury, and York; and the university cities of Oxford and Cambridge. In total, perhaps thirty communities had populations exceeding 5,000 residents. Naturally, a wide swath of society populated these cities, from beggars and servants to artisans, tradespeople, government officials, and the aristocracy.

Most of society, about 80 per cent, lived in the rural countryside, in communities ranging from 50 to perhaps 1,000 inhabitants. The larger of these were market towns, in which farmers, artisans, and merchants bought and sold crops and supplies in exchange for ready money or barter. Smaller communities – villages, hamlets, or parishes (because their inhabitants worshipped at the same church) – numbered in the thousands. The church, the house of the manorial lord, and the village square were the main features in these villages and were often very vibrant places. They hosted festivals and markets during certain times of the year, traveling troupes and tradesmen, the administration of law and order, weddings and funerals, and news of goings-on beyond their small communities, often proclaimed in church on Sundays by the priest or landlord. Several of these villages were grouped together into administrative units known as "hundreds," presided over by mayors, reeves, and elders ("aldermen").

* * *

Discussion Question 1.2: Why do you think that England was so insular from Europe and the world at the end of the medieval period?

The English Social Structure

England in 1485, like most of Europe, was a late-feudal society. Although feudalism no longer shared many characteristics with its origins hundreds of years earlier (vassals providing homage, rent, and service to lords in exchange for personal protection), early modern England maintained the orderly hierarchy that feudalism created. This hierarchy was also taught and enforced by the Roman Catholic Church, which placed man within a larger "great chain of being" including God, angels, animals, plants, stones, and the damned. Other than the omnipresent God, each link in the chain was subdivided into, for example, nine ranks of angels; noble (lions) and ignoble (snakes) animals; and mighty (trees) and lowly (weeds) plants, et cetera.

Man was also subdivided, particularly between what later commentators such as Sir Thomas Smith and William Harrison would refer to as "men who rule" and "men who do not rule." At the top of the men who rule was the king, a ruler who, by God's divine authority, was the fount of all wisdom and justice and a natural ruler of lesser men. Monarchs usually came to their position by right of succession through male primogeniture, which entitled the former king's eldest son or closest male heir (a brother or uncle) to inherit.[1] The monarch was believed to be endowed with what political commentator John Fortescue referred to in the late fifteenth century as "angel intelligence," or intellectual powers that could not be attained by other mortals. These powers enabled the monarch to rule effectively in the best interests of his people and commonwealth.

Next were the nobles, starting with the temporal nobility: dukes, marquesses, earls, viscounts, and barons.[2] The king granted these titles to those who made valuable contributions to the realm through military or administrative service, or they were inherited by right of male primogeniture. In the traditional feudal system, these men were "tenants-in-chief," which means they held land directly from the king and owed him homage, allegiance, and certain financial obligations. Historically, at the time of their creation, dukes, of which there were only four in 1485, were usually closely related by blood to the king (as uncles, brothers, or sons, for example). Marquesses, at least initially, governed the English "marchlands" separating England from Wales and Scotland. Earls – known as counts in the rest of Europe – governed the counties and were often named after the major city in the county where they held their property. Viscounts, once a title given to sheriffs (*vicecomes* in Latin), and barons, lesser landholders, could hold their title from the king, but many also held them as courtesy titles, assumed by the eldest sons of greater nobles until they inherited their father's loftier titles.

In 1485, there were about fifty noble families, whose income came from the rents paid by their many feudal tenants. They also often possessed considerable wealth, sometimes accumulated over centuries, which allowed these families to live in splendor (although there were many poorer barons among them).[3] Their lands and estates were often vast, and they retained large affinities, gentlemen and servants who served the needs of these great lords. Among this group were also the younger sons of nobles, who would not inherit their father's title but

---

1   As already seen, right of conquest was also a means of accession to the monarchy, although in England this was rare.

2   Their wives were, respectively, duchess, marchioness, countess, viscountess, and baroness. Upon the death of their husbands, wives were referred to as "dowager" (e.g., the "dowager countess of …") in order to distinguish them from current title holders.

3   We shall have the opportunity in Chapter Ten to discuss the material wealth and culture of the various ranks in English society.

who were, nonetheless, wealthy because they were well placed into professions such as law, the military, the church, and government service.

The spiritual nobility included the leaders of the English branch of the Roman Catholic Church, including cardinals, archbishops, bishops, and abbots (who headed the monasteries), totaling about sixty clerics. These men were appointed by the pope on recommendation from the king, but in practice it was the king's decision. Although less wealthy, generally, than their temporal counterparts (but some, like Cardinal Wolsey during the reign of Henry VIII, were extremely wealthy), spiritual lords also lived extravagantly, from the tithes collected from their parishioners, the rents paid by tenants who lived on church lands, and the fact that church lands were not taxed. Both the temporal and spiritual lords were entitled to sit in the House of Lords, the upper branch of the English parliament, and many also assumed the roles of royal advisors and great officers of state.

Beneath the nobility was a larger group of men, numbering approximately 3,000 in 1485, known as the landed gentry. At the top of this group were knights, whose title was created by the king and was not, technically, inheritable, although heirs commonly paid a fee to the king in exchange for knighthood. Achieving knightly status was often the result of important military, administrative, or other service to the king or government. Next were esquires, which were usually courtesy titles rather than individually bestowed; they were adopted by men who served certain political offices and by the eldest sons of nobles and knights.

The largest group among the gentry were "mere" gentlemen, men with sufficient wealth to apply for a coat of arms from the heralds at the College of Arms. These men were "landed" because they held lands either directly from the king or from the nobles and rented the land to tenants, with the rent serving as their main source of income. Most gentlemen – and their wives, sons, and daughters – lived lives of plenty and often could afford to keep numerous servants. They were also the "natural rulers of society" because they served in various local offices – justice of the peace, sheriff, mayor, alderman – and were thus a regular presence in rural governance. They could also stand for election as members of the House of Commons, the lower branch of parliament. In total, the nobility and gentry – or the aristocracy – composed about 2 per cent of society.

Below the gentry was a larger group, about 10 per cent of society, known (depending in part on whether they lived in urban or rural environments) as citizens and yeomen. These men had enough wealth (40 shillings in freehold property) to own property and to vote,[4] though they might themselves not have enough income to run for such a position. In the cities (or boroughs, whose parliamentary representatives were known as "burgesses"), these men included what

---

4   The right to vote constitutes citizenship. Most people in early modern England, therefore, were subjects but not citizens.

would later be termed the professionals, or middling sort. They included university professors, lawyers, physicians, clergymen, teachers, merchants, master artisans, and, by virtue of their offices, certain members of the royal administration. These professionals often had similar wealth and authority to the gentry, but their lack of "landed" status generally placed them lower on the social hierarchy of English society, which was not based solely on economic wealth.[5] Yeomen were farmers who held their land in freehold tenure, roughly equivalent to modern notions of private property ownership. They farmed enough land or raised enough livestock to sell the surplus at market for profit, rather than merely living a subsistence lifestyle, and were able to employ farm laborers (though, unlike most gentlemen, they also worked their land themselves) and some household servants. Their position in society required citizens and yeomen to serve in various local capacities, such as constables and jurymen.

At the lower ranks of the English social hierarchy were those "who do not rule," comprising about 75 per cent of society. These people were known as copyholders and cottagers, who rented modest parcels of land from those higher in the chain. Many of these men, their wives, and children, also worked in what was known as the "cottage industry," performing various low-skilled artisanal activities (such as spinning) during slow times in the farming calendar to make extra money and support their subsistence lifestyle. Lower still on the chain were apprentices and journeymen, who worked for many years to develop the skills that might enable them to become master artisans and climb into the ranks of the citizenry. At the very bottom of the recognized hierarchy were field laborers, who typically worked daily or seasonally and lived in extremely modest dwellings, and menial servants, men and women who served others and usually lived in the homes or outbuildings of their lords and masters. All of these lower-ranking people were commonly, and not derisively, referred to as the "laboring poor," and were respected because their labor was essential to maintain the lifestyle of those higher up the chain.

Officially unrecognized in English society, though possibly comprising about 5 per cent of its inhabitants, were the "sturdy beggars." Mostly living in the larger cities, these were the vagrants, vagabonds, and other unwanted members of society, who, it was argued, had the ability to work but chose not to do so. Instead, they traveled the countryside seeking alms and handouts, living under bridges and pitching temporary tents in forests and fields. They were deemed "strangers" because they did not have a community that acknowledged them or masters to rule over them. These men, women, and children had virtually no

---

5   Although both contemporaries and historians use the word *class* to describe ranks of people in the Tudor and Stuart period, the modern understanding of class as a strictly economic construct is anachronistic. A poor earl was still higher in status than a rich merchant.

legal status and, in a society that lacked any form of social welfare and, later, distinguished between the deserving (or the "laboring") and undeserving (or the "idle") poor when determining where to direct charity, were badly mistreated in early modern English society by both the official legal system and by vigilante justice.

Perhaps surprisingly to the modern reader, those who lived in early modern England were, by and large, satisfied with the social hierarchy, although there were at times uprisings and rebellions that suggested otherwise. There was little talk of equality, of ranks or genders. People were often more concerned about falling down the ladder due to poor circumstances than climbing up it through hard work or advantageous marriages, although improvement did happen for some, especially among the nobility and gentry. Moreover, the rulers of society were visually distinguishable, a perpetual reminder of the great chain of being. The wealthy wore robes, satin, silk, velvet, gold, and swords, while the poor wore cheap wool and muted browns. In fact, a series of English "sumptuary laws" passed in the sixteenth century prohibited men and women from wearing certain types of clothing, fabrics, or accessories unless they were of a certain social rank or earned a minimum amount of money annually. Forms of address also depended on a person's rank and position. The king and queen were "your majesty"; a duke, "your grace"; nobles, "my lord" and "my lady"; gentlemen, "sir" and "squire"; citizens and professionals, "doctor," "professor," or "master"; yeomen, "goodman" and "goodwife"; servants, "sirrah," forenames ("William"), or surnames ("Jones"), depending on their age and position.

* * *

Discussion Question 1.3: To what extent did English people's belief in the great chain of being reinforce the rigid social hierarchy?

Securing the Tudor Crown

Given the dubious legitimacy of his elevation to the kingship by right of natural succession, Henry Tudor relied on his victory at Bosworth to claim the crown by right of military conquest and also by God's will and favor, which Henry claimed had allowed his smaller army to prevail. Henry's first parliament, which met on November 7, 1485, dutifully acknowledged both these claims and recognized their new king as Henry VII (see Figure 1.2). Henry was careful, however, to ensure that parliament recognized his title rather than granted it to him. According to the standards of medieval and early modern monarchy, as we have seen, kings were selected *rex dei gratia* (by the grace of God), rather than by men or by institutions of government. Parliamentary selection of a king would set a poor precedent for the notion of natural succession by male primogeniture.

Even divine intervention and parliamentary support were not enough to ensure that the Yorkist faction or the English nobility would accept Henry VII without challenge. The weakening of the power and wealth of the monarchy over the previous century had resulted in English nobles having virtually king-like powers in their own counties, a condition that was of some concern to the new king, who (1) wanted to secure his crown against possible usurpers and (2) wished to restore the monarchy to its earlier prestige under powerful rulers such as Edward I. It can be argued that Henry's reign was, above all else, about achieving these two goals.

One potential problem facing Henry was solved when, five months after becoming king, he followed through with an earlier promise to marry Elizabeth of York, daughter of Edward IV. This marriage served a number of key purposes. It restored Edward IV's children to legitimacy; removed Elizabeth as a potential claimant to

Figure 1.2 *Henry VII, circa 1505, by an unknown artist.*

the throne; united the Yorkist, Lancastrian, and Tudor factions together (the Tudor emblem later became a small white rose nestled inside a larger red one); and placed into question the legitimacy of Richard III's rule and, thus, that of anyone later claiming to be the heir of Richard. The birth of Prince Arthur – a name intended to remind people of Henry's Welsh lineage and his ancestry back to the fabled King Arthur – in September 1486 ensured that the heir to the throne was of mixed Yorkist and Lancastrian blood. By employing Yorkists in his administration and continuing the policies and practices of his predecessors, Henry managed to secure the loyalty of many Yorkists without having to resort to extreme measures, although he found it necessary to do this as well. Nobles and gentlemen who fought against Henry at Bosworth were attainted by parliament, which means they were found guilty of crimes against the king and were subject to the loss of their lands and titles. Henry stayed most of the attainders on condition of loyalty and good behavior.

Still, a series of challengers for the throne emerged over Henry's first decade as king. The main contenders were the heirs of the siblings of Richard III. Had Richard died a natural death, the crown would have descended to ten-year-old Edward, earl of Warwick, Richard's nephew by his brother George, or to John de la Pole, earl of Lincoln, son of Richard's sister Elizabeth and possibly, given Warwick's youth, Richard's own choice of heir. Warwick was swiftly apprehended and placed into the Tower of London, but in 1487 a boy named Lambert Simnel claimed, at the behest of his tutor, that he was Warwick, having escaped from the Tower. Simnel was brought into Ireland and was crowned in Dublin as "Edward VI." Meanwhile, Lincoln schemed with his aunt Margaret, duchess of Burgundy (sister to Edward IV and Richard III), and sailed to Ireland with 2,000 mercenary troops. The Yorkist army arrived in Lancashire, England, in June 1487 but was defeated by the king's army at the Battle of Stoke. During the battle, Lincoln was killed and Simnel was captured. When it became clear that Simnel was merely a puppet in the whole affair, he was pardoned and employed as a scullery boy in the royal kitchen, eventually rising through the ranks to become the king's falconer.

A few years later, another imposter appeared, this time in the person of Perkin Warbeck, who was alleged to be Richard, duke of York, the younger of the princes in the Tower and second son of Edward IV. In a conspiracy once again hatched by Margaret of Burgundy, Warbeck was widely touted as the legitimate king and was recognized as such in several European courts, including that of Holy Roman Emperor Maximilian I. Warbeck and his supporters staged several rebellions between 1495 and 1497, but none were successful. In 1497, Warbeck was captured, confessed to his subterfuge, and was initially granted a reprieve by Henry and placed under a light guard. After Warbeck attempted to escape to the Continent, however, he was recaptured and placed into the Tower of London, in a room next to the real earl of Warwick, who had then been imprisoned for more than a decade. By 1499, Warbeck and Warwick managed to escape. They were quickly recaptured, convicted of high treason, and executed in November; Warwick, by virtue of his high station, was beheaded, while Warbeck, a mere commoner, was strangulated by hanging (see *Voices of the Past*: **The Execution of Perkin Warbeck**).

Although he had managed to deal effectively with individuals with potential Yorkist claims to the throne, Henry had go to further to secure the crown for his children. One key step was ensuring that he was accepted by other important dignitaries in Europe. Henry managed to obtain from Pope Innocent VII a papal bull that excommunicated all pretenders to the throne of England. Additional foreign support came through the Treaty of Medina del Campo with the Spanish monarchs Ferdinand of Aragon and Isabella of Castile in 1489. Spain was in the process of emerging as a united nation through the marriage of Ferdinand and Isabella and the final stages of the Reconquista, by which Christians finally managed to repel the Muslims who had dominated the Iberian Peninsula since the Middle Ages. An alliance with England was a good way to provide security for both nations, particularly with regard to France, no friend of England or Spain. The treaty ensured that both nations would, if needed, provide military support against France. It also arranged a marriage between Henry's eldest son and heir, Arthur, to Ferdinand and Isabella's daughter Catherine of Aragon. The two were married by proxy in 1499, not coincidentally the same year that Henry had managed to rid himself of the final two potential rivals to the throne, Warwick and Warbeck. The marriage rites were completed two years later, in November 1501, when both parties were deemed old enough to consummate the relationship.

By April 1502, however, Arthur was dead from an unknown illness, most likely tuberculosis. The new heir was Henry, the second son of Henry VII and Elizabeth of York. Almost immediately plans were put into motion to marry Prince Henry to his brother's widow, Catherine, which involved securing a papal dispensation from Pope Julius II. For various reasons, the wedding did not take place until shortly after Henry inherited the crown in 1509. Nonetheless, the marriage was important, as it upheld the spirit of Medina del Campo and maintained a key relationship between England, Spain, and the Holy Roman emperor, a significant political figure to have as an ally. Additional foreign support for Henry VII's crown came from King James IV of Scotland. James had supported Warbeck's efforts to claim the throne and his close association with France meant that he was a threat to the security of the Tudor dynasty. Rather than meet this threat with force, James and Henry agreed to the Treaty of Perpetual Peace, which also involved an arranged marriage between Henry's eldest daughter, Margaret, and James, from whom the Stuart dynasty, beginning in 1603, would descend.

Early Tudor Kingship

With his Yorkist rivals dead or assuaged, a young and healthy heir to the throne, and key alliances with other European royal families, Henry VII managed to secure his crown. But it was also necessary for the king who had brought an end to the Wars of the Roses to strengthen the power and wealth of the English monarchy, the weaknesses of which had been the cause of the conflict in the first place. By most accounts, Henry was well suited for kingship. He was tall, slender, and strong; he was intelligent and hardworking and sought advice from his advisors; and he was willing to punish his enemies but also to reward loyalty.

Henry also recognized that a king and his court must be magnificent. The king should live in greater splendor and dress more richly than the wealthiest of his subjects, and the court's main purpose should be to celebrate the majesty of the king and his family. Henry ensured that the Tudor coat of arms was emblazoned on buildings, charters, and the liveries of those who served him. He undertook regular progresses throughout the countryside, so that he could be seen and adored by his subjects, and issued large coins that showed him sitting on his throne, wearing his crown. He brought about improvements to several royal residences, such as Windsor Castle and the Tower of London, building new towers and making the royal lodgings more comfortable and more resplendent. These royal palaces were adorned with new tapestries, jewels, and silver and gold plate that cost many thousands of pounds. Henry also regularly issued royal proclamations that emphasized both his right to rule and his obligations as king.

Part of realizing the Tudor concept of kingship was to ensure that loyalty was given to the king, rather than to great nobles of the realm. A century of weak and impoverished kings enabled aristocrats throughout England to rule their counties as virtual kings, a practice known as provincialism. Nobles amassed large affinities composed of men who swore fealty to them and were willing to wear their noble's crest on their liveries (uniforms) into battle when needed. Furthermore, the provincial aristocrats had managed to use their power, wealth, and patronage to sway various judicial proceedings in their favor and in that of their supporters. The very rule of law and the concept of impartial justice were in jeopardy as parties in disputes resorted to the whims of provincial despots rather than to the king and his institutions of justice. Some of the problems of provincialism were eased by 1485 because a number of noble families died off during and in the aftermath of the Wars of the Roses. Throughout his reign, Henry also managed to keep the problem in check by limiting creations to the nobility (by the end of his reign the number of noble families had dropped to about forty), which also meant that much Yorkist land that had reverted to the crown over the course of the wars remained in Henry's hands. These could be used for judicious distribution to nobles who proved themselves loyal, or they could be kept by the king to help finance his new monarchy, as he retained the rents they brought in.

Henry's first step to limiting provincial power of nobles was through the parliamentary Statute against Liveries (1487). This law made it illegal for nobles to amass private armies for the primary reason that these armies could be directed against the king. Instead, Henry arranged for the use of Commissions of Array, which required aristocrats appointed by the king in each county to, when so ordered, recruit and train an army in the king's name, although, consistent with ancient feudal practice, they were to pay for the men at their own expense. Henry also required his nobles to swear fealty directly to him, promising to uphold royal proclamations and not to support or attempt any riots or foment violence against the king. He forced those of the nobility whose loyalty was not entirely clear to enter into recognizances promising that they would, in essence, be of good behavior and follow the king's instructions, otherwise they would forfeit large fines. Henry also issued additional commissions to county gentlemen, later known as lords lieutenant, in order to distribute power in the provinces more broadly and limit that of a smaller number of great nobles.

In addition to limiting provincialism, the new monarchy required a sophisticated infrastructure to ensure the smooth running of the court and proper display of royal majesty. Under Henry VII, the court came to number several hundred employees, whose job was to provide for all the possible needs of the king and his family, courtiers, and guests. The king enhanced the three household departments that already existed. The "household above stairs" was run by the lord chamberlain, who was nearly always a member of the aristocracy. He ran the Presence Chamber, where the king officially met dignitaries, courtiers, and petitioners while enthroned. He was also in charge of a new creation of Henry, the Privy Chamber, which was also staffed by numerous ushers and grooms. This was a private apartment for the king to meet with his royal advisors. The chamberlain also had authority over the king's living quarters and bedchamber, which was run by the Groom of the Stool, a gentleman who had the intimate privilege of assisting in the king's toileting. The Privy Chamber also housed the king's private treasury, overseen by the Keeper of the Privy Purse, and clothes, furniture, weapons, and armor, procured and maintained by a department known as the Great Wardrobe. In both chambers, Henry was protected by another creation of his, the Yeomen of the Guard, his corps of personal bodyguards. This guard protected the king from assassination and had the added benefit of emphasizing the grandeur of monarchy.

The "household below stairs" was operated by the lord steward, also a noble, who had numerous masters working under his supervision. The steward and his deputy – the comptroller, usually a knight – were responsible for ensuring that the physical needs of the members of court were met and, therefore, had hundreds of staff who butchered, cooked, cleaned, laundered, sewed, and performed dozens of other mundane but necessary tasks. Low-ranking members of this household would rarely, if ever, set eyes on the king or powerful courtiers, and a series of private, narrow staircases and doors hidden behind walls and tapestries ensured that these court employees could move unobtrusively throughout the palaces to undertake their duties.

The third major unit at court was the "outside department," run by various masters, such as those of the horse, hound, and falcons; these men were usually knights or gentlemen. The outside department was responsible to keep the stables, erect tents, organize revelries and hunts, and run tournaments that became especially important with the Tudor recovery of chivalric games, such as jousting and sword-fighting. As the king was peripatetic, moving among various palaces and county progresses throughout the year, many members of the court traveled with his entourage, a large gathering that also demonstrated the king's great majesty. Although Henry VII did not create any of these three branches of the royal household, each experienced a degree of innovation that reflected a newer and stronger approach to kingship that continued throughout the Tudor period.

Government under Henry VII

Henry VII's approach to the workings of government was also critical to his success in restoring luster and authority to monarchy. Ever since the statute of *Prerogativa Regis* in the reign of Edward I (circa 1300), the king had been endowed with a wide range of royal prerogative rights that enabled him to govern in the best interests of the commonwealth. He had the authority to create nobles and knights, declare war and peace, select and dismiss councillors and magistrates, engage in foreign affairs, call and dismiss parliament, issue proclamations, and enforce feudal obligations between the king and his tenants. Despite his divinely granted status and his "angel intelligence," the king was expected to rule with respect to the ancient laws of the land and, as much as possible consistent with his rights of sovereignty, with the consent of the governed. Assisting the king in the exercise of these prerogatives, within the confines of the law, were several important governmental bodies.

One of these bodies was the king's royal council. Whereas the council before 1485 tended to be a large and unwieldy body composed of nobles, knights, and crown officials – numbering one hundred or more – Henry limited its membership to about twenty active councillors, a smaller and more effective body that could remain loyal to the king, though not so small that individual members would be able to wield exceptional power. It was composed of the heads of the royal household, other branches of government and the church, and the law courts, together with individuals specifically appointed by the king to serve as his councillors. The council was responsible for the day-to-day administration of the realm. It handled a wide range of issues, such as drafting royal proclamations, issuing charters and orders to administer royal lands, overseeing county affairs and local officials, assisting in matters of diplomacy and peace, hearing petitions and appeals from the king's subjects, and issuing "orders in council" in the name of the king. It also oversaw two subsidiary bodies, the Council of Wales and the

Marches, and the Council of the North, both initially established by Edward IV and strengthened under Henry VII, to improve governmental control over the west and north parts of England.

At some point, the council began meeting as a Court of Star Chamber and heard legal disputes, usually ones directly involving the security of the realm, such as riot, conspiracy, treason, forgery, and perjury.[6] Many nobles were brought before the council's court and questioned, often by the king himself, about their compliance with royal orders. Because it was technically part of the king's household, the council also regularly moved about with the court. It quickly became the administrative arm of the crown and the practical source of sovereign authority for the English state. By the mid-sixteenth century, it was routinely referred to as the privy council.

Two other important branches of government were the Chancery and Exchequer. Chancery was run by perhaps the most important royal official in England, the lord chancellor, also a key member of the king's council. The chancellor possessed the Great Seal of England, which was applied to land charters, parliamentary legislation, and royal proclamations, thereby giving them the force of the king's authority. By 1485, Chancery had also developed into an "equity court," which was responsible to provide remedies for legal issues that could not be addressed in a common law court, in theory using the residual powers possessed by the king as the "fount of all justice." The Exchequer, run by the chancellor of the Exchequer, was responsible for all royal finances that were not part of the king's personal treasury, primarily the collection and accounting of taxation money.[7] The Exchequer also held its own law court, to collect monies owed to the crown. One of the problems Henry observed with the Exchequer was the ponderous slowness with which accounting was completed. The inability of the Exchequer to keep Henry fully aware of his financial situation at any given time compelled the king to place more and more authority in the hands of his personal treasurers to handle the finances that helped fund the court.

The two royal common law courts, the Court of King's Bench and Court of Common Pleas, each staffed by their own chief justices (who were usually members of the king's council) and lesser (or puisne, pronounced "puny") judges, were also institutions of government that had, by 1485, come into some disrepute as a result of provincialism and archaism. King's Bench, in theory, handled criminal and civil cases touching the king or the physical bodies of his subjects, such as

---

6   The Court of Star Chamber was so named because it sat in a room at Westminster Palace known as the *camera stellata*, which had decorative stars painted on the ceiling.

7   The Exchequer was so named because accounting was initially done by placing counters on a checkered cloth, a method used because many tax collectors and crown appointees had limited literacy and numeracy skills.

treason and murder. Common Pleas focused on civil cases involving ordinary subjects, including property, contract, debt, and injury. Both these courts applied a rigorous form of the common law, which was based on precedents created by previous court cases. By the beginning of the Tudor era, these courts had gained reputations for being tediously slow, overly technical in their procedure, and extremely expensive to initiate a lawsuit. It was these problems that caused the creation of the equity courts of Chancery and, in about 1494, a subsidiary court of the council, later known as the Court of Requests.

The final major branch of government that assisted the king in governing was the bicameral parliament. As we have seen, the House of Lords consisted of all members of the temporal and spiritual nobility, about one hundred men in total. The House of Commons was a body elected by forty-shilling freeholders (3 to 5 per cent of the male population) and consisted of two "knights of the shire" from each county and two "burgesses" from each of about 120 incorporated towns and cities, totaling about 300 members of parliament.[8] The right to summon, prorogue, or dissolve parliament fell to the king's prerogative.[9] Unlike modern parliaments, which sit regularly with a body of professional politicians, early modern parliaments met on average every three to five years, such that its members did not develop professional status or institutional memory. As its members, in theory, represented their constituents by attorney, parliament was the primary institution of government that ensured the king ruled through consent of the governed.[10] Meetings of parliament enabled its members to challenge or question royal policies made through proclamation or otherwise, and to petition the king for redress of grievance.

Parliament had two primary functions in the early modern period: legislation and taxation. Legislation was usually passed to this body by the king's council for discussion and ratification in each of the two houses before it was ultimately approved by the king and sealed by the chancellor, at which point it became statute law that was subject to enforcement. In theory, either house was free to initiate its own legislation, even if it was against the wishes of the king or his government, but the king was equally free to exercise his prerogative right to veto the bill before it became an act, in which case it never became law. Because, at

---

8 Some towns that had the right to elect members of parliament had, by 1500, become virtually deserted, but the landowners still sent representatives; these came to be known as "pocket boroughs" because they were, in essence, in the pocket of wealthy aristocrats.

9 When summoned, a new election was required for parliament to sit. When prorogued, parliament was suspended but the same members returned when recalled. When dissolved, the members were sent back to their counties and new elections were required when parliament was again called.

10 The term *attorney* was from Law French, the legal language used in the English law courts. It meant an individual who "stood in" for absent clients, or in the case of parliament, for absent constituents.

this time, the king had the power to issue proclamations (within certain limitations), legislation served the purpose of gaining "everyman's consent" to some
of Henry's and his successors' more contentious practices. An excellent example
of this is the passage of the Statute against Liveries: because it was ratified by
the very men it was most likely to affect (nobles, knights, and gentlemen), it had
stronger force than an edict from the king might have had. The second function
of parliament was to approve taxation among the people of England. Although
the king had wide-ranging powers to issue proclamations on nearly any subject,
common law severely restricted his ability to exact taxes, which in theory were
only needed in times of emergency, such as war.

Naturally, a king who emulated a new theory of Tudor kingship such as Henry
VII was not one to be questioned too thoroughly about his policies, but he still
recognized the importance of gaining at least a semblance of consent by calling parliament on a fairly regular basis. In all, Henry called seven parliaments
between 1485 and 1509, which was broadly consistent with the frequency with
which parliament had been called for two centuries, although none lasted more
than a single session (that is, there were no prorogations). A sign of Henry's and
his council's increasing authority – and what has been referred to as "Tudor
despotism" – is the fact that he called only two parliaments in his last fourteen
years as king, and each lasted only about eight days. In his last parliament, in
1504, Henry asked its members to renew and strengthen the Statute against
Liveries, once again forcing its members to, in effect, legislate against their own
personal interests.

Fiscal Feudalism

One reason Henry called so few parliaments in the second half of his reign
has to do with his approach to crown finances. Over the previous century,
provincialism, corruption of local officials, and war had led increasingly to
the impoverishment and indebtedness of the crown, a condition that Henry
worked hard to improve. In this he was very successful; his ability to live off
his own means also meant that he needed to rely less and less on parliament's
powers of taxation, or "extraordinary" income. In theory, a king should have
been able to fund his entire court on his "ordinary" income, which derived
from several sources. The king owned large parcels of property that he did
not distribute to tenants, which provided him with an annual income through
rents. As a result of lands that reverted to the crown after Henry had dealt with
his noble enemies, crown lands yielded much higher profits than previously.
The king was also entitled to the revenue collected by the customs office, from
goods both imported into and exported from England. During the Wars of the
Roses, trade had declined considerably, as had customs revenue. With peace

came prosperity and the ability to renew trade with foreign powers and increase this important revenue source.

Henry's greatest, and most controversial, financial triumph came from the recovery of what was known as "fiscal feudalism." Historically, as head of the feudal society, the king could exact from his tenants-in-chief (nobles and knights) various feudal fees. These collections had fallen into abeyance over the previous century, or, because of provincialism, had fallen into the hands of nobles rather than the king's treasury. The king recovered, for instance, his rights to wardship, or the right to administer and collect the profits and rents from land held by minor or female heirs until they reached the age of majority or married. He also collected reliefs, aids, and incidents, or fees associated with land transferred upon the death of its occupant, the marriage of his wards, and the creation of a deceased knight's son to his father's title. The king also had the feudal right to collect fees when his eldest son was knighted or when his daughter was married; Henry demanded both in 1504 when his daughter Margaret married King James IV of Scotland, even though Arthur had been knighted fifteen years earlier and had been dead for two years. Parliament offered Henry £40,000, a considerable sum at the time, if he would refrain from inspecting ancient land tenure obligations to determine his feudal entitlements. Finally, Henry had parliament pass penal statutes that allowed him to collect fines for various infractions and employed commissioners to tour the counties looking for victims of his strict fiscal feudal policies.

In total, Henry managed through these various means to increase crown annual finances from about £50,000 when he claimed the throne to closer to £120,000 by 1509. This enabled him to live an extravagant life while relieving himself of the need to call parliament for regular infusions of cash. It is his financial avarice that has given Henry a poor reputation among early modern commentators, although Henry operated within the confines of the law to increase revenues that helped to strengthen his reign and secure his dynasty. As a result, when the crown passed to Henry VIII in 1509 – his father having died of tuberculosis that April – the new king inherited a full treasury. To appease his noble subjects who thought his father excessively avaricious, however, Henry started his reign by imprisoning and later executing two of his father's more successful revenue collectors, Edmund Dudley and Sir Richard Empson. Like his father's, Henry VIII's reign started in bloodshed.

* * *

Discussion Question 1.4: In what ways did Henry's reforms in government and his use of fiscal feudalism help to secure the Tudor dynasty from further challenges?

VOICES OF THE PAST
THE EXECUTION OF PERKIN WARBECK

The claims of Perkin Warbeck represented the last significant challenge to Henry VII's crown. Warbeck arrived in England in 1491 claiming that he was Richard, duke of York, the younger of the princes believed to have been murdered in the Tower of London by Richard III. Henry initially spared Warbeck after his capture in 1497, but when Warbeck tried to escape to the Continent, Henry committed him to the Tower of London. An attempted escape in 1499, coupled with rumors of Warbeck's renewed plans to claim the throne, finally forced the king to order the imposter's execution. The following extract records Warbeck's history from his first attempt at escape until his execution.

* * *

Now began the fateful day of the death of Perkin Warbeck ... to approach.... Perkin, whether it grieved him to be kept inward [at close guard], or else that he was instigated and enlisted by some of his old friends to stir more coals, and begin some new seditious faction, ... studied how to escape and fly away ... and convey himself out of the Englishmen's hands.... And so deceiving his keepers, [he] took him to his heels, by which he brought himself into a straighter custody and prison, and wrapped himself into tortures and punishments. For ... when the rumor of his flight was spread abroad, every byway and lane was set ... with the king's guard.... Wherefore he being sore abashed with the clamour of them that searched and made inquiry of him, and being in manner destitute of wit and counsel, altered of necessity from his pretenses [plans]

and came to ... the Priory of Shere beside Richmond ... and committed himself to the prior of the monastery, requiring him for God's sake to ask and desire his life and pardon of the king's majesty.

The prior, ... moved with the calamity and unfortunate state of this man, came to the king and showed him this Perkin, whose pardon he humbly craved, and frankly obtained it.... Perkin was brought to the courts again to Westminster with many a curse and reproach, and was one day set fettered in a pair of stocks, before the door of Westminster Hall, and there he stood a whole day, not without innumerable reproaches, mocks, and scornings. And the next day, [he] was carried through London and set upon the ... stocks as he occupied the day before, and there stood all day and read openly his own confession written by his own hand....

When night of the same day ... was come (partly because the king had pardoned him his life, and partly because he should no more run away and put the king in doubt of any mistrust or misfortune to come) he was committed to the Tower of London, where his wickedness boiling so hot within his ... stomach would not suffer him to escape the punishment and vengeance of God.... Perkin being now in hold, ... began to study which way to fly and escape. For he by false persuasions and liberal promises, corrupted [his gaolers] in so much that they (as it was at their arraignment openly proved) intended to have slain [Sir John Digby, lieutenant of the Tower] and to have set Perkin and the earl of Warwick at large, which earl was by them made privy of this enterprise, and thereunto ... to his destruction assented.

But this crafty device and subtle imagination [was] open and disclosed, ... he being repulsed and put back from all hope and good luck with all his accomplices and confederates. And on the three and twenty day of the same month [November 23, 1499], Perkin [was] drawn to Tyburn and there ... standing on a little scaffold, read his confession, ... asked the king's forgiveness, and died penitently.[11] This was the reward of ... Perkin Warbeck, which as in his life, with false persuasions and untrue surmises, had brought many noble personages to death and utter perdition, so at his death he brought with him other of the same sort to their not undeserved punishment.

Source: Edward Hall, *The Union of the Two Noble and Illustre Families of Lancastre & Yorke* [commonly known as *Hall's Chronicle*] (London, 1548), volume VII, fols. xlix–xli.

* * *

Discussion Question 1.5: Why do you think that, despite Perkin Warbeck's treasonous acts, his detailed confession, and an escape attempt, Henry VII initially had the imposter imprisoned instead of executed?

---

11 Tyburn was then a village located at the northeast corner of present-day Hyde Park, most famous for the public gallows used to hang criminals in London until 1783. See Chapter Nine.

CHAPTER TWO

HENRY VIII AND REFORM, 1509–1547

DEATH AND DISORDER:
THE EVIL MAY DAY RIOT

Among the few legitimate occasions for disorder in otherwise orderly early modern England were the days of celebration associated with ancient pagan festivals, when commoners exercised some freedom of expression. During Saturnalia, for example, which occurred just before Christmas, the Greek god Saturn was figuratively released from the wool that bound his feet for the remainder of the year. When Saturn was liberated, workers were likewise freed from their obligations, and a local "lord of misrule" was chosen to preside over a day of harmless revelry. The next day, with Saturn rebound, order was restored.

Another occasion for revelry was May Day, a holiday celebrated on May 1 to herald the arrival of spring and the beginning of the agricultural cycle. In the rural countryside, young, virgin women were selected to dance around a maypole, symbolically representing fertility and the readiness of the earth to be implanted with seed. In the cities, where agriculture was less important, May Day was more commonly associated with a celebration of the labor provided by

apprentices, journeymen, artisans, and merchants, and with appeals to justice, fairness, and redistribution of wealth among the rich and the poor. The myth of Robin Hood, in this context, was sometimes invoked.

Normally, May Day was another harmless event causing minor disorder, but the celebration of 1517 was anything but. It was triggered by an Easter sermon given by an Augustinian canon named Thomas Bell. In the sermon, Bell railed against the "aliens and strangers" who lived in London, stole jobs from hardworking laborers and artisans, took business from English merchants, and became rich as Londoners became impoverished. There was also some suggestion that "aliens" were seducing English wives and daughters, placing the future of English families – and perhaps the purity of English blood – in jeopardy. Bell called on all Englishmen "not to suffer the said aliens so highly in their wealth, and the natural born men of this region to come to confusion."[1] Fueled by xenophobia, Bell's sermon was a call to action against the immigrants of London.

---

1   For a contemporary account, see Edward Hall, *The Union of the Two Noble and Illustre Families of Lancastre & Yorke* (London, 1548), volume VIII, fols. lx–lxiii.

Over the next two weeks, as May Day approached, apprentices and journeymen began distressing immigrants. Aliens were beaten and thrown into rivers and canals and their property was damaged, actions that forced the mayor to commit several of the aggressors to gaol. Perceiving the city's government to be unduly affectionate toward immigrants, at some point it was decided that, on May Day, "the city would rebel and slay all aliens," which caused many immigrants to flee out of fear. The privy council soon became involved, commanding the mayor and aldermen to enforce a curfew on May Day eve. In defiance, starting around nine in the evening, Londoners violently freed their fellow artisans from the gaols, gathered weapons, and moved into immigrant parts of the city, such as the area north of St. Paul's Cathedral, where especially Dutch and French aliens lived. The rioters sacked homes, workshops, and businesses and threw the strangers' goods into the street.

It did not take long to restore order. Although the rioters had not killed anybody nor caused significant damage to person or property, a greatly exaggerated version of the events was sent to the king, who ordered the duke of Norfolk and 1,300 troops into London to suppress the rioters. By three in the morning, most of the rioters either had been arrested or had returned to their homes. About 180 men, women, and boys were apprehended and sent to various gaols awaiting their fate. The courts acted quickly. By May 2, thirteen men were charged with treason against the king on the somewhat spurious

grounds that the king was, at that time, at peace with the victims' home countries. The judges – the mayor of London, the duke of Norfolk, and the earls of Shrewsbury and Surrey – found each of the accused guilty. The executions occurred at various gallows erected throughout London on May 4.

A couple of weeks later, the remainder of the rioters (including eleven women) stood before the king; his queen, Catherine of Aragon; chief minister Cardinal Thomas Wolsey; and several nobles. "The poor younglings and old false knaves" were joined together with lengths of rope, wearing shirts, with halters around their necks, all imminent signs of execution.[2] As a group, the prisoners declared their guilt, admitted that they deserved to be hanged, and pled for mercy. In a highly orchestrated event, the nobles and Wolsey got on their knees and pleaded for a pardon, as did the queen, who appealed on behalf of the prisoners' wives and children. The king announced the pardon and sent the accused home. For Henry VIII, this was a rare sign of mercy in a reign that saw the death of many other rebellious subjects.

The Evil May Day Riot speaks to a number of key themes in Tudor England: the importance of order, limits on how much disorder was tolerated even during days of revelry, the intense insularity and xenophobia that characterized England at this time, and the crown's swift and harsh treatment against perceived enemies of the realm.

* * *

Discussion Question 2.1: Why do you think the Tudor state executed more than a dozen people after the Evil May Day Riot even though the riot itself had not resulted in any deaths?

---

2   Shirts at this time were worn as undergarments. Before an execution, the condemned would be stripped of his outer clothes, which became the property of the executioner. The halter was used to drag the condemned to the place of execution, then served as the noose by which he or she was hanged.

Thomas More and English Humanism

Sir Thomas More was perhaps the greatest intellectual in the court of Henry VIII. More was one of the earliest beneficiaries of the "new learning" associated with the adoption of Renaissance humanism in England during the late fifteenth century. Humanist education (the *studia humanitatis*, or study of the humanities) emphasized the importance of reading and writing the classical languages of Latin and Greek, and a curriculum that focused on liberal arts subjects such as ethics, rhetoric, logic, history, law, and religion, with particular emphasis on the writings of classical authors from Rome, Greece, and the early Christian church. Humanists also disapproved of citizens leading a contemplative life, often characterized by monastic isolation, rather than an active life, which required becoming involved in public affairs. To an extent, the adoption of humanist education and ideas in England represented a key transition from the medieval to the early modern worldview.

At the age of eleven, More left grammar school to join the household of Archbishop of Canterbury John Morton, who also happened to be England's lord chancellor. More's intellect quickly came to the attention of Morton, who sent the youth to Oxford to further his studies. There, More came into contact with leading humanists of the day, including Thomas Linacre and William Grocyn, who taught More Latin and Greek. After two years, More entered Lincoln's Inn, one of England's four Inns of Court[3] to become a common law lawyer, but he still maintained close ties with the Oxford humanists and came into contact with Grocyn's friend Desiderius Erasmus, a Dutch Christian humanist who is often considered to have been England's leading scholar and theologian at the time. More's marriage in 1505 made it clear that his career track would be law, not the priesthood, as priests were not allowed to marry.

While working as a lawyer, More produced translations and editions of classical and humanist works, sat as a member of parliament, became a justice of the peace and undersheriff, and wrote a biography of Richard III. In 1516, More produced his best-known work, *Utopia*, a quintessentially humanist rhetorical dialogue, written in Latin, that fictionally and satirically described More's and many humanists' desires for a world that was less corrupt and avaricious, more pious in religion, and fairer in law, especially regarding England's harsh treatment of criminals and its system of private property ownership that heavily favored the wealthy. Ultimately, the book was about encouraging active, virtuous citizens, such as More, to become involved in worldly affairs in order to limit noble excess, injustice, and potential royal misrule. Ironically, More was London's undersheriff

---

3   These central London schools – Gray's, Lincoln's, the Inner Temple, and the Middle Temple – had trained common law lawyers since the fourteenth century.

at the time of the Evil May Day Riot, where he implored the rioters to return peacefully to their homes.

It was shortly after the writing of *Utopia* that More became a trusted advisor to Cardinal Thomas Wolsey, lord chancellor of England, and a chief councillor to Henry VIII. More's training in law and religion made him a vital member of the king's council. When the king decided to write a treatise criticizing Martin Luther, the *Assertio septem sacramentorum* (*Defense of the Seven Sacraments*, 1521), More was a leading advisor. When Luther wrote a vituperative response, More, as a key figure in the English Catholic humanist movement, penned the *Responsio ad Lutherum* (*Response to Luther*, 1523). More was also heavily involved in suppressing English heretics who supported Lutheranism or any other form of church reform, particularly those who wanted to read a new English-language Bible produced by William Tyndale. By 1529, More had written his masterful *Dialogue Concerning Heresies*, in which he defended the institutional nature and doctrinal correctness of the Roman Catholic Church and its theology. Despite his value to the English state, More would, as we shall see, suffer for these beliefs.

The King and the Cardinal

Henry VIII was seventeen years old when he ascended the English throne. Handsome, exceptionally tall for the time (six feet two inches), athletic, charming, and extroverted, Henry was an imposing figure (see Figure 2.1). Like many elite boys of his generation, Henry had been trained to be a superior archer, horseman, swordsman, and huntsman. He had a profound love of showing off these skills during chivalric tournaments, which, owing largely to Henry's passions, achieved something of a rebirth during the sixteenth century. Contrary to how he is often represented in modern times, Henry was also a gifted student blessed with a sharp intellect. Trained in the same humanist intellectual tradition as More, and guided in his efforts by Erasmus and other leading humanists, Henry was well versed in philosophy, law, religion, and mathematics. He was both artistic and musical and composed and played songs on a variety of instruments. He was also skilled at languages, especially Latin and French (the two most common languages of literature and diplomacy), but also Italian and Spanish. It was this wide-ranging humanist education that enabled Henry, with a little help from More, to pen his rebuttal to Lutheranism.

Henry was, however, a young man who preferred pleasure to business and lacked the work ethic of his father. Whereas Henry VII was routinely involved in the day-to-day governance of the realm and devoted himself to being an effective administrator, his son was lazy, arrogant, and self-centered, acted impulsively on his desires with little thought to the consequences of his actions, and traveled extensively for pleasure with a massive body of servants and courtiers, paying the least possible attention to affairs of state. Also unlike his father, who had relied on experienced military leaders at Bosworth and otherwise preferred peace within Britain and Europe, Henry wanted to prove that he was a man capable of leading his kingdom in war. In particular Henry wanted to recover losses from the Hundred Years' War (1337–1453), which saw England's claim to extensive French territories dwindle down to only the port of Calais. Finally, Henry quickly became overwhelmed by the sheer number of men who offered him counsel, in part because he lacked his father's decision-making skills and attention to detail. Only a couple of years into his reign, therefore, Henry required a chief executive officer, or principal minister, to run the English state, help manage his military campaigns, and relieve the king of the burdens of his office.

Figure 2.1 *Henry VIII, circa 1536, after Hans Holbein the Younger.*

Credit: IanDagnall Computing/Alamy Stock Photo.

The minister Henry turned to was Thomas Wolsey, the son of a butcher whose intellect, like More's, managed to get him into Oxford University. At the start of Henry's reign, Wolsey had been working as a royal almoner, a chaplain who distributed charity to the king's subjects. Henry quickly appreciated Wolsey's administrative skills and employed him to manage a military campaign into France (1512–14) in support of the Empire and papacy. This campaign resulted in Henry personally leading an army into combat and winning the Battle of the Spurs. Wolsey had, in effect, turned his king into a legitimate military victor. This naturally raised Wolsey in the esteem of a king who prided himself on military prowess that had, up to that point, been demonstrated only through the sporting spectacles of his youth.

Numerous honors soon followed for Wolsey. By 1514 he was archbishop of York, and in 1515 he was elevated by the pope to cardinal, the highest rank in the Roman Catholic Church. Wolsey was also granted several other church positions, including several bishoprics. Although Wolsey could not, of course, attend to all these clerical positions (a practice known as pluralism) and employed others to serve in his stead, he retained the revenues that they brought in, which soon made him the richest man in England besides the king himself. In total, his income has been estimated at greater than £30,000 per year, roughly five times that of the wealthiest nobleman and one-third or so of the king's own income, which was used to run a royal court consisting of several palaces and hundreds of people. Wolsey was fond of conspicuously displaying his wealth, dressing in magnificence and building palaces in London (York Place) and Surrey (Hampton Court), both of which eclipsed the king's own palaces.

Wolsey was a commanding presence in both domestic and foreign affairs. Henry made Wolsey lord chancellor in 1515, a position that put him at the head of the royal council and gave him the ability to use the Court of Chancery and the Court of Star Chamber against those who challenged his authority. He was immensely disliked by the nobility, who saw him as a usurper, and his access to coercive tribunals afforded him the opportunity to bring the great men of the realm into conformity.[4] As chancellor, Wolsey also had exclusive use of the Great Seal, which was necessary to issue most important documents of state and meant that virtually no government policy – from parliamentary legislation to treaties – could proceed without Wolsey's explicit knowledge and approval. Wolsey was also chiefly responsible for advising the king on appointments to key positions in the realm. Candidates for judgeships, university professorships, episcopal benches, and royal councillors, among many others, all depended on Wolsey to pass their name to the king, who invariably took his chancellor's

---

4   It did not help his reputation that Wolsey, a Catholic priest, also publicly maintained a mistress, who bore him two illegitimate children.

advice. All these activities involved the collection of fees, further enriching the wealthy cardinal.

In foreign matters, Wolsey proved somewhat less successful, in part because England's remoteness and smaller population meant that it was hardly a major player in European politics, especially when compared to juggernauts such as the united France that emerged from the Hundred Years' War and the vast Holy Roman Empire. Nonetheless, he brokered a number of key deals for England that proved, at least in the short term, beneficial. The Treaty of London (1518), for example, designed by Wolsey, was a nonaggression pact signed between France, England, the Empire, the Papal States, and Spain to come to the aid of any party who was attacked, especially if that attack came from another signatory or, of greater concern at the time, the Ottoman Empire. Wolsey also engineered a meeting between Henry and Francis I of France known as the Field of the Cloth of Gold (1520), so named because both kings attempted to outdo each other's extravagance and had their clothing and tents made of silk sewn with gold thread. When the amiable relationship between England and France soured, Wolsey allied England with Emperor Charles V, a relationship that also soured when imperial forces sacked Rome in 1527 and took the pope captive.

Although Wolsey managed to make Europe aware of England's existence, his various diplomatic strategies on behalf of Henry VIII managed, more than anything, to drain the royal treasury that Henry VII had worked so hard to fill. Making war in Europe, even if it pleased a bellicose king, was an expensive proposition. The shortcomings of royal revenue to pay for these enterprises forced Wolsey to rely on parliament for taxes. When these funds still proved insufficient, Wolsey surveyed the country and used its data to levy "forced loans" and "benevolences" against landholders. This was an extension of Henry VII's fiscal feudalism, as these methods during wartime were historically valid, but they were naturally unpopular. It was, possibly, a cold and calculating move by the king that he could claim ignorance of Wolsey's revenue-gathering schemes.

The King's Great Matter

For nearly fifteen years, from 1515 to 1529, Wolsey was the virtual ruler of the realm – or at least that was the impression held by contemporaries and promoted by the king. But there was one thing that even the great cardinal could not accomplish: securing an annulment for Henry VIII from his wife, Catherine of Aragon. By 1527, Catherine was in her mid-forties, and, though healthy, was probably no longer fertile. She had provided Henry with a daughter, Mary, in 1516, but only four of her seven pregnancies were brought to term, and none produced a male heir who lived more than a matter of weeks. Henry believed it was essential that the heir to the Tudor throne be a male, as the rule of a woman would subvert the great chain of being and quite possibly place the new dynasty at risk of usurpation by a male claimant.[5] Henry also accepted that his own fertility was not at issue; he had successfully fathered an illegitimate son, Henry FitzRoy (literally "son of the king"), with his mistress Elizabeth Blount, in 1519. This son, however, could not inherit the throne by virtue of his bastardy. The only solution, to Henry, was remarriage to a younger woman who could provide him with a legitimate son.

Although divorce, as the term is generally understood today, was illegal by canon law, it was not unusual especially for wealthy families to secure annulments, in essence a declaration from the church that the marriage had not been validly contracted and was, therefore, illegitimate. Gaining such a concession would have meant that Henry could remove Mary from the line of succession and was free to remarry. He had already set his sights on a young lady-in-waiting named Anne Boleyn, who had refused to become his mistress but was quite content to become his new wife, should the opportunity arise. Henry also had a reasonably valid legal argument, perhaps presented to him by Wolsey. According to Leviticus 20:21, a man who had sexual relations with his brother's wife, as Catherine had been for a matter of months, would be childless, which it was easy to interpret meant incapable of producing a living, male heir. In fact, because of this biblical injunction, Henry's marriage to Catherine had required a papal dispensation which, Henry and Wolsey would later argue, the pope did not have the authority to give, as it was a matter of divine rather than canon law. Catherine would later claim that she and Arthur had not consummated their marriage, which meant she was never technically his wife, although this argument had little effect.

To handle the logistics of what should have been a fairly straightforward annulment (both of Henry's sisters had secured annulments before these events), Henry turned to Wolsey, his lord chancellor, leading churchman, and papal representative, a position which he was granted in 1518. There was, however, a pressing diplomatic problem. In 1527, imperial forces on behalf of Charles V sacked Rome and took the pope, Clement VII, captive. Emperor Charles V, the pope's jailor, also happened to be the nephew of Catherine of Aragon and consequently disapproved of the annulment. So long as this situation continued, the pope could not permit the usual procedure in a case such as this, which would have been to allow Wolsey to hear the case in England. Instead, to slow down the proceedings and appease the emperor, in 1528 the pope sent his own representative, Cardinal Campeggio, to London to hear the case. Following his orders, Campeggio prevaricated and delayed the hearings until May 1529, at which point Catherine – who had plenty of time to prepare her case – made a powerful argument against the

---

5   Arguably, England had only once before been ruled by a woman, Matilda, in 1141, although she was never formally crowned.

annulment and, as a royal personage, demanded the right to have the case heard by the pope himself, rather than a mere representative. Before that issue could be resolved, Campeggio ordered a stay in the proceedings, arguing that it was necessary for the court to follow the papal court calendar, which did not sit during the summer months. As the imperial forces continued to make gains in Italy, the pope recalled the case to Rome, another delay tactic that would not, Henry had become convinced, result in an annulment from Catherine.

Campeggio's departure also signaled the end of Wolsey. He had failed to accomplish the one thing that, as cardinal and legate, should have been an easy victory, and pressure from the Boleyn faction plus immense pressure from Wolsey's detractors began breaking down the king's support of his principal minister. The final straw came when Wolsey advised Henry not to ally with France against the Empire, which Henry saw as the only sure way to secure his annulment. He allowed Wolsey to be charged at the Court of King's Bench with *praeminure*, a medieval statute that prevented foreign powers from interfering with the king's authority. With a new parliament summoned for November 1529, Wolsey became concerned that he would be convicted by attainder, the consequences of which would have been execution. Instead, he pleaded guilty to the *praeminure* charge and was dismissed as chancellor and stripped of all other offices except the archdiocese of York. Hampton Court was seized and became Henry's main residence for the remainder of his reign. Wolsey traveled to Cawood Castle, near York, but evidence that he was negotiating with agents in Europe soon brought a charge of treason. On his way back to London to answer the charge, Wolsey fell ill and died, saving himself from the indignity of beheading that would have been the probable outcome otherwise.

The Reformation Parliament

Wolsey's failure to secure the king's annulment and developments in European politics had, by 1529, convinced Henry VIII that if he was to secure his divorce it would take more aggressive, nonconventional measures. It is in these measures that we see the beginnings of the reformation of the English church. Wolsey's replacement as chancellor was Thomas More who, for several reasons, preferred not to get involved in the divorce proceedings. Henry instead relied on the advice of another protégé of Wolsey's, Thomas Cromwell, who like More came from humble beginnings to make his name in law, serving as a member of parliament and councillor to the king. In both capacities, Cromwell became a leader of parliamentary religious reform.

Henry called parliament, his first in five years, in November 1529, with the intention that it help resolve various financial issues, but also that it address abuses allegedly committed by the English clergy. For good reason, this

parliament, which sat intermittently for seven years, is known as the "Reformation Parliament." In the early stages of reform, there were no plans to break with
Rome, nor, except for a vocal few – such as Simon Fish in his *Supplication for
the Beggars* (1530) – to move toward a "heretical" religion such as Lutheranism.
But there were plenty of concerns about the church that could be addressed. As
seen in the example of Wolsey, many clergymen were pluralists, serving multiple
dioceses and parishes, which also caused absenteeism, because a priest holding
multiple positions could only be in one place at a time. There were also criti-
cisms about the number of priests and nuns in monastic orders, who cloistered
themselves off from society. Together, pluralism, absenteeism, and monasticism
made some members of the clergy immensely wealthy, while also ensuring that
many priests did not actively minister to the English people. It was argued that
priests also charged excessive fees for their services in probating wills, arranging
funerals, and exacting fines in ecclesiastical courts. The Latin mass and absence
of an English-language Bible also meant that few commoners could actively
participate in their religion.

There was also the fact that the entire priesthood was, in Henry's mind, guilty
of *praeminure*, by listening to the orders of Cardinal Wolsey and the church in
Rome, and by paying annates, the first year's revenue of a new ecclesiastical position, to the pope. Henry charged the entire English clergy with *praeminure* and
only pardoned them when they submitted to his authority and paid a substantial
fine. In their submission of 1532, the clergy, through its legislative body known
as convocation, also acknowledged that Henry was "singular protector, only and
supreme lord and, as far as the law of Christ allows, even supreme head." This
submission provided Cromwell with the ability to push a flurry of legislation
through parliament, signaling something of a change in parliament's historical
practices – by legislating matters relating to religion – that would become an
issue in later decades.

Henry and Cromwell were helped in their efforts by the death in 1532 of
Archbishop of Canterbury William Warham. This allowed Henry to place the
acquiescent Thomas Cranmer, who was more favorable to the annulment, into
the position of being the highest prelate in the realm. To ensure that Cranmer
had the unfettered power to hear the annulment case, Cromwell had parliament pass the Act in Restraint of Appeals. This act declared that "this realm
of England is an empire, ... governed by one supreme head and king having
the dignity and royal estate of the imperial crown." In essence Henry claimed
"imperial" – absolute – authority to govern his realm without deference to any
other being except God. Convocation duly submitted to this authority, prompting More to resign the chancellorship, ostensibly because of his health but
clearly in protest. More was humanist enough to seek reform of clerical abuses
and other deficiencies of the church, but he could not so easily throw off the
authority of the Roman Catholic Church in England and accept his king as its

head. Although Cromwell did not step into the chancellorship, he indisputably became Henry's principal minister.[6]

The passage of the Act in Restraint of Appeals had the immediate effect of denying Catherine the ability to appeal her case to Rome, as she had attempted during the Campeggio hearing. This meant that Cranmer now had the authority to hear the case and issue the annulment that Henry and the Boleyn faction had sought for nearly six years. Cranmer promptly assembled a tribunal that declared the marriage illegitimate. This was just in time, as Cranmer had already secretly married Henry and Anne in January 1533 and by the time Anne was crowned queen, she was already six or seven months pregnant. Unfortunately for Henry, the child born in September was a girl, Elizabeth Tudor. But Anne was young, healthy, and obviously fertile, so although Henry was initially despondent, he had every reason to believe that she would bear him a healthy boy to inherit the crown. As we shall see, this did not turn out to be true.

Four parliamentary acts followed in 1534: those of Succession, Supremacy, Treason, and Annates. These acts declared Mary illegitimate, placed the succession into the children born of Anne, made the king the supreme head of the English Church, made it an act of treason to deny these facts, and abolished the payment of annates to Rome. The supremacy, in particular, was quite radical for the time. The idea that the pope was not the head of the church and that the church was instead headed by the king – a secular authority – was not one that everybody could accept. The requirement for all clergy, professionals, gentlemen, and nobles to swear oaths that acknowledged the succession and supremacy was a bitter pill for many to swallow. Most did swear the oaths: out of fear for their lives, offices, titles, and lands; because they held a genuine belief that the church needed reform; or because they did not much care who headed the church. The clergy, of course, had already acknowledged Henry's superior position two years earlier.

Thomas More refused to swear to the supremacy and the succession, which enabled his enemies to charge him under the treason act. He was tried before a panel of judges that included Anne's father, brother, and uncle in July 1535. Although More elected not to respond to certain questions, hoping that his silence would not be viewed as an explicit denial of the supremacy, Cromwell produced a witness, solicitor general Richard Rich, who claimed he had personally heard More deny that the king was supreme head of the church. Given the composition of the tribunal, this was sufficient evidence to secure a conviction. More was sentenced to be hanged, drawn, and quartered – a common method of capital punishment used for traitors – but in deference to his former offices, the sentence was commuted to beheading, a swifter and more dignified death

---

6   Cromwell was the precursor to a position that became known later in the sixteenth century as secretary of state.

normally reserved for members of the nobility. More's head was placed on a pike over London Bridge as a warning to other would-be traitors.[7] By the end of Henry's reign, many others – mostly clerics decrying the supremacy from the pulpit – would follow him into martyrdom. A final act of 1536 extinguishing any and all authority of the pope in England brought the momentous Reformation Parliament to an end.

* * *

Discussion Question 2.2: What purposes were served by the English Reformation occurring by acts of parliament, rather than being ordered by the king?

The Reforms of Cromwell and Cranmer

Although the Reformation Parliament had accomplished a great deal, the reform of the church was not yet over. Cromwell was named to the new position of vicegerent in ecclesiastical matters, in effect becoming the king's deputy head of the church. With Cranmer, Cromwell supported the printing in 1536 of the Ten Articles, which contained both Lutheran and Catholic elements. For example, the Articles accepted the Catholic doctrine of transubstantiation, whereby the bread and wine consumed at the altar during the eucharist take on the "whole substance" of Christ's body and blood, while the outward appearance remained unaltered. Lutherans, by contrast, explicitly rejected transubstantiation, arguing that the bread and wine comingled with Christ's body and blood, in what was known as a "sacramental union."

But the Articles also accepted the necessity of only three sacraments – the eucharist, baptism, and penance (confession) – without mention of the other four sacraments required by the Catholic Church – confirmation, last rites, holy orders, and matrimony – which in Lutheranism were considered rites that were not necessary for salvation. Taking another Lutheran stance, the Articles accepted that images and statues of saints were symbolic for remembrance, but that they should not, in and of themselves, be venerated as objects of worship. Finally, the Articles claimed that prayers for the dead were useful to speed their time in purgatory, but that papal pardon had no utility. This was a position that reflected Luther's attack against granting of indulgences, which England adopted because of its anti-papal position.

---

7   On the four-hundredth anniversary of his martyrdom (1935), More was canonized by Pope Leo XIII. His feast day is celebrated each year on July 6, the day of his execution.

Using the Ten Articles as his marching orders for reform, but in fact going well above their mandate, Cromwell issued a series of injunctions, enforced by several traveling commissions and visitations, in which he initiated a number of ecclesiastical reforms. These included the introduction of the "Great Bible" in 1539, an English-language version written by Miles Coverdale, and instructions that ordered parents and masters to teach their subordinates the Lord's prayer and the ten commandments. In essence, Cromwell's reforms could be seen to have placed the interpretation of scripture into the hands of laypeople, a Lutheran idea that was not preferred by Catholics. Books and treatises that were too "popish" were outright destroyed; this action had devastating effects on the university libraries, which were populated primarily by orthodox religious texts. Several sets of injunctions and visitations by commissioners occurred over the next few years, during which there were various outbreaks of iconoclasm. Images, icons, statues, shrines, and relics – especially those that smacked of popery and idolatry – were removed from churches and sometimes destroyed. The issuance in 1537 of *The Institution of a Christian Man*, better known as the *Bishops' Book*, supported a number of these initiatives, while also better explaining the role of the four sacraments left out of the Ten Articles.

Perhaps the most significant of Cromwell's reforms as vicegerent involved the dissolution of the monasteries, beginning in 1536. As noted, one of the grievances against the clergy was their tendency to cloister themselves off from the world. By the mid-1530s, there were nearly 900 religious houses in England, including monasteries, convents, and friaries, housing about 12,000 men and women who did not provide religious services to laypeople. One of the chief critics of monasticism was Erasmus. He argued that members of religious houses were lazy and self-centered, contributed little to the spiritual needs of the laity, and lived in shrines that contained idols and relics that were either false or deserved to be seen by ordinary people. All these concerns were confirmed, and probably somewhat exaggerated, by Cromwell's servants who visited the monasteries and other religious houses. Because monasticism often involved the copying out of canonical Catholic texts, it was also believed to be a chief cause of the older brand of education, scholasticism, which was being increasingly challenged by the new form, humanism.

Moreover, these institutions sat on about 15 per cent of the land in England, land that brought in a tremendous fortune for the cloistered clergy but was not taxed in the usual manner, nor was enough of it used to distribute as charitable alms. In dissolving the monasteries, therefore, Henry could send the clergy out among the people while at the same time claiming all their considerable property and land as part of the crown's possessions. Another significant impact of the dissolution was the removal of the abbots from the House of Lords, which reduced the spiritual lords to about twenty-five and – importantly for the reforms yet to come – ensured that the temporal peerage had numerical supremacy in that body. Those monastic houses that were allowed to remain were required to pay substantial fines to the crown in exchange for exemption from dissolution.

Cromwell even created a new government body, the Court of Augmentations, to administer the financial windfall that roughly doubled Henry's royal revenues and enabled him, for a time, to live the life due a great Renaissance prince in a now-enlarged Hampton Court Palace, which became a prime symbol of a wealthy and powerful Renaissance monarchy. By the end of his reign, however, Henry had been forced to sell a large portion of monastic lands to pay for wars and campaigns, with the result that he ultimately died in debt.

Reactions to Reform

These changes to religion caused some reaction among the English populace, though not as much as one might expect. From a doctrinal and ceremonial perspective, few ordinary people in England would have noticed much difference in their religious observance, and most would not have much cared that the king, rather than the pope, was now the head of their church. Besides the supremacy, the key changes – reducing clerical abuses, limiting the gluttonous and avaricious lives of the senior clergy, as exemplified by Wolsey's lifestyle, and introducing vernacular texts – were reforms that most laypeople would have seen as practical and necessary. Bursts of iconoclasm were surely noticed, but these efforts at reform did not, as we shall see, last very long. Indeed, reform in the church had been ongoing, on a slow evolutionary basis, for more than a century. Although the Reformation under Henry was decidedly an act of state, carried out by the king, his councillors, and parliament, rather than a groundswell popular movement that developed from widespread discontent over the church, the common people were also not so fervently faithful that they could not accept change and compromise, especially in areas of worship that did not jeopardize their salvation.

The major exception to the otherwise muted reaction to religious reform came in the form of an uprising known as the Pilgrimage of Grace. By the end of 1536, when the reform-minded Ten Articles had recently been published and the monasteries were being dissolved and their property claimed by the crown, discontent fomented in the northern parts of England. The participants in the uprising, led by a country gentleman named Robert Aske, wore badges depicting the Five Wounds of Christ and produced a list of grievances known as the Pontefract Articles. The articles listed twenty-four demands made by the pilgrims, including restoration of the pope, the legitimization of Princess Mary, the return of the monasteries and their property, and the impeachment of Cromwell. All of these would suggest that the pilgrims had serious concerns about the religious reforms that had taken place since 1531.

In fact, however, the majority of the articles cited demands that had nothing to do with religion, such as bringing about changes in how members of parliament were elected and grievances about new methods of taxation and the ongoing process of enclosing common lands, which negatively affected the gentry and yeomanry. Despite the pilgrims' ostensible purpose of reversing religious reforms, the Pilgrimage of Grace was mostly an indictment of the many Tudor policies that managed, over the past half century, to centralize royal authority, increase crown revenue streams, and limit provincialism that had been especially strong in the remote northern part of the kingdom. Although the king's representative, the duke of Norfolk, failed to suppress the uprisings in 1536, another series of outbreaks in the spring of 1537 was decisively handled by the king and resulted in the execution of Aske and nearly 200 other rebels.

Despite the secularized concerns of the Pilgrimage, it did encourage Henry to reflect on the changes to religion that Cromwell and Cranmer had brought about. At Henry's direction, parliament issued the Six Articles (1539) – otherwise known as An Act Abolishing Diversity in Opinions – to reverse some of the more evangelical elements and affirm that England, though without a pope, was still Catholic. Henry was, after all, the principal author of *Defense of the Seven Sacraments*, which had earned him the title of *Fidei defensor* (Defender of the Faith) from Leo X, a title still used in the English monarch's full styling to the present day.[8] The fact that the Six Articles was issued not as a statement of faith so much as a penal statute threatening felony punishment for those who refused its directions shows that the king was serious both about restoring traditional Catholicism and about impeding subsequent reform. In the ensuing years, a number of Protestant reformers, such as Anne Askew, were burned at the stake for heresy because of this statute (see **Voices of the Past**: **The Execution of Anne Askew**). The Six Articles, together with the *King's Book* (1543) – a highly revised version of the *Bishops' Book* – serves as a reminder that Cromwell, ultimately to his detriment, leaned more toward doctrinal reformation than the king and court had ever intended.

The brand of religion in England after 1538, therefore, was what might be referred to as "Henrician Catholicism," because whatever efforts certain people took to move the nation toward Protestantism in the ensuing decade were thwarted by a king who was decidedly of the old faith, even if he had thrown off the yoke of Rome. It is possible that Henry was merely being cautious, and that his effort to retain Catholicism was more about appeasing the powerful conservative nobility and certain foreign powers, such as the emperor, than about his personal religious beliefs. Some evidence that he was involved in early drafts of the Ten Articles lends support to that argument. But Henry was also a monarch used to getting his way; had he truly wanted reform, he very likely would have worked hard to achieve it and dealt decisively with those who challenged his authority, so it seems most likely that he was, after all, of a Catholic mindset. Whatever the case, especially

---

8   The title was revoked upon Henry's excommunication but was restored by parliament in 1544, with the monarch now seen as defender of the English church.

after 1538, Henry refused to allow Lutheran reforms to enter England, even though he later considered a military alliance with the Lutheran princes of Germany.

The Fall and Legacy of Cromwell

By 1536, Henry VIII was forty-five years old, the age at which, by the standards of the early modern period, adults entered their elder years. Henry also appeared older than he was. He had by then taken on the physical characteristics that, today, have come to be most associated with him – morbid obesity and serious gout because of extravagant living – such that he sometimes had to be carried about on a litter. More seriously for the aging monarch, Henry still did not have a legitimate son to inherit his throne. Queen Anne had miscarried a boy in January of that year and, at thirty-five years old, her chances of producing a live male heir were decreasing. Anne had also developed some enemies at court, not least of whom was Cromwell, who, at Anne's instruction, had been recently attacked in a sermon given by the queen's chaplain because of his approach to dissolving the monasteries.

At Henry's instigation, Cromwell undertook an investigation of Anne that soon led to a charge of adultery. Although adultery was not a particularly serious crime and was not unusual among the upper ranks of English society, Anne and her alleged lovers were charged with treason, because of the threat to the realm if Anne had become pregnant with another man's son. Using strong interrogation methods, Cromwell managed to get one of Anne's court musicians, Mark Smeaton, to confess to an illicit affair with the queen. Within days, several other courtiers were rounded up and interrogated, including Anne's own brother, George, viscount Rochford. After a brief trial, Anne, her brother, and four others were beheaded at the Tower of London in May 1536. Henry's marriage to Anne was declared invalid and Princess Elizabeth was bastardized.[9]

Eleven days later after the execution, Henry wed his current infatuation, Jane Seymour, who had been one of Anne's ladies-in-waiting. The marriage was short lived. Jane gave birth, much to Henry's delight, to a son, Edward, in October 1537, but she died from complications associated with the birth a few days later. With an heir to the throne firmly, and finally, established, Cromwell saw the opportunity for a political marriage and arranged for Henry to court Anne of Cleves. Anne was the sister of a powerful German duke who, though himself Catholic, was entertaining the idea of joining a league of Lutheran princes to protect himself against the pope (who had recently excommunicated Henry) and emperor. Cromwell dispatched Hans Holbein, England's most famous portrait painter, to travel to

---

9   Conveniently for Henry, Catherine of Aragon had died in January 1536, which prevented her supporters from advocating for a remarriage or from challenging the king's marriage to Jane.

Germany and return with a painting of Anne. On the basis of the painting, which was evidently too flattering, Henry agreed to marry Anne, but upon seeing her in person in Rochester in 1540, the king was repulsed. He went through with the marriage because it was already contracted and because the success of a foreign treaty depended on it, but Cromwell was now in the line of fire. The association of the marriage and treaty with Lutheranism, plus Cromwell's effecting of broader religious reform than Henry was comfortable with, and the efforts of his many enemies at court, ultimately led to his arrest for treason and heresy in June 1540. Cromwell was attainted by parliament, convicted, and executed at the Tower in July. As was common of traitors, his head was placed on a pike on London Bridge.

Cromwell's execution brought an unfortunate end to a man who, according to historian G.R. Elton, engineered a "revolution in government" in the 1530s.[10] Although most historians today see Cromwell's contributions as less revolutionary than they appeared to Elton, nonetheless under Cromwell's leadership the English state did become more bureaucratic and professional and began exhibiting modern characteristics. For example, the administration of the erastian (state-run) church and the increased royal revenues from crown lands required more rigorous national infrastructure. In addition, Henry's council became a smaller and more private body of officeholders, rather like a modern ministerial cabinet. Cromwell also tightened the relationship between the central government and the provinces by appointing hundreds of local office holders who owed allegiance to the crown and further reducing the ability of nobles to retain affinities. However, many of these reforms were initiated under the Yorkists and especially under Henry VII, making them evolutionary rather than revolutionary developments. Furthermore, the degree to which Cromwell himself was involved in these changes and how deliberate he was in introducing them are still questions engaged by historians.

Cromwell was also instrumental in ensuring that the authority of Tudor kings reasserted under Henry VII remained supreme. A good illustration of this is the passage in 1539 of the parliamentary statute known formally as the Proclamation by the Crown Act and informally as the *Lex regia* (Law of the Crown). Although the king had always had the power to issue proclamations on various subjects, normally this reflected prerogative powers of the king that were outside of parliamentary jurisdiction, such as the regulation of trade and the declaration of war and peace. *Lex regia*, by contrast, allowed the king's proclamations – provided they were issued with the advice of his council and did not extend to the taking of life or property – to have the force of statute and be enforced by the government and courts as if they were passed by parliament. In a continuation of the "abuse" of parliament that had begun when it was called to reform

---

10 G.R. Elton, *The Tudor Revolution in Government* (Cambridge: Cambridge University Press, 1967).

religion, this act furthered the process of what has been referred to as "Tudor despotism." Although the act was repealed shortly after Henry's death in 1547, possibly because the new king was a child, it set the tone for the controversial nature of proclamations that would lead to crisis in the seventeenth century.

In the few years before his death, Cromwell had also initiated policies that sought to bring unity to Britain and establish Henry as an imperial monarch. In theory, the rulers of Ireland, Scotland, and Wales all owed allegiance and homage to the king of England, primarily as a result of various gains during the reign of Edward I (r. 1272–1307). Their remoteness, combined with a century or more of weak kingship and strong provincialism, had resulted in limited English authority in these far-flung parts of the historical empire. Regarding Wales, Cromwell initiated a series of laws that abolished the "Marcher lordships" – borderland English authorities that governed Wales – and united England and Wales together. English laws became operative in Wales, and Welsh subjects were given positions in the English parliament, to represent their constituencies. To administer Wales, parliament passed an act that gave legislative recognition to a less formal body that had been operating since 1472, the Council of Wales and the Marches.

Following a series of uprisings, Cromwell and Henry decided in 1535 that Ireland would be governed by an English deputy, who maintained a well-equipped and expensive garrison in Dublin to limit further violence. Following Cromwell's execution, the deputy in Ireland helped to steer the issue of the religious supremacy through the Irish parliament and had that body, in 1541, recognize Henry as "king of Ireland." Irish Gaelic chieftains were required to surrender their lands and titles to Henry, who would then regrant them using his regal authority. In Scotland, Henry's nephew King James V (the son of Margaret Tudor and James IV) refused to break from Rome and accept Henry's supremacy. This refusal forced Henry to send an army into Scotland, where the Scots suffered defeat at the Battle of Solway Moss. James died shortly thereafter, leaving the throne to his six-day-old daughter, Mary, Queen of Scots. Scotland was, until Mary came of age, ruled by regents who agreed in the Treaty of Greenwich (1543) that Mary would, at the age of ten, wed Henry's heir, Edward, which would dynastically unite the realms. When Scotland repudiated the treaty, Henry sent his former brother-in-law, Edward Seymour, earl of Hertford, to invade Scotland, a campaign known as the "Rough Wooing." In sum, by the end of Henry's life, imperial authority, albeit in a fashion that still needed strengthening in subsequent decades, had been reasserted after two centuries of apathy.

***

Discussion Question 2.3: Henry VIII ultimately expressed regret for allowing Thomas Cromwell to be executed, yet he did little to prevent it. Why do you think this was the case?

Succession, Death, and Legacy

In 1540, with the political situation in Europe altered and an alliance with the Lutheran princes no longer an issue, Henry swiftly secured an annulment from Anne of Cleves, a matter made easier by Henry's claim that the marriage was never consummated. Once again, he had fallen in love with a younger woman, this time Catherine Howard, niece of the powerful Thomas Howard, duke of Norfolk. Henry and Catherine were married in July 1540, but this was yet another brief marriage. By spring 1541, Catherine began a romance with a courtier, Thomas Culpeper, which was revealed by Lady Rochford, the former sister-in-law to Anne Boleyn, and later by a letter found in Culpeper's private quarters. Catherine was imprisoned, Culpeper and another lover from before the marriage were identified and executed for high treason – the usual punishment for which was being hanged, drawn, and quartered – and Catherine was convicted by parliamentary attainder in January 1542. The fifth of Henry's wives was executed at the Tower the following month.

Henry married for the last time in July 1543, to Catherine Parr, who managed to outlive him.[11] A little older than thirty at the time of the marriage, Catherine was probably Henry's best match as wife. She was patient with her husband, served as an effective regent while Henry was away fighting a costly war in France, and encouraged the king to reconcile with his daughters and return them to the line of succession. In 1544, another succession act declared Edward heir to the throne, which merely respected the historical precedent of male primogeniture (first-born son), but made Mary and Elizabeth second and third in line. Henry presumably anticipated that Edward would grow into a man, marry, and have children of his own, making the succession of his daughters merely a matter of form. He could not have known that, ultimately, both of his daughters would take their turns as regnant queens of England. If all his children died without issue, the crown was to pass to the children of his sister, Mary, whose husband was Charles Brandon, duke of Suffolk. Importantly, the succession conveniently passed over Henry's sister Margaret even though she was older than Mary. Margaret's granddaughter, Mary Queen of Scots, was, therefore, silently removed from the line of succession, although ultimately her son would assume the English throne.

By the end of 1546, it was clear that Henry was near death. In December, one month before he finally succumbed, he revised his last will and testament. It restated the restored order of succession and, because Edward was a nine-year-old boy, established a regency council to rule England until the king came of age. The council consisted of sixteen men, including Thomas Cranmer and the two chief

---

11 Thus the mnemonic to remember Henry's wives: "Divorced, beheaded, died/divorced, beheaded, survived."

justices of the law courts. The composition of the rest of the council was very unusual. It included five Catholics, several men who were considered religiously neutral, and six men who were almost certainly Protestant, or at any rate of a humanist-reformed disposition. This was an unexpected move for a king who, several times between 1536 and 1543, took active steps to ensure that doctrinal reform was not introduced into the English church. Perhaps Henry felt that reform was inevitable and wanted to place into power the men most likely to bring about a religion he could tolerate. Perhaps he perceived the noble Catholic families to be a greater threat to his son's minority than the reformed men he named to the council, or that his two greatest legacies as king – the royal supremacy of the church and emergence of the king as emperor within his own kingdom – would be reversed by a council that had the power to invite the return of the pope. It is also possible that Henry saw the council as so perfectly balanced in terms of faith that they would maintain the status quo he had worked so hard to achieve.

Henry VIII has often been described as the model Renaissance monarch. By the end of his reign, England had emerged as an imperial, centralized nation that had been run by secular authorities, such as More and Cromwell. Its royal house was secure, celebrated the magnificence of divine-right monarchy in palaces such as Hampton Court, and was wealthy and powerful enough to reward loyalty and punish enemies, both of which Henry did prodigiously. These characteristics combined to create what is often referred to as the rise of the early modern "nation state," a status also achieved at this time by, for example, France and Spain, as opposed to the disunity and provincialism that came to characterize Italy and the Holy Roman Empire by the late sixteenth century. Henry also displayed numerous characteristics that reflected Niccolò Machiavelli's ideal "prince." He was intelligent, religious, gave the appearance of being merciful, and employed wise, secular councillors. But he was also selfish, deceitful, militant, and ruthless to his enemies. He was, in short, both feared and loved, outwardly wise and kind, inwardly shrewd and plotting. It is possible that Henry was given a copy of Machiavelli's *The Prince* by Thomas Cromwell around the time of its first printing, in 1532. Whether Henry saw himself reflected in Machiavelli's words, or actively sought to emulate them in the last fifteen years of his reign, there is little doubt that Henry's style of rule would have pleased the Italian statesman.

* * *

Discussion Question 2.4: Can you think of reasons why Henry VIII chose a regency council to govern during his son's minority, rather than appoint a single lord protector, as had happened in the past?

VOICES OF THE PAST
THE EXECUTION OF ANNE ASKEW

In the last decade of Henry's reign, England was divided between religious traditionalists, who preferred Catholic rituals despite the break from Rome, and reformers, who sought Lutheran-minded Protestantism. At the royal court, the traditionalists held sway, largely because of political and diplomatic considerations, and began arresting and examining men and women who strongly advocated reform. One such reformer was Anne Askew, a poet who had become estranged from her husband because of her religious views. After her arrest in June 1546, Askew was tortured in the Tower but she refused to recant her beliefs. She was then convicted of heresy and condemned to be burned at the stake, making Askew one of the first English women to be executed in the name of religious reform. The following extract describes Anne's torture and death.

* * *

Touching the order of her racking in the Tower, thus it was. First she was led down into a dungeon, where Sir Anthony Knevet, the lieutenant, commanded his gaoler to pinch her with the rack. Which being done so much as he thought sufficient, [he] went about to take her down, supposing he had done enough. But [Thomas] Wriothesley [pronounced "Risley"], the lord chancellor, not contented that she was loosed too soon confessing nothing, commanded the lieutenant to stretch her on the rack again. Which because he denied to do, tendering the weakness of the woman, he was threatened therefore grievously of the said Wriothesley, saying that he would signify his disobedience unto the king. And so,

consequently, upon the same, he and Sir John Baker throwing off their gowns, would needs play the tormentors themselves, first asking her if she was with child. To whom she answering again, said, "Ye shall not need to spare for that, but do your evils upon me." And so quietly and patiently praying unto the Lord, she abided their tyranny, till her bones and joints almost were plucked asunder, in such sort, as she was carried away in a chair....

Now it remaineth that we touch somewhat as concerning her end and martyrdom. After that she, being born of such stock and kindred that she might have lived in great wealth and prosperity, if she would rather have followed the world than Christ, now had been so tormented, that she could neither live long in so great distress, neither yet by her adversaries be suffered to die in secret. The day of her execution being appointed, she was brought into Smithfield in a chair, because she could not go on her feet, by means of her great torments. When she was brought unto the stake, she was tied by the middle with a chain, that held up her body. When all things were thus prepared to the fire, Dr. Shaxton, who was then appointed to preach, began his sermon. Anne Askew, hearing and answering again unto him, where he said well, confirmed the same; where he said amiss, "There," said she, "he misseth, and speaketh without the book."

The sermon being finished, the martyrs [Anne, John Lacelles, John Adams, and Nicholas Belenian], standing there tied at three several stakes ready to enter their martyrdom, began their prayers. The multitude and concourse of people was exceeding; the place where they stood being railed about to keep out the press. Upon the bench under St. Bartholomew's church sat Wriothesley, chancellor of England; the old duke of Norfolk, the old earl of Bedford, [and] the lord mayor, with divers others. Before the fire should be set upon them, one of the bench, hearing that they had gunpowder about them, and being alarmed lest the faggots [bundles of sticks], by strength of the gunpowder, would come flying about their ears, began to be afraid; but the earl of Bedford, declaring unto him how the gunpowder was not laid under the faggots, but only about their bodies, to rid them of their pain, which having vent, there was no danger to them of the faggots, so diminished that fear.[12]

Then Wriothesley, lord chancellor, sent to Anne Askew letters, offering her the king's pardon if she would recant; who, refusing once to look upon them, made this answer again, that she came not hither to deny her Lord and Master. Then were the letters likewise offered unto the others, who, in like manner, following the constancy of the woman, denied not only to receive them, but also to look upon them. Whereupon the lord mayor, commanding fire to be put unto them, cried with a loud voice "Fiat Justitia" [let justice be done].

And thus the good Anne Askew, with these blessed martyrs, being troubled so many manner of ways, and having passed through so many torments, having now ended the long course of their agonies, being compassed with flames of fire, as a blessed sacrifice unto God, she slept with the Lord A.D. 1546, leaving behind her a singular example of Christian constancy for all men to follow.

Source: John Foxe, *Acts and Monuments* (London, 1570), 1419–20.

* * *

Discussion Question 2.5: Why was it important that the execution of Anne and the others be witnessed by a "multitude" of people? Why were the condemned first offered the opportunity to recant?

---

12 Pouches of gunpowder were often strapped to the bodies or necks of those about to be burned, in order to hasten their death and, therefore, reduce suffering.

CHAPTER THREE

PROTESTANTS AND CATHOLICS, 1547–1558

DEATH AND DISORDER:
THE PRAYER BOOK REBELLION

With the exception of the Pilgrimage of Grace, which, as we have seen, was not entirely motivated by religion, reactions to religious reform under Henry VIII had not brought about much disorder in England. The same cannot be said of reforms during the mid-Tudor period. Almost immediately upon the accession of Edward VI, both church and state moved decisively toward Protestant religious reform. These reforms were met with considerable resistance, especially in the Catholic stronghold of Cornwall, in southwest England. For instance, in 1548, the task of removing Catholic symbols throughout Cornwall was given to Archdeacon William Body. When, in April of that year, Body tried to confiscate church property in Helston, he was confronted by an angry mob and stabbed to death. The two men most directly involved in Body's murder, William Kylter and Pascoe Trevian, were found guilty of treason and hanged, drawn, and quartered, while several others were merely hanged.

The following year, Archbishop Cranmer's English-language and Lutheran-leaning *Book of Common Prayer* became England's official book of worship and was required to be used in all parishes beginning on Whitsunday, in early June. This order prompted hundreds of Cornish men – who feared for the loss of their religion and their Cornish language – led by Sir Humphrey Arundell, to gather and protest the government's policy and demand that the traditional Catholic mass be spoken in Latin. As the rebels grew in number and conviction – marching under the motto "kill all the gentlemen" because the gentry were charged with enforcing new government policies – they ransacked several gentry homes, moved east into Devon, and presented their *Demands of the Western Rebels* to Cranmer, who promptly dismissed them.

As the rebels moved past Plymouth, the government sent Sir Peter Carew to negotiate with the rebels in Crediton, near Exeter, but his men were forced to retreat after being attacked by rebels wielding longbows. As the rebels laid siege to Exeter, John Russell, England's lord high steward, arrived in early July with a force of about 1,200 soldiers and arquebusiers (who carried matchlock rifles) and engaged in an inconclusive battle with Arundell's rebels that resulted in about 600 deaths. By August, Russell's force had grown to more than 5,000 men, which met Arundell's contingent of 6,000 at the Battle of Clyst St. Mary. More than 1,000 Cornish and Devonian men were killed and, at Russell's command, an additional 900 prisoners were massacred, allegedly in the course of ten minutes, by having their throats slit. The following day, at the Battle of Clyst Heath, Russell's men killed another 2,000 rebels; two weeks later, at the Battle of Sampford Courtenay, with Russell's forces outnumbering Arundell's at least five to one, they killed another 1,200, either during the battle or when Russell's forces pursued the retreating rebels. Arundell was eventually captured and executed by public hanging in January 1550.

At least 5,000 West Country men lost their lives during the Prayer Book Rebellion. For his part in the rebellion, Russell was created earl of Bedford the same month that Arundell was hanged, and two years later he was made lord lieutenant of Devon. Four hundred and sixty years later, in 2007, Bill Ind, bishop of Truro, criticized the handling of the Prayer Book Rebellion, stating that the English government had acted "brutally and stupidly and had killed many Cornish people" and calling the state's response "an enormous mistake."[1] Although the Prayer Book Rebellion was not to be the last rebellion to arise because of religious reform, it was certainly Tudor England's bloodiest and most disorderly uprising.

✳ ✳ ✳

Discussion Question 3.1: Why do you think that Russell, acting on behalf of the Tudor state, reacted so harshly to the West Country rebels, rather than trying to end the rebellion through more peaceful means?

---

1   "Bishop of Truro Says Sorry for Prayer Book Conflict," Cornwall For Ever/Kernow Bys Vyken, accessed January 2020, https://www.cornwallforever.co.uk/history/bishop-of-truro-says-sorry-for-prayer-book-conflict.

Reform and Rebellion under Somerset

When nine-year-old Edward VI ascended the throne in 1547, he also inherited several problems left behind by his father (see Figure 3.1). War with France and Scotland had depleted crown resources and required the selling off of land that had come from the dissolution of the monasteries, which further reduced annual revenues. The economy was in turmoil because wool was the nation's major export, and the trade was at the mercy of a European market that had many competitors and was in the throes of war. Despite Henry's efforts, religion was still in a state of uncertainty, evidenced in part by the diversity of faith represented on the new king's regency council. It was, naturally, also a problem that Edward, though the recipient of an advanced humanist education and as intellectually and artistically gifted as his father, was nonetheless a boy not yet old enough to rule in his own stead.

With the appointment of a regency council that would make decisions by majority vote, Henry made the deliberate decision not to appoint a single lord protector of the realm during his son's childhood. Lord protectors had been used in England as regents for minor or incapacitated kings since the early fifteenth century, most notably for Henry VI during his minority. Almost immediately, however, Henry's wishes were disregarded and the king's uncle, Edward Seymour, now duke of Somerset, managed to secure letters patent from Edward making him lord protector.[2] In that role, Somerset had virtually regalian powers equal to those of the king, including the right to appoint and dismiss councillors, determine issues of war and peace, and issue proclamations, the latter of which he did prodigiously.

Somerset had no Tudor blood flowing through his veins, nor the intelligence or political shrewdness of a Tudor monarch – the ability to secure loyalty through any means necessary and act decisively when called upon to do so – which quickly threatened the power that the monarchy had managed to acquire since 1485. Government under Somerset degenerated into factionalism, disobedience, and corruption, both because Somerset was the king's maternal uncle rather than a member of the royal family and because he lacked political acumen. An early victory for Somerset was a successful battle against the Scots in a continuation of the Rough Wooing but here, and elsewhere, he proved incapable of following through to bring an end to the conflict and pacify the Scots. As his troops remained garrisoned in Scotland, the Scots managed to move their queen to France, where she married the heir to the French throne (the dauphin), bringing further unity to two of Tudor England's greatest enemies.

Another major initiative of Somerset was religious reform. It is unclear precisely what Somerset's personal religious outlook was, but it is evident that he was well trained in reformist ideologies. Like Henry VIII, Somerset used parliament to secure further reform, giving the changes a semblance of the consent of the governed. Parliament repealed the Six Articles, Henry's restatement of the Catholic faith, in addition to the various laws about heresy. These measures provided a haven for Continental reformers to arrive in England and enabled operators of printing presses to distribute English-language versions of the Bible and the central writings of Protestant reformers, which soon came to dominate debate in the English universities. In 1547, parliament also dissolved the chantries, the religious houses whose priests were responsible to pray for those souls in purgatory.

In 1549, parliament passed an Act of Uniformity, which ordered parishes to use a new *Book of Common Prayer* produced by Archbishop Cranmer. Priests were also allowed to marry, a tenet of Lutheranism that had been explicitly

---

2　Letters patent (always in plural) are documents issued by the king conferring a right or privilege. They are open documents, and their contents are public, as opposed to letters close, whose contents are private.

forbidden by Henry. Somerset also purged the episcopal bench of Catholics, such as Stephen Gardiner, one of the chief supporters of Henrician supremacy and the Catholic-leaning Six Articles, who had provided a counterpoise to the more aggressive reform measures of Cranmer and Cromwell. Gardiner was imprisoned in the Tower of London for the remainder of Edward's reign. New bishops with reformist tendencies, such as Nicholas Ridley, were appointed to fill the bench, while other reformers, such as Hugh Latimer, were given prominent positions as court preachers. Ultimately, these new measures, though causing little disruption among the majority of the populace, pleased few on the extremes: Catholics wanted, at the very least, a return to the religion of Henry VIII, while Protestants imbued with Continental ideas emanating from Switzerland and Geneva pushed for additional reform along Calvinist lines.

The changes in religion merged with various economic concerns to realize two key rebellions in 1549. The first of these was the Prayer Book Rebellion

Figure 3.1 *Edward VI, circa 1547, from the workshop of Master John.*

Credit: Pictorial Press Ltd./Alamy Stock Photo.

that took place in Cornwall and Devon, which, as we have seen, was dominated by Catholics who wanted the traditional Latin mass and Bible, the return of the Six Articles, and the end of renewed bouts of iconoclasm caused by the recent reforms. Another series of rebellions fomented in Norfolk, caused largely by the ongoing process of enclosure. This was the effort of landlords, with the permission of parliament, to fence in common lands, denying tenants the ability to graze animals or gain access to water to irrigate their crops. As farmers increasingly could not survive without these resources, the wealthy began engrossing (buying up) land so that they could raise sheep. Wool was still one of England's few profitable enterprises, but it was also one that did not help to feed the increasing population of sixteenth-century England nor stem the rise in inflation caused by the food shortage resulting from poor harvests. These grievances led, in July 1549, to Kett's Rebellion. Its leader, Robert Kett, was actually a landlord who had enclosed his land, but upon hearing of his tenants' grievances, he joined their cause and tore down his own fences before moving onto those of others. The rebels – numbering around 16,000 – wanted better rental terms, the end of enclosure, and restoration of traditional common rights of grazing, and in some instances a radical demand to end private land ownership.

The simultaneity of the West Country and Kett's rebellions revealed the ineptitude of Somerset, who, it was believed by his detractors, lacked the strength of character to put the uprisings down. Somerset initially appeared sympathetic toward the rebels, encouraging a series of negotiations, with offers of amnesty and redress of grievances in exchange for the laying down of arms. This pacifist response was particularly galling to John Dudley, the earl of Warwick, who claimed that Somerset's cowardly actions bordered on treason. With the help of other privy councillors, Warwick secured a commission from Edward to command a 14,000-men army to deal with the Kett rebels in a manner Somerset seemed unable or unwilling to do. In the end, more than 3,000 rebels were slaughtered in battle, around 50 were executed, and Kett was hanged in chains, a common punishment for treason. As we have seen, the West Country rebels were treated in a similarly heavy-handed manner. By the end of August 1549, both rebellions were over, the rebels decisively defeated.

Warwick's rise also signaled Somerset's fall. Once the rebels had been dealt with, Somerset was arrested largely because of his incompetence and his passive response to the uprisings, and, though allowed to remain on the council, was stripped of his title as protector in 1549. In all but title, Warwick, who soon became duke of Northumberland, essentially stepped into the protectorship through his appointments as lord president of the council, which placed him at the head of the king's body of advisors, and master of the household, which gave him control over the functioning of the royal court. In October 1551, Somerset was accused, probably unjustly, of scheming to overthrow Northumberland and was executed for treason in January 1552.

* * *

Discussion Question 3.2: Why do you think Somerset chose to negotiate with the rebels rather than, in typical Tudor fashion, violently ending the rebellions?

Reform and Succession under Northumberland

Northumberland's biggest challenge was placating a young king who, though uncommonly frail of body and frequently ill, was now a precocious and head-strong teenager within a few years of coming into his majority. In particular, Edward had made it clear that he was a Protestant and wanted even further reform than Somerset had accomplished. This expectation resulted in another rash of religious reforms, starting with the Ordinal of 1550, a book containing the procedures used in the ordination of priests and consecration of bishops. Taking a distinctly Calvinist position, the Ordinal ensured that priests became mere ministers, who were now expected to wear a simple black gown that signified their position as teachers of the gospel. This visibly contrasted with the ornate vestments worn by Catholics. A new prayer book and Act of Uniformity removed stone altars from the church, to be replaced by simple wooden communion tables. Nonconformity and failure to attend church regularly was punishable by fines and imprisonment. Finally, Northumberland saw to the production of the Forty-Two Articles of Faith (1553), a reformed document that supported Luther's justification by faith alone and the Calvinist doctrine of predestination,[3] emphasized the end of mass and the symbolic rather than transubstantiative nature of the lord's supper, and reduced the sacraments to those of baptism and eucharist.

The Forty-Two Articles, written by Cranmer with some consultation, was not issued by royal decree until June 1553, by which time the king's health was in serious decline. He had contracted consumption (tuberculosis) in 1552, followed by a bout of measles, which enabled the tuberculosis to increase in virulence. By March 1553, the king was dying. This presented problems for Northumberland, who had invested a great deal of effort and political capital pushing through Edward's religious reform, which was still so new that it had

---

3   Briefly, Calvinist predestination holds that an individual's election (admission into Heaven) was determined by God before the beginning of time. Thus, the performance of good works, fortune, or chance, do not determine salvation, but one must have faith in God's wisdom in his choice of the elect.

not even taken effect throughout most of the country. Edward's heir, of course, was Princess Mary, who was devoutly Catholic and, given her and her mother's treatment under Henry VIII, would, it was believed, show little mercy to Northumberland, Cranmer, or the Protestant reformers now dominating the episcopal bench and universities. To prevent a return to Catholicism, Mary needed to be removed from the line of succession.

Historians are uncertain about the precise actions taken by Northumberland and Edward in devising a new line of succession to the crown. Some suggest that Edward felt strongly about preserving Protestantism in the realm; believed his two sisters were, in fact, illegitimate, regardless of their return to legitimacy in 1543; and recruited Northumberland to help effect his desires for a Protestant heir to the throne. Others hold that Northumberland styled himself as a kingmaker and created a master plan that he presented *fait accompli* to Edward. Whatever the case, the king appears to have been persuaded that the accession of either of his sisters would cause problems for the realm and the reformed religion. Mary's case, as a Catholic, was rather obvious, but there was also concern that Elizabeth, who was more likely to support Protestantism, would marry a foreign prince, probably a Catholic, who would become king (as was then the custom) and place both the laws of the realm and the reform of religion in jeopardy.

Edward, therefore, drafted a "Devise" for the succession that made Mary and Elizabeth illegitimate and designated Lady Jane Grey – the granddaughter of his aunt Mary – as heir. In doing so, Edward deliberately passed over not only his half-sisters, but also Mary, Queen of Scots (daughter of his aunt Margaret) and Jane's mother, Frances, duchess of Suffolk. In many ways, Jane was a good choice. She was intelligent, a daughter of Tudor blood, and educated in the style of Protestant humanism. At sixteen years old, she was also young, easily managed, and a suitable age for marriage. In May 1553, Northumberland contrived a marriage between his son, Guildford, and Jane, which lends some support to the argument that the "Devise" was of the duke's making. The union would have made Guildford king of England *jure uxoris*[4] upon Jane's accession, establish their children as heirs to the throne, and position Northumberland well in the new administration. Jane, in all likelihood, was unaware of the master strategy at work and was innocent of later claims that she actively sought the throne. On June 21, Edward issued the "Devise" by letters patent, making it a public document, and it was signed by more than one hundred important men, including the entire privy council, judges, nobles, and bishops.

Edward died on July 6 but his death was kept secret for four days, allowing Mary sufficient time to escape into the arms of Catholic supporters. Meanwhile,

4   Men who were *rex jure uxoris*, or "king by right of his wife," shared rule, but the title was extinguished upon the death of the queen.

Jane was proclaimed queen by her supporters in London on July 10 and resided in the Tower of London awaiting her coronation. What Edward, Northumberland, and many of England's officers of state did not anticipate was the widespread support for Mary throughout the country. To most people, Mary was the legitimate heir, so named by Henry VIII, whereas Jane was little known and did not fit naturally into the line of succession. Moreover, Mary was Catholic, which, given the relative novelty of Protestantism and the protests it had caused in certain parts of the realm, was considered to be a significant factor in her favor, especially by the nobility. In the sixteenth-century mindset, Mary's only negative quality was that she was a woman in a society that generally deemed women unfit to rule. But she was only thirty-seven years old, for the first time in her life an excellent candidate for marriage, could be supported in her rule by a husband, and still had a chance of producing a male heir.

Armies in support of Mary and Jane moved to intercept each other. In the meantime, the privy council and many others reversed their position, disregarded the "Devise," and gave their support to Mary. At Cambridge, Northumberland learned of the council's reversal and offered his support to Mary, but it was too late. Northumberland was arrested, as were Guildford and Jane, and Mary entered London triumphantly as queen on July 19. The "reign" of Lady Jane Grey, which is not officially recognized in the English royal line, was only nine days. Northumberland was executed for treason the next month. Although Jane and Guildford were both convicted of treason, their death sentences were suspended, at least for a while.

* * *

Discussion Question 3.3: What reasons might explain why England under Edward VI transitioned from Lutheranism, then to Calvinism, rather than simply adopting Calvinism in 1549?

England's First Female Monarch

Though possessed of her father's intelligence and temper, Mary's disaffected childhood as the estranged and illegitimate daughter of Henry VIII, tucked quietly away from court in disgrace, also meant that she lacked several early advantages enjoyed by her siblings (see Figure 3.2). Before about 1527, Mary was well educated along humanist lines, reading the works of More, Erasmus, and others, after which her education declined. She was humiliatingly forced to submit to the parliamentary acts that bastardized her, removed her from succession in favor of her half-sister and then half-brother, and recognized her father as supreme head of the church. Even upon her return to the succession in 1544, Mary was a poor candidate for marriage because no foreign potentate could take a chance on her potentially tainted bloodline. During her brother's reign, Mary navigated a treacherous path as she steadfastly refused to accept Protestant reform, especially in her own household. At one point, she contemplated fleeing the realm for a Catholic refuge, but she was persuaded that such an action would forfeit her claim to the throne.

Once Mary became queen, she knew she needed a strong and practiced council by those supportive of her Catholic faith, but also that she needed to show some restraint in removing all of Edward's officers of state. She appointed Stephen Gardiner, the bishop of London who had been languishing in the Tower, as her lord chancellor. This appointment brought Henrician experience to an inner circle that, for stability, also continued to employ some Edwardians. When Mary called parliament, its first step was to reinforce the 1544 succession and declare the

Figure 3.2 *Mary I, circa 1554, by Antonio Moro.*

Credit: PRISMA ARCHIVO/Alamy Stock Photo.

validity of her parents' marriage. These measures served to suppress any doubters who might continue to question her right to rule.

At the outset of her reign, Mary faced two pressing issues: marriage, in order to produce an heir but also to add a male voice to the weight of the crown, and the restoration of the church. At thirty-seven, Mary was still of child-bearing age, but just barely, and her health was poor, so marriage was a top priority. Although there were a number of eligible suitors in England of noble rank and with sufficient royal blood running through their veins, Mary instead chose to pursue marriage to a European Catholic. She turned for advice to her cousin, Emperor Charles V, also the king of Spain, who promptly suggested his own son, Philip. Both Mary's council and her parliament vehemently disapproved and a groundswell movement under the command of Sir Thomas Wyatt, leading several thousand men, rose up in opposition to the "Spanish match" and the related threat of a return to Catholicism. With the active support of the residents of London, who repelled Wyatt's forces at London Bridge and prevented the rebels from taking the capital, the rebel army eventually broke up. Wyatt surrendered and was executed along with nearly one hundred followers, who were hanged, drawn, and quartered. Because her father and uncles had joined the rebels, Lady Jane Grey and her husband were also executed, on February 12, 1554.

Wyatt's Rebellion caused Mary to strengthen her resolve both to marry Philip and to prevent possible usurpation of her crown. She imprisoned Elizabeth, her Protestant-leaning half-sister, in the Tower on suspicion of conspiracy with Wyatt. Elizabeth survived only because there was no direct evidence of complicity. The despised marriage to Philip took place in July 1554. Philip remained in England as king (*jure uxoris*) for about a year, during which time there were excited rumors of a pregnancy, which turned out to be false. Philip went back to Spain in 1555 and returned to England only once, in 1557. By then king of Spain, Philip had declared war on France and demanded English support. Despite parliament's objections to the war, and an economic situation that could ill afford it, Mary obeyed her husband and sent an army into an expensive conflict that, ultimately, saw the loss of the port of Calais, England's last vestige of empire on the Continent.

The second major issue of Mary's reign was the restoration of the Roman Catholic pope and the mass to England, an eventuality that was signaled by the appointment of Gardiner as chancellor and when her marriage plans to Philip were announced. Mary, after all, had been raised Catholic, and her cousin, Emperor Charles V, was an extremely active figure in the "universal Roman inquisition" that saw the persecution of thousands of Protestant heretics. There was no possibility that Mary would tolerate the Edwardian religion, especially the radical version created in 1552–3, and the arrival into England of Cardinal Reginald Pole, an English exile returning as papal legate, in 1554 sealed the deal. Following the precedent of her predecessors, Mary knew that she needed to rely on parliament to gain the consent of the governed. Parliament dutifully repealed the Edwardian legislation that introduced the *Book of Common Prayer* and Act of Uniformity, reversals that do not appear to have caused the legislature much concern. But there was a problem with the restoration of monastic lands, as most of these had new owners, many of whom were parliamentarians themselves. As a concession, Pole secured a papal dispensation that allowed the owners to retain their lands, in exchange for a restoration of Roman Catholicism.

As usual, there was little opposition from the general populace to the return to Catholicism. Edwardian reforms had been slow to creep into many parts of the realm, such that a number of churches experienced little or no change. Elsewhere, the restoration was cheered by those who had begrudgingly accepted the changes wrought by Edward's councillors. Altars were restored and vestments and images returned. The bigger problem was the hardcore Protestant reformers who had taken up key posts in the episcopacy and the universities. None could be allowed to remain in their current positions, because their ability to spread sedition would have undermined the restoration. There was also a requirement that these men recant their beliefs and convert back to the true faith, Catholicism, and that they acknowledge the supremacy of the pope. Here, Mary was merciful, in that she allowed about 800 Protestants to leave England voluntarily rather than convert, an exodus known as the "Marian exile." Many leaders of English Protestant reform left for Geneva, Zurich, and Strasbourg, where they worshipped freely, in communion with others of the reformed faith, using the 1552 *Book of Common Prayer*.

Yet some chose not to leave and others needed to be made an example of. Among the best known of these are the "Oxford martyrs," Nicholas Ridley and Hugh Latimer. After refusing to recant, they were burned at the stake in 1555 (see *Voices of the Past*: **The Burning of the Oxford Martyrs**). Thomas Cranmer expressed several recantations of his Protestant views and fully accepted Catholicism after his trial and conviction, but later regretted his recanting, which resulted in him being burned at the stake six months after the executions of Ridley and Latimer. Following Cranmer's death, Pole was appointed archbishop of Canterbury. Another 290 or so heretics were burned in the ensuing two years, many at Smithfield Market in London, in what have come to be known as the "Smithfield Fires." Many, such as Ridley and Latimer, died with extraordinary grace and the unwavering belief that their faith would bring everlasting life, which had the unanticipated effect of enlisting more to the cause of reform rather than thrusting waffling evangelicals back into the arms of the Roman Catholic Church.

Death and Reputation

In 1558, Mary believed that she was pregnant, the result of a spousal coupling when Philip had briefly returned to England in 1557. Mary was so convinced of her pregnancy that she decreed in her will that Philip would serve as regent during the minority of their child. It turned out, however, that Mary was probably suffering from ovarian or uterine cancer that gave false symptoms of pregnancy. Convinced that Mary was dying and hoping to avoid another dynastic struggle for the throne that had inaugurated Mary's reign, her councillors urged her to acknowledge Elizabeth as her successor, which she did. Between May and November 1558, Elizabeth slowly gathered courtiers and began preparing for the day when she would become queen. Mary died on November 17, 1558, and, fortunately for Elizabeth, Cardinal Reginald Pole, England's last Catholic archbishop, died the same day.

As a result of ordering the burning of Protestants, Mary has been given the epithet "Bloody," a title that, when viewed in the broader context of the history of the inquisition, was unearned. Elsewhere in Europe, the numbers of executions were far higher, and even Henry VIII (often through Thomas More) and later Elizabeth took their fair share of heretics' lives. Mary, by contrast, has suffered at the hands of both historians and early modern antiquarians, most notably the martyrologist John Foxe in his famous *Actes and Monuments*, better known as the *Book of Martyrs*. Foxe became Protestant in 1545 and spent the period of Marian exile in reform-minded Strasbourg and Frankfurt, where he began writing the history of English people who died for their faith. Published early in the reign of Queen Elizabeth, Foxe's book recounted in horrid detail the execution of Protestants such as Anne Askew, Jane Grey, and the Oxford martyrs, complete with woodcut images showing the burning of women and unborn, innocent children. In the face of such claims, which in fact reflected careful research undertaken by Foxe, it was nearly impossible for Mary's reputation not to be irreparably damaged.

Historians sometimes refer to Edward VI and Mary I – a sickly child king and a sterile queen – as the "little Tudors," a term that has the effect of diminishing the accomplishments of their reigns. This is, perhaps, understandable when considering the long and titanic reigns of the Tudors who preceded and succeeded them, Henry VIII and Elizabeth I. However, these two reigns, though short, should not be so readily dismissed. The swift introduction of Protestantism under Edward, followed by the equally swift restoration of Catholicism under Mary, provided a good sense of what the English church and people were willing to tolerate when it came to subsequent reforms, and also how quickly such reforms could take place in order to be accepted with minimal appetite for rebellion. Mary's actions in persecuting Protestants, amplified by Foxe, increased the reformist zeal of some while decreasing the conservatism of others, providing an opportunity for Elizabeth to explore a "middle way" religion during the early stages of her reign. In addition, the tumult associated with Mary's accession to the throne paved the way for Elizabeth's unchallenged accession in 1558.

* * *

Discussion Question 3.4: In what ways did Mary's gender work for and against her during her lifetime?

VOICES OF THE PAST
THE BURNING OF THE OXFORD MARTYRS

Among the first to die during the Marian persecution of Protestants were the so-called Oxford martyrs – Nicholas Ridley, bishop of London; Hugh Latimer, bishop of Worcester; and Thomas Cranmer, archbishop of Canterbury – who were all prominent leaders of the Protestant Reformation. All three were tried by Catholic officials at the University of Oxford and were burned at the stake at Broad Street, Oxford, where a metal cross still marks the site of their martyrdom. Ridley and Latimer were burned in October 1555, and Cranmer went to the stake in March 1556 (see Figure 3.3). Their deaths were famously described in John Foxe's Book of Martyrs.

The following extract recounts the deaths of Ridley and Latimer.

* * *

Mr. Latimer, after remaining a long time in the Tower [of London], was transported to Oxford, with Cranmer and Ridley.... He remained imprisoned until October, and the principal objects of all his prayers were three: that he might stand faithful to the doctrine he had professed, that God would restore his Gospel to England once again, and preserve the Lady Elizabeth to be queen; all of which happened....

Dr. Ridley, the night before execution, was very facetious, had himself shaved, and called

Figure 3.3 *The execution of Ridley and Latimer, from John Foxe,* Book of Martyrs.

his supper a marriage feast; he remarked upon seeing Mrs. Irish (the keeper's wife) weep, "Though my breakfast will be somewhat sharp, my supper will be more pleasant and sweet."

The place of death was on the north side of the town, opposite Baliol College. Dr. Ridley was dressed in a black gown, and Mr. Latimer had a long shroud on, hanging down to his feet. Dr. Ridley, as he passed Bocardo,[5] looked up to see Dr. Cranmer, but the latter was then engaged in disputation with a friar.

When they came to the stake, Mr. Ridley embraced Latimer fervently, and bid him: "Be of good heart, brother, for God will either assuage the fury of the flame, or else strengthen us to abide it." He then knelt by the stake, and after earnestly praying together, they had a short private conversation. Dr. Smith then preached a short sermon against the martyrs, who would have answered him, but were prevented by Dr. Marshal, the vice-chancellor. Dr. Ridley then took off his gown and tippet [fur scarf], and gave them to his brother-in-law, Mr. Shipside. He gave away also many trifles to his weeping friends, and the populace were anxious to get even a fragment of his garments. Mr. Latimer gave nothing, and from the poverty of his garb, was soon stripped to his shroud, and stood venerable and erect, fearless of death.

Dr. Ridley being unclothed to his shirt, the smith placed an iron chain about their waists, and Dr. Ridley bid him fasten it securely; his brother having tied a bag of gunpowder about his neck, gave some also to Mr. Latimer. Dr. Ridley then requested of Lord Williams ... to advocate with the queen the cause of some poor men to whom he had, when bishop, granted leases, but which the present bishop refused to confirm. A lighted fagot was now laid at Dr. Ridley's feet, which caused Mr. Latimer to say: "Be of good cheer, Ridley; and play the man. We shall this day, by God's grace, light up such a candle in England, as I trust, will never be put out."

When Dr. Ridley saw the fire flaming up towards him, he cried with a wonderful loud voice, "Lord, Lord, receive my spirit." Master Latimer, crying as vehemently on the other side, "O Father of Heaven, receive my soul!" received the flame as he were embracing of it. After that he had stroked his face with his hands, and as it were, bathed them a little in the fire, he soon died (as it appeareth) with very little pain or none.

But Master Ridley ..., because the wooden faggots were ... over high built, the fire burned first beneath, being kept down by the wood. Which, when he felt, he desired them for Christ's sake to let the fire come unto him. Which when his brother-in-law heard, but not well understood, intending to rid him of his pain ... heaved faggots upon him, that he clean covered him, which made the fire more vehement beneath, that it burned clean all his nether parts, before it once touched the upper, and that made him leap up and down, under the faggots, and often desired them to let the fire come unto him, saying "I cannot burn." Which indeed appeared well, for his legs were consumed by reason of his struggling with the pain....

Yet in all this torment he forgot not to call unto God still, having in his mouth, "Lord have mercy upon me, let the fire come unto me, I cannot burn." And when the flame touched the gunpowder, he was seen no more.... Surely it moved hundreds to tears, to behold the horrible sight. For I think there was none, that had not clean exiled all

---

5   The Oxford prison that housed the martyrs until their executions.

humanity and mercy, which would not have lamented to behold the fury of the fire so rage upon their bodies....

Well! dead they are, and the reward of this world they have already. What reward remaineth for them in Heaven, the day of the Lord's glory, when he cometh with His saints, shall shortly, I trust, declare.

Source: John Foxe, *Actes and Monuments* (London, 1563), chapter XVI.

* * *

Discussion Question 3.5: Considering also the execution of Anne Askew, discussed in the last chapter, what purposes were served by Foxe's detailed descriptions of these burnings?

CHAPTER FOUR

ELIZABETH, THE VIRGIN QUEEN, 1558–1603

DEATH AND DISORDER:
THE LONDON PLAGUE OF 1603

Disorder came in many forms in early modern England, such as the havoc caused by frequent outbreaks of medieval and early modern Europe's greatest pestilence, the bubonic plague. The plague was caused by a bacterium known as *Yersinia pestis*, which was carried by black rats and transmitted to humans from a flea bite. Once contracted by humans, the plague could spread pneumatically (by air) and was, therefore, particularly severe in large, urban areas, such as London. Physical signs of the plague included coughing and sneezing; enlargement of the lymph nodes (buboes) in the armpits, groin, and throat; a ring of sores around the neck; and acral necrosis, which causes the blackening of infected body parts and gave the plague its more common name, the "black death." A horrible and painful death occurred within a mere few days.

Although today we know that the cause of the disease was bacterial, its cause was not known in the early modern period. Contemporaries speculated that God was unhappy, either with the Catholic church or with ongoing reforms. Others blamed astrological and astronomical phenomena; still others blamed natural disasters, such as earthquakes, for releasing poisonous gases from deep within the earth. Various scapegoats also came under suspicion, including witches and Jews, all of whom suffered at least social estrangement and, frequently, death at the hands of angry mobs or the criminal justice system. Nor was early modern medicine up to the task of dealing with plague. Traditional treatments to cure the body – sweating, bloodletting, vomiting, the application of pigeon blood, and poultices – failed to slow death or the spread of the disease.

The London plague of 1603 was the most severe since the medieval period, claiming 30,000 to 40,000 souls in the city. In *The Wonderful Yeare*, the writer Thomas Dekker lamented that infected corpses were either burned or buried in mass graves, covered in lye (see Figure 4.1). In this final state of rest, the deceased, "buried like dogs," were denied the dignity of a proper Christian burial. Dekker went on to describe, in detail, the impact of the plague in London. The state closed theaters to limit the presence of large crowds and forced the infected and their families into isolation, with painted markings on their doors and windows to warn others.

Figure 4.1 *The burial of plague victims in mass graves, circa 1665.*

Credit: Science History Images/Alamy Stock Photo.

Fear drove some to burn the buildings that housed the sick. Those who could flee to the less-populous countryside did so, although naturally this was a privilege only available to the wealthy.

Dekker also describes the sorrow felt by those who survived:

> Lend me art ... to paint and delineate to the life the whole story of this mortal and pestiferous battle, and you the ghosts of those more (by many) than 40,000 that with the virulent poison of infection have been driven out of your earthly dwellings. You desolate hand-wringing widows, that beat your bosoms over your departing husbands. You woefully distracted mothers that with disheveled hair fallen into swoon, whilst you lie kissing the insensible cold lips of your breathless infants. You outcast and downtrodden orphans, that shall many a year hence remember more freshly to mourn.... Join your hands together, and with your bodies cast a ring about me; let me behold your ghastly visages, that my paper may receive their true pictures. Echo forth your groans through the hollow trunk of my pen and rain down your gummy tears into mine ink, that even marble bosoms may be shaken with terror, and hearts of adamant melt into compassion.[1]

Dekker's was merely one of several dozen accounts of the last Elizabethan plague that described its

inhumanity, the loss of family and neighborliness, the "sins" of flight and fear, and the failure of physicians to treat the afflicted and of priests to respect the dead. The plague took on a literary genre of its own, shaping the *carpe diem* (seize the day) and *danse macabre* (dance of death) themes that characterized much seventeenth-century poetry.

During the outbreak of 1603, for example, the playwright and poet Ben Jonson lost his seven-year-old son, Benjamin, and lamented on this tragedy in the poem "On My First Son":

> Farewell, thou child of my right hand, and joy;
> My sin was too much hope of thee, loved boy,
> Seven years thou were lent to me, and I thee pay,
> Exacted by thy fate, on the just day.
> O, could I lose all father now! For why
> Will man lament the state he should envy?
> To have so soon escaped world's, and flesh's rage,
> And, if no other misery, yet age?
> Rest in soft peace, and, asked, say "Here doth lie
> Ben Jonson his best piece of poetry.
> For whose sake henceforth all his vows be such,
> As what he loves may never like too much."[2]

Jonson's poem speaks both to the pain parents felt for the loss of a child and to the joy that survivors were, according to church teachings, supposed to feel for the deceased's escape from earthly troubles

---

1   Thomas Dekker, *The Wonderful Yeare* (London, 1603), sigs. C3r to D4v. Adamant was a legendary stone believed to be impenetrable.

2   Ben Johnson, *The Workes of Benjamin Johnson* (London, 1616), 780–1.

and their beginnings of everlasting bliss in heaven. The boy was Jonson's "best piece of poetry," his most significant creation, and the author ends the poem by vowing not to get too attached to the things he loves, to reduce future grief. As Dekker attested, however common death by plague was in early modern England, it created a heavy burden for its survivors.

* * *

Discussion Question 4.1: Why do you think plague narratives, which were often quite gruesome in their details, became so prevalent throughout the seventeenth century?

The Virgin Queen and the Cult of Elizabeth

The accession of Elizabeth Tudor to the English throne in November 1558 went smoothly. In contrast to recent events such as Somerset's eclipsing of Edward's appointed regency council and Lady Jane Grey's brief usurpation of Mary's throne, this time the wishes of Henry VIII for succession were respected. Elizabeth's path to queenship was made easier by an elaborate and expensive coronation, held on the day prescribed by the royal astrologer, John Dee, as the day that would lead to a long and happy reign. Elizabeth was also strengthened by being possibly the best educated and most intelligent of the Tudor monarchs. Especially after her return to the succession in 1544 and placement into the household of Catherine Parr, she was given excellent humanist tutors. One such tutor was Roger Ascham, author of *The Scholemaster* (1570), which described the ideal humanist education as it was provided to Elizabeth. The new queen's knowledge of the classics was exceptional for the time, as was her mastery of Latin, Greek, French, and Italian. Nor did Elizabeth's education end in her teen years; even as queen, she continued advanced studies in Greek and produced translations as late as 1598.

At the outset of Elizabeth's reign everybody – likely even the queen – assumed that she would marry, and sooner rather than later. This was still a society that believed women were incapable of possessing or exercising the intelligence or strength of men, which were necessary in interpreting law, carrying out constitutional responsibilities, leading armies into battle, and deciding delicate matters of state with sound reason and good judgment. Mastering the art of double-translating[3] Greek was one thing; running an early modern European monarchy was quite another. While few questioned the queen's right to rule, many doubted the fitness of a women to do so well, and the recent specter of Mary's reign did not help this perception. A king consort, therefore,

---

3   This process involved translation from the original language into another, then back again, in order to confirm the accuracy of the translation.

could provide Elizabeth with much-needed male advice and possibly relieve her of some or all of the burdens of rule. More importantly, marriage was the only sure way for Elizabeth to produce an heir, preferably male, to secure an orderly succession to the throne. Recent history of premature royal death by sickness and disease had taught Elizabeth's advisors that the queen could die at any time. These feelings only intensified when she was nearly carried away by smallpox in 1562.

Parliament and the privy council first approached the queen about marriage in 1559. Elizabeth prevaricated, either out of concern for the good of the realm or for the stability of her own crown. Various foreign suitors presented themselves, which served the valuable purpose of legitimizing her reign in the eyes of Europe. However, most of these men were Catholic and, therefore, could not be considered by Elizabeth at such a delicate time in the reformation. The sting of Mary's wedding to Philip and the rebellions that it spawned were in very recent memory. Another potential suitor was Elizabeth's childhood friend, Robert Dudley, for whom the queen had developed genuine affection. Marriage became a distinct possibility when Dudley's wife, Amy, fell down a flight of stairs to her death in 1560, leaving Dudley – whatever his suspected role in his wife's death – a widower free to remarry. Her council was strongly against the marriage and at some point, Elizabeth, too, decided that she could not marry one of her own subjects. Parliament continued to press the queen to marry, in 1563, 1566, and again between 1578 and 1582. Elizabeth entertained two candidates during this time, archduke Charles of Austria and François, duke of Anjou, but after the marriage negotiations began, both enterprises failed on the grounds of religion. By the time the Anjou match was being considered, the queen was nearly fifty years old, was unlikely to bear a child, and had effectively governed her realm for a quarter century. A Catholic marriage, even if it had diplomatic advantages, was not popular if an heir was no longer a possible outcome of the union.

In the end, as is common knowledge, Elizabeth never married. By the 1580s, she began to style herself as the Virgin Queen, married only to her people. Her chaste state was promoted by numerous writers of the age, not least Edmund Spenser, whose *Faerie Queene* (1596) memorialized the aging monarch as Gloriana, the leading character and a clear allegory of Elizabeth. William Shakespeare also celebrated the virgin theme in *A Midsummer Night's Dream* (circa 1596):

> I saw … Cupid all armed. A certain aim he took
> At a fair vestal [virgin] throned by the west, …
> But I might see young Cupid's fiery shaft
> Quenched in the chaste beams of the watery moon,
> And the imperial votaress passed on,
> In maiden meditation, fancy-free. (II.i.142–49)

Not even Cupid's powerful arrow, "loosed … smartly from his bow," could claim the chastity of the queen who gave a vow (thus making her a "votaress") to remain a virgin and serve her people.

Portrait artists also celebrated her virgin state. In Quentin Metsys the Younger's *Sieve Portrait* (1583), Elizabeth is depicted holding the symbol of the vestal virgin Tuccia, who, with God's assistance, carried water in a sieve to vindicate herself after her chastity was questioned. Near the end of Elizabeth's life, Isaac Oliver painted the *Rainbow Portrait* (1600), which depicted the queen as Astraea, the virginal Greek goddess who was to return to Earth and bring with her a golden age that would end human suffering (see Figure 4.2). In the face of such literary and artistic outpouring, whether Elizabeth was, in fact, a virgin – her youthful and affectionate dalliances with Dudley perhaps suggesting otherwise – was immaterial.

In spite of the "cult of Elizabeth" that enshrouded the last Tudor monarch, the virgin queen was at least as Machiavellian as her father. She was vain, arrogant, and unpredictable, possessed a famously fiery temper, and did not hesitate to rebuke publicly (and occasionally physically) important men who failed to

Figure 4.2 *The Rainbow Portrait of Elizabeth I, circa 1600, by Isaac Oliver.*

Credit: World History Archive/Alamy Stock Photo.

follow her instructions, assumed authority they were not explicitly granted, or treated her like a mere woman. Elizabeth deliberately employed councillors who disagreed with each other, expecting both that disunity within the council would require regular consultation with her and that the council would not unite in a single voice against her. She did not hesitate to imprison men who criticized her or her closest councillors, and became incensed when her council or parliament discussed certain matters without her permission. At court, Elizabeth was patron to a number of "favorites," such as the handsome Dudley, who became earl of Leicester in 1564, Sir Walter Ralegh, and Sir Christopher Hatton, who later became lord chancellor. She affectionately gave these men nicknames – Leicester was "eyes," Hatton "lids" – and bestowed numerous titles on them that brought both wealth and power. Yet these men could also be the victims of her famous wrath, as was Leicester when he married without permission in 1578, although the two later reconciled.

Elizabeth also selected wise councillors with experience at statesmanship. This is illustrated especially in her appointments for the position of secretary of state, the role once held by Thomas Cromwell. At the outset of her reign, she appointed Sir William Cecil – a longtime servant under Edward and Mary – into this position. In one of Elizabeth's few elevations to the peerage, Cecil was created baron Burghley in 1572, which placed him into the House of Lords, and took on an even greater role as lord treasurer. Another key secretary was Sir Francis Walsingham, the brilliant "spymaster" whose intelligence gathering averted several dynastic crises during the Elizabethan era. For good reason, Elizabeth deeply mourned the loss of Walsingham in 1590 and Burghley in 1598. Still another important secretary was Burghley's son and Walsingham's mentee, Sir Robert Cecil (whom the queen nicknamed "pygmy" due to his small stature), who served in that role beyond Elizabeth's death. All these men brought credibility and experience to the government and were fiercely loyal to the queen.

Elizabeth's court was also as magnificent and as peripatetic as the early Tudors'. She surrounded herself with women – mostly from noble and gentle families – who attended to her every need, dressed in exquisite clothing, and allegedly spent up to two hours each morning in the privy chamber dressing, and another two each evening undressing. The queen divided her time between several palaces, especially Whitehall, St. James's, Placentia, and Windsor,[4] and undertook lengthy and expensive summer progresses throughout the countryside, depending on wealthy nobles to provide for her extensive entourage while in residence. Elizabeth

---

4   Whitehall, the official royal residence, was located in Westminster; most of it was destroyed by fire in 1698, although Banqueting House remains today. St. James's, built by Henry VIII as a less formal residence in Westminster, currently houses several members of the royal family and is used for royal functions. Placentia, in Greenwich – the birthplace of Henry VIII, Mary I, and Elizabeth – no longer exists, while Windsor is still used regularly by the British royal family as a weekend retreat and a place to hold state banquets.

also enjoyed masques, dancing, and music, and especially during holidays the court was abuzz with these activities.[5] Her preference for entertainment and the attention of her favorites sometimes meant that, also like her father, Elizabeth could not always be relied upon to attend to matters of state efficiently, which was a cause of consternation for her councillors, whom she often kept waiting inordinate amounts of time for decisions. In sum, the virgin queen was truly her father's daughter, and a consummate Tudor monarch.

The Elizabethan Settlement

Much to the satisfaction of many, including the Marian exiles who flooded back into England, Elizabeth was Protestant thanks to her childhood relationship with Catherine Parr and the fact that she was born of a union that could be deemed legitimate only if the break from Rome was *fait accompli*. Beyond Elizabeth's general embrace of the royal supremacy of the church and a certain degree of Protestant-leaning reform, however, it is difficult to define precisely what the queen's personal religious views were. This was possibly because, unlike the other Tudor monarchs, she viewed religion as a matter of political expediency rather than personal faith. To this end, Elizabeth dismissed all Catholics from her privy council and appointed several men – including Cecil, who probably had the single greatest role in designing the reform package – with moderate reformist desires. The new council was virtually devoid of religious officials. This meant that the proposals for religious reform ultimately put to parliament in February 1559 were designed by secular individuals for whom religion was also largely a political matter.

The religious settlement had two main goals: restoration of the royal supremacy of the church and movement toward Protestant reform. Neither of these goals was easily achievable give the current composition of parliament. A vocal minority of the House of Commons was strongly Catholic, but more vitally the House of Lords was dominated by Catholics, including the Marian bishops and abbots, who still held their positions. To achieve their goals, Elizabeth and the council arranged for the "Westminster disputation" in March. In theory, the meeting was an opportunity for Protestants and Catholics to debate the issue of supremacy, but in practice it was a subterfuge that resulted in the imprisonment of two bishops and an abbot, just enough to upset the majority opinion in the Lords. The queen also agreed to a concession to satisfy the conservatives by making herself "supreme governor" rather than "supreme head" of the church.

The second goal of the settlement was movement toward Protestant reform. Here, too, Elizabeth and her council made compromises to satisfy parliament. Many

---

5   Courtly entertainment will be discussed in greater detail in Chapter Ten.

in both houses were concerned with the extremism of the second *Book of Common Prayer*, which was strongly Calvinist with regard to images, vestments, and the interpretation of the eucharist. This liturgy was repugnant not only to Roman Catholics and anti-papal Henrician Catholics but also to many of the more conservative Protestants, such as Lutherans. To appease these conservatives, a new Act of Uniformity promised a revised version of the 1552 prayer book that retracted some of its perceived radical elements but retained predestination, establishing what has been referred to as a *via media* (middle way) religion. The communion service, which had become a commemorative event in 1552, was ambiguously restored as a mass, so that conservatives who wanted a sacrificial ceremony during the eucharist were satisfied. The act also included a proviso that authorized the use of "ornaments" – vestments, crosses, candles, altars, and others – according to the terms of the 1549 Lutheran-oriented prayer book, which would also appease centrist views. This proviso was, however, subject to review by the queen and her religious officials and gave hope to Calvinists that further reform was forthcoming.

Naturally, despite seeking a compromise on the issues of greatest concern to the conservatives in parliament, which allowed the Elizabethan religious reform package to pass through that body successfully, the settlement was not satisfactory to those on the religious extremes. This applied especially to the current episcopal bench, which was filled entirely with Catholics. In the summer of 1559, the Marian bishops were obliged to resign and the episcopacy was quickly filled with Protestants. About half of these bishops, including the new archbishop of Canterbury, Matthew Parker, had remained in England in seclusion during the reign of Mary. The other half had been former Marian exiles who had resided primarily in two locations, Strasbourg and Zurich. These were reformed communities that took a "middle way" position between Lutheranism and Calvinism. Zurich reformers, for example, supported erastianism, clerical hierarchy within the church, and a largely Lutheran approach to their understanding of the eucharist (as established in the 1540 *Consensus Tigurinus*). There is evidence that supporters of this religious position were present on the privy council and that leading members of the Zurich reformed tradition corresponded with Elizabeth and other officials in the events leading up to the parliamentary passage of the settlement.

Although the new episcopacy could, therefore, agree with many aspects of the new brand of Anglicanism, there was still disagreement about the use of ornaments, about which the Zurich reformed tradition was less tolerant. Some bishops supported their use provided they could make decisions on these matters within their own dioceses, while others remained opposed on the grounds that these devices were too Catholic and superstitious. In an episcopal visitation of 1560, some of the visitors went so far as to order the removal of images from churches, an act of iconoclasm that went against the ornaments proviso and provoked reaction from the queen, whose own Chapel Royal displayed a crucifix. Ultimately, after two controversies over vestments in the 1560s, the dissenting bishops decided that it was better to accept the proviso than resign their positions and possibly be replaced by extremists. In fact, one of these bishops, John Jewel, became the Church of England's leading defender in the immediate aftermath of the settlement. He produced several treatises, likely commissioned by Cecil, designed to explain the current state of the church and contradict claims that the English clergy was rife with factionalism. Jewel's *Apology of the Church of England*[6] (1562) became the unofficial confession of faith for the new religion.

The final major step toward the acceptance of the religious settlement was its passage through convocation, the religious body that met simultaneously with parliament. Although the precedent had been set under the earlier Tudors for parliament to legislate for religion, this was a comparatively new phenomenon. In 1559, the Catholic-dominated convocation had not been asked for its opinion with respect to religions reform, so the more Protestant 1563 body took the opportunity to voice its opinions. Here again the key issue was the ornaments proviso in the uniformity act. Various members of the lower house of convocation, later termed "precisians" by Parker, supported further reform, such as the end of vestments and that the communion table not be positioned "altarwise." Some of the bishops also supported further reform, although ultimately convocation accepted the version of the settlement as explained by Jewel. It also passed the Thirty-Nine Articles, the church's official statement of faith. This was a more conservative version of the Edwardian Forty-Two Articles, although the articles continued to accept the doctrine of predestination.

For the next two decades, Puritans, as the precisians came to be called, continued to push for further reforms, sometimes quite aggressively. One example of this is the pamphlet war of Cambridge professor Thomas Cartwright in the early 1570s. After his removal from his position because of his critical stance against bishops, Cartwright resorted to the medium of print to support his belief that the church should be neither erastian nor episcopal. Instead, it should be Presbyterian, meaning that religious decisions should be made by elected assemblies of clergymen and laymen. Unsurprisingly, the queen bristled at the idea that the church should be governed without the royal prerogative. The religious situation in England was far too delicate, too needful of uniformity, and too married to politics, diplomacy, and the very concept of royal authority to rely on the whims of men who had already proven too radical for the queen. Elizabeth relied primarily on her three archbishops of Canterbury – Parker, Edmund Grindal, and John Whitgift – to ensure conformity to church policies. This practice met with limited success as Grindal, for instance, tended to side with the Puritans and was suspended from his duties during his term in office.

---

6   At this time, the word *apology* meant a defense of something rather than an admission of wrongdoing.

The stronger efforts of Whitgift, who used a special court to punish Puritans and took active measures against the printers of the anti-episcopal, anonymous "Martin Marprelate" tracts (1588–9), managed finally to alienate some dissenters from the church. Led by a nonconformist minister named Robert Browne, who had established an independent congregation in Norwich, a number of Puritans separated from the Church of England and fled to the Netherlands to escape persecution. Some later traveled to America in hopes of a more reformed religious society. In general, however, most Puritans (who were by no means ideologically monolithic) tolerated the settlement and did their best to worship within its guidelines, possibly because they were not so fervent as to flirt with sedition. Despite regular agitation, the middle way religion established between 1559 and 1563 has withstood the test of time. With some minor revisions, this reformed Church of England – only later to be known as Anglicanism – continues to be the national religion of England to the present day.

❊ ❊ ❊

Discussion Question 4.2: Despite criticism from Puritans, many characteristics of the "Elizabethan settlement" continue to exist today. Why do you think the settlement was so successful in creating an enduring reformed religion?

Mary of Scots and the Catholic Menace

While Puritanism was a thorn in the side of Anglicanism and Elizabeth's authority to govern the church, the Catholic menace was their predator. Some Catholics of the Henrician stripe were sufficiently satisfied with the "middle way" settlement to worship within the bounds set by the supreme governor. Others simply could not accept the new religion, a situation made worse by Pope Pius V's injunction in 1566 that true Catholics must not worship in Anglican churches. Two years later, a series of Catholic problems was initiated by the arrival into England of Mary, Queen of Scots, Elizabeth's cousin by her aunt Margaret. As a child queen, Mary had been sent to France, while Scotland was ruled by regents; she returned in 1561, following the death of her husband, Francis II. By this time, Scotland was Presbyterian, which Mary, though a Catholic, tolerated with the help of her Protestant half-brother, the earl of Moray, and a reform-minded council.

Mary's second marriage, to her cousin and fellow Catholic Henry, Lord Darnley, in 1565, was despised by her Protestant subjects and quickly turned sour. Darnley demanded to reign equally with Mary, which would have made him heir to the throne upon her death, and accused her of having an affair with her secretary, David Riccio. After arranging the murder of Riccio, Darnley reconciled with the now-pregnant Mary, and she gave birth to Prince James in 1566. The reconciliation did not last long. Within a year, Darnley was killed under suspicious circumstances and rumors spread that the assassination had been arranged by Mary and her new lover, James Hepburn, earl of Bothwell. Fearing for his life, Bothwell ran away with (and possibly kidnapped) Mary and the two were married. All this intrigue was too much for Mary's nobles, who promptly detained the queen, denounced her as an adulteress and murderer, and placed her in prison. In July, Mary was forced to abdicate her throne in favor of baby James, under the regency of Moray, and in 1568 she fled to England seeking Elizabeth's protection.

The presence of the usurped Scottish queen on English soil presented problems. First, Mary had a legitimate claim as Elizabeth's heir. Although the heirs of Henry VIII's sister Margaret were not mentioned in his last will and testament, in favor of his sister Mary Tudor, the line stemming from Mary had become tainted. Until her death in January 1568, the presumptive (though never acknowledged) heir to the throne had been Catherine Grey, Mary's granddaughter (and Lady Jane's younger sister). Catherine left behind two sons, but her marriage to their father, Edward Seymour, earl of Hertford, had infuriated Elizabeth and could not, at any rate, be proven and had been annulled. With the line legally extinguished, Mary of Scots had the best, if still unacknowledged, claim as Elizabeth's heir. Elizabeth, therefore, found it necessary to give Mary lodgings in England as her "guest," and although Mary was accorded the privileges that her rank and position demanded, she was, nonetheless, kept under close guard.

The second complication was that Mary was Catholic. This meant that Elizabeth's death – by natural or unnatural means – could easily have led to the restoration of Catholicism. This concern became heightened when the plan of Thomas Howard, duke of Norfolk and head of England's wealthiest and most powerful Catholic family, to wed Mary was announced. Along with several other northern peers, Norfolk had come to believe that Cecil was the principal cause of England's problems, including its religious settlement. They also disapproved of the secular and reformist composition of the remainder of the council. When these concerns came to Elizabeth's attention, she supported Cecil and her council, forbade Norfolk's marriage to Mary, and demanded his presence at court for a stern rebuke. With Norfolk chastened, the earls of Northumberland and Westmorland rose in rebellion and began marching south. The 4,500 or so rebels met approximately 19,000 troops loyal to the queen, which caused the retreat and dispersal of the earls' forces. Although Westmorland escaped to the Continent, Northumberland was captured by the Scots, handed over to the English, and promptly executed, along with hundreds of the rebels.

While the Northern Rebellion was underway, the pope attempted to lend his support for the uprising by issuing a papal bull excommunicating the "pretended Queen of England" and releasing all subjects from her allegiance. One of the reasons given for issuing the bull was Elizabeth's choice to fill her council with "obscure … heretics," lending clear support for the goals of the northern earls. When the rebellion was suppressed, one of its supporters, Roberto Ridolfi, plotted to invade England with an army from the Netherlands and Spain, free Mary from her prison, ensure her marriage to Norfolk, and murder Elizabeth so that Mary could succeed and restore Catholicism. The plot ultimately failed because of the inability to foment sufficient support from English Catholics, who were far less numerous than Norfolk and Ridolfi believed. When the entire conspiracy was discovered and reported to Cecil, Norfolk was arrested, convicted of high treason, and executed in 1572.

Elizabeth resisted her advisors' recommendation that Mary be prosecuted for her part in the plot, but otherwise showed little tolerance for Catholics from the 1570s onward. In part, this was a reaction to an underground movement initiated by the arrival of Jesuits into England, who could operate incognito and spread dissent without easy discovery. A series of parliamentary acts made it treason to call the queen a heretic and illegal to say or attend Catholic mass, convert to Catholicism, attempt to convert others, absent oneself from Church of England services, or harbor Catholic priests. These "recusancy" acts prescribed penal measures ranging from crippling fines to imprisonment or even death. They also often resulted in the use of torture to extract confessions. This involved the body being broken on the rack, in which the prisoner was stretched on a wooden frame until his or her ligaments and muscles separated. The polar opposite of the rack was the "scavenger's daughter," employed in the Tower of London. It was either a metal ring of about two feet in diameter, or a metal A-frame, into which the legs and body of a kneeling prisoner were savagely compressed. Sometimes, prisoners were placed into tight cages, which were suspended from buildings, where their bodies were preyed upon by birds and rats.

It has been estimated that upwards of 200 people were executed in Elizabethan England because of their Catholicism. One particularly famous example is that of Margaret Clitherow. In 1586, after a decade of having run afoul of parliamentary legislation leading to fines and imprisonment, Clitherow was accused of harboring Catholic priests and enabling them to hold mass. At trial, she refused to plead, probably to protect her three children and others from being subjected to torture and trial. Her refusal led to *peine forte et dure*, commonly known as "pressing," which was the standard procedure when an accused felon refused to plead at court. Normally, the accused was stripped of his or her clothes (save a cloth over the genitals) and laid out on the bare floor. Each limb was stretched taut with a rope, and large stones or plates of iron were gradually placed on the prisoner's torso until he elected to plead or until he died. Clitherow was pressed to death using this method, even though she was then pregnant with her fourth child (see Figure 4.3). Clitherow's martyrdom led to her canonization by the Catholic church nearly four centuries later.

A leading figure in the persecution of Catholics was Francis Walsingham, a committed Protestant and Elizabeth's principal secretary, who managed through espionage and torture to uncover various Catholic plots. The most significant of these was the Babington Plot of 1586. Walsingham had, for some time, read with Mary's knowledge all her incoming and outgoing correspondence. He entrapped

Mary into believing that she could covertly send correspondence using encrypted letters smuggled by a brewer in beer kegs. Through this means, Anthony Babington wrote to Mary about a plot to kill Elizabeth, and Mary responded with encouragement and sanction. All the correspondence passed through Walsingham, who in fact had arranged the cipher code used to encrypt the letters. In July 1586, Walsingham was finally in possession of concrete evidence of Mary's complicity in a plan to assassinate Elizabeth that earlier plots had failed to provide.

Mary's actions ran afoul of a "Bond of Association" produced in 1584, which ordered the execution of any person who plotted against the queen. The major obstacle to trying Mary under this device was Scotland's possible reaction to the execution of their king's mother, no matter how much she had disgraced herself. To allay these concerns, while the Babington Plot was unfolding, Walsingham arranged the Treaty of Berwick with James VI, promising him an annual pension of £4,000 – a substantial sum to a poor king – and, without directly saying so, implying that James was heir to the English throne, provided that peaceful

Figure 4.3 *The pressing of Margaret Clitherow, from a contemporary woodcut.*

Credit: Science History Images/Alamy Stock Photo.

relations were maintained. With proof of Mary's guilt and the acquiescence of James VI, Walsingham and Cecil arranged a tribunal, during which Mary was found guilty and a warrant was prepared for her execution. Elizabeth signed the warrant, allegedly instructing that it not be put into action until she gave direct authorization. Notwithstanding, the privy council ordered that the sentence be carried out, and Mary was executed on February 8, 1587, with two strokes of the axe (see *Voices of the Past*: **The Execution of Mary, Queen of Scots**). Although Elizabeth was allegedly furious that her orders had been disobeyed, it is also possible that the whole affair was designed to give her plausible deniability as to her role in the regicide of her cousin and immediate heir.

War with Spain

The final two decades of Elizabeth's reign witnessed war with Spain, of which there were several causes. Since the 1560s, English ship captains had been distressing Spanish colonies in the New World. Sir John Hawkins undertook several slaving expeditions, collecting Africans from the West Coast of Africa, transporting them across the Atlantic Ocean, and selling them to Spanish colonies in the Caribbean and South America. All these activities challenged Spanish authority in the region, which saw all foreign trading in the Americas as illegal. In 1577, Sir Francis Drake began his famous three-year circumnavigation of the Earth, making his way around South America and, in the process, raiding numerous Spanish colonies and claiming ships, cargo, and gold as his prize. Despite official Spanish complaints about Drake's piratical activities, Elizabeth had him knighted him on the deck of his ship for his services to the nation. In addition, in 1585 the earl of Leicester was sent to the Spanish Netherlands in command of several thousand men to aid in the struggle of the Protestant Dutch against their Catholic overlord, Philip II. When Spain responded by seizing English merchant ships in Spanish harbors, a state of war was unofficially declared and would continue until 1604.

In the early stages of the war, Hawkins, Drake, and others became English "privateers," operating with English royal letters of marque to distress the Spanish enemy in the Americas. The situation became far more serious after the execution of Mary of Scots, who for two decades had been the focal point of attempts to restore a Catholic monarch to the English throne. In retaliation, Philip II threatened to send an armada of ships to invade England, a plan that was initially thwarted when Drake, during the Cádiz expedition, managed to burn thirty-seven Spanish ships and return to England with a booty exceeding £100,000. Drake's raid delayed the armada for about a year. In May 1588, 130 ships carrying 26,000 men (two-thirds of them land soldiers) departed Lisbon under the command of the duke of Medina-Sidonia, who unfortunately lacked military command experience at sea and on land. The plan was for Medina-Sidonia to join with an additional 30,000 troops under the command of the duke of Parma in the Netherlands, land an army in England, and engage in a land battle.

The armada sailed into the English Channel in July, its progress slowed by the presence of several troop-carrying merchant ships that had limited speed, which gave the English plenty of time to prepare its naval forces. After several brief engagements with the English, Medina-Sidonia managed to bring the majority of his armada to Calais, where it was expected Parma's troops would be waiting. It turned out, however, that the army was days away. In the meantime, on July 28 the English sent eight fireships[7] across the Channel, which, assisted by the weather, forced the armada to raise anchor and make sail. Superior forces, better maneuverability, greater experience at sea battle, and the weather all favored the English as they closed in for battle at Gravelines, Flanders. The Spanish ships were not well supported by cannon, and Medina-Sidonia had expected to succeed with boarding parties rather than firepower. Instead, the English ships kept their distance and fired repeated, damaging broadside volleys into the enemy ships. Thousands of Spaniards died, several ships were lost, and many more were severely damaged. All Medina-Sidonia could do was limp back to Spain by sailing around Scotland and Ireland, a long and treacherous journey that saw the loss of dozens of ships. In the end, about 65 ships and 15,000 lives were lost, mostly from disease and starvation caused by the unexpectedly long trip home.

In an age that viewed military victory as a sign of God's favor, the overwhelming English success at the Battle of Gravelines naturally provided a significant boost in the fight between Protestantism and Catholicism in England. Before news of the battle's success reached England, the queen gave a speech to the assembled troops at Tilbury, Essex, that is considered to be her most famous oration. Arriving on a white horse, wearing a helmet and military breastplate, and carrying a sword or baton, Elizabeth supposedly said,

> Let tyrants fear, I have always so behaved myself that, under God I have placed my chiefest strength and safeguard in the loyal hearts and good-will of my subjects; and, therefore, I am come amongst you as you see in this time, not for my recreation and disport, but being resolved, in the midst and heat of battle, to live or die amongst you all…. I know I have the body but of a weak and feeble woman, but I have the heart and stomach of a king and of a king of England too – and take foul scorn that Parma or Spain, or any other prince of Europe, should dare to invade the borders of my realm; to which, rather than any dishonor should grow by me, I myself will take up arms.

---

7   Old warships covered in tar and gunpowder and set alight.

However accurate the reporting of Elizabeth's appearance and speech was, the arrival of the fifty-five-year-old queen among a sea of soldiers preparing for battle surely had great impact on its audience.

Although the defeat of the armada was the most significant event of the Anglo-Spanish War, the conflict continued for another fifteen years. An English armada roughly equal in size to the Spanish one was sent to distress the king of Spain and his possessions in the Americas and the Azores, under the command of Hawkins and Drake, but its successes were limited. Continued support of the Protestants in the Netherlands led to the conscription of nearly 100,000 young men. In 1596, the earl of Essex and Sir Walter Ralegh brought an Anglo-Dutch fleet to Cádiz and sacked and burned the city, with devastating consequences for the Spanish, who burned their own naval fleet rather than let it fall into the hands of the enemy. By 1604, when peace was achieved in the Treaty of London, there was little doubt that England had been considerably more successful during the course of the war. But the terms of the treaty called for *status quo ante bellum* – the state that existed before the war – which meant that England's efforts during these conflicts were mostly an expensive diversion. England made no political or territorial gains in Europe and still struggled for legitimacy in the Americas.

Elizabeth and Her Parliaments

As we have seen, meetings of parliament were an occasional occurrence throughout the Tudor period, typically called when the monarch wanted support for contentious policies, such as the changes to religion, and when extraordinary income in the form of taxation (then known as subsidies) was necessary to supplement the royal treasury. Otherwise, the monarch's extensive prerogative powers, including the ability to issue proclamations, and the powers held by the privy council were sufficient for the day-to-day administration of the realm. During the first quarter-century of Elizabeth's reign, only four parliaments met for seven sessions, averaging one session every three and a half years. This contrasts sharply with the first three-quarters of the century, when parliament met, on average, every year and a half.

This infrequency of Elizabeth's parliaments was the result of the fact that the queen's treasury was kept reasonably full from the ordinary revenues of the crown. Despite some uprisings in the north and Ireland, England was not at war between 1559 and 1584, which meant that military expenses were kept to a minimum. Although Elizabeth maintained the grandeur of majesty at significant expense, she was, after all, a single woman; unlike her father, she did not have to maintain households for other immediate members of the royal family, which also kept costs down. When funds were short, Elizabeth could still sell off some of the crown lands that remained from Henry's monastic dissolution, rely on some of the feudal dues resuscitated by her grandfather, and distribute various grants and commissions that provided her with additional income. These factors combined to limit the need for parliaments, a condition that was generally favorable to the populace, as meetings of parliament almost always meant the approval of new taxes.

Perhaps most importantly, Elizabeth had learned during her early parliaments that its members were not as submissive as she preferred. Although parliament was primarily tasked with addressing the legislation put to it by the queen and her council, the House of Commons, especially, often took the opportunity to discuss issues that Elizabeth held to be personal in nature and part of her prerogative rights to determine. For example, parliament frequently attempted to discuss the issues of religion, the queen's marriage, and the succession of the crown, all of which Elizabeth generally held were outside of its jurisdiction. Such discussions sometimes led to the prorogation or dissolution of parliament, which allowed Elizabeth to make speeches upbraiding its members for their obstinacy and temerity. Under these conditions, Elizabeth felt compelled to call parliament only when it was needed.

Elizabeth's views were somewhat at odds with contemporary writings about the role of the English parliament. Sir Thomas Smith, secretary of state from 1572–6, wrote in his *De Republica Anglorum* (written 1562–5, published 1583) that

> the most high and absolute power of the realm of England, is in the Parliament.... The Parliament abrogateth old laws, maketh new, ... establisheth forms of religion, ... giveth forms of succession to the crown, defineth of doubtful rights, whereof is no law already made, appointeth subsidies, ... and impositions, giveth most free pardons and absolutions.... For every Englishman is intended to be there present, either in person or by procuration and attorneys, of what preeminence, state, dignity, of quality soever he be, from the Prince (be he King or Queen) to the lowest person of England. And the consent of the Parliament is taken to be every man's consent.[8]

Smith's views were evidently not shared by a queen who, in 1563, wasted no time arresting and imprisoning several members of parliament who colluded to discuss marriage and succession before the session began, even though the session was ultimately dominated by these issues. Even parliament, however, recognized limitations on its independence, as evidenced by its detainment of fellow member Peter Wentworth in 1576 for arguing that members had absolute freedom of speech. In 1593, Wentworth was imprisoned for discussing the succession, never regaining his freedom before dying in the Tower in 1596.

---

8   Thomas Smith, *De Republica Anglorum* (London, 1583), book II, chapter 1.

If it was possible, Elizabeth probably would have continued the infrequency of parliament until the end of her reign. However, beginning in 1585 she was forced to work more closely with parliament because her ordinary income was no longer adequate to fund the needs of the nation. England was at war with Spain and in Ireland (to be discussed), both of which extended beyond Elizabeth's death. A series of agricultural crises in the 1590s caused impoverishment, unemployment, and inflation of food prices, a situation that was not helped by the severe plague outbreak of 1593. The result of these and other events was a financial shortfall exceeding £100,000 per year, which could only be met by parliamentary subsidy. Consequently, after 1584, parliament met more often and for longer periods of time.

The frequency of parliament during these years brought about several discernible changes to its composition. Because of the rising population, the number of parliamentary seats under the Tudors had increased membership in the House of Commons from about 300 in Henry VIII's time to closer to 450 in Elizabeth's later parliaments. This made meeting of the Commons, which occurred after 1547 in the modest-sized St. Stephens Chapel at Westminster Palace, extremely loud and crowded affairs. By contrast, the House of Lords had dwindled to about seventy-five, owing to Elizabeth's frugality in creating peerages and the drop in the number of ecclesiastical members. With six times as many members in the Commons than in the Lords, the Commons began assuming greater authority with regard to law-making.

In addition, a number of members returned over several sessions, which gave the Commons an institutional memory with regard to residual issues from previous sessions and the members' and queen's general disposition about certain matters. Some members became, in essence, professional politicians and sometimes banded together in ways that had not been seen in the past. Many members of parliament also increasingly came to be better educated, partly the result of humanism, with more than half the members in the later parliaments possessing university or law degrees. This gave them better knowledge of their historical rights and responsibilities in the mixed "king-in-parliament" constitution described by Smith, which had developed since the start of parliament in the late thirteenth century. Thus, for instance, the abuses of parliament caused by the privy council forcing reformation legislation through that body were becoming increasingly evident as Elizabeth's reign wore on.

All of this is not to say that the relationship between queen and parliament was entirely antagonistic, but as the Commons did what it was asked in approving subsidies and legislation to deal with the problems of poverty, drought, and war, it was also becoming more self-aware and, consequently, more vocal and opinionated. Sometimes Elizabeth avoided confrontation by letting parliament openly discuss issues and pass its bills, only to exercise her prerogative right of veto before they were enacted, which she did more than sixty times. At other times, she fiercely guarded her prerogative rights to determine certain issues by executive authority.

The issue of monopolies serves as the best example. To raise crown revenue outside of parliamentary subsidies, and as a way to reward loyalty among her favorites, Elizabeth began in the 1580s to issue letters patent granting individuals the right to hold monopolies on certain products. Monopolists, such as Walter Ralegh, paid the crown for licenses and then collected a percentage of sales from their commodities, which forced merchants to pass the additional cost on to their customers. By 1601, there were literally hundreds of monopolies: on salt, sugar, soap, silk, tobacco, beer, timber, wine, and almost anything else that was not considered among life's most basic necessities. Because these monopolies involved the regulation of trade, they were within the ambit of the royal prerogative, but parliament viewed the additional cost to the consumer as a form of taxation.

The issue of monopolies came up during several parliamentary sessions, and it became heightened in 1601 when the Commons attempted to make the practice illegal. Before they could do so, Elizabeth indicated her intention to speak with parliament and gave her Golden Speech:

> We have heard your declaration and perceive your care of our estate. I do assure you there is no prince that loves his subjects better, or whose love can countervail our love. There is no jewel, be it of never so rich a price, which I set before this jewel: I mean your love.... Of myself I must say this: I never was any greedy, scraping grasper, ... nor yet a waster.... [H]ad I not received a knowledge from you [about monopolies], I might have fallen into the lapse of an error, only for lack of information.... That my grants should be grievous to my people and oppressions to be privileged under color of our patent, our kingly dignity shall not suffer it.... [I]f my ... grants [have been] turned to the hurt of my people contrary to my will and meaning, ... I hope God will not lay their culps [blame] and offenses in my charge. I know the title of a king is a glorious title, but assure yourself ... that we also are to yield an account of our actions before the great judge. To be a king and wear a crown is a thing more glorious to them that see it than it is pleasant to them that bear it.... And I pray ... that before these gentlemen go into their countries, you bring them all to kiss my hand.

Coming from the mouth of a woman of nearly seventy years, who had been queen for more than four decades, this speech must have been a powerful one to listen to. That Elizabeth took this opportunity to dismiss her last parliament without giving it a chance for further discussion on monopolies, and gave only a vague indication that she would do anything about them, is a perfect reflection of how well Elizabeth had learned to manipulate her parliaments. Ultimately, monopolies and most of parliament's perceived gains during Elizabeth's reign would return with a vengeance under the early Stuarts.

※ ※ ※

Discussion Question 4.3: Given the Tudors' tendency to use (or abuse) parliament to support religious reform and the royal succession, why do you think the queen was so resistant to allow parliament to discuss these matters?

Rebellion, Coup, and Death

Toward the end of her life, Elizabeth was forced to deal with one final rebellion. Overlordship over Ireland had been reasserted by Henry VIII and Thomas Cromwell in the 1530s, leaving the island under the control of deputies with martial powers and well-staffed English military garrisons. In the early to mid-Elizabethan period, following a series of rebellions that were brutally suppressed by the English, large portions of Munster in southern Ireland had been granted to English Protestants in what has been referred to as the "conquest of Ireland." These "plantations" caused the displacement of many Gaelic Irish clans, or septs. These regions operated under English law and religion, but were also forced to adapt to Ireland's customary Brehon law and the fact that the majority of the Irish were still Catholic despite the adoption of supremacy and uniformity laws similar to England's.

By the early 1590s, English authorities in Ireland attempted to extend their powers into the Ulster region of northern Ireland, which was under the control of the wealthy and powerful Irish lord, Hugh O'Neill, earl of Tyrone, and also into the Pale, a region dominated by the Catholic "Old English," who had settled during the Middle Ages and generally disassociated themselves from the Protestant newcomers in the south. A series of major skirmishes, coupled with the attempt of O'Neill to seek assistance from Spain, forced Elizabeth – whose resources had been stretched by the Anglo-Spanish conflict – into action in 1599. She sent a 17,000-strong army into Ireland under the command of Robert Devereux, the earl of Essex, Leicester's stepson and a favorite at court since Leicester's death in 1588. The handsome young courtier turned out to be a poor general. Thousands of his troops died of typhus and dysentery while Essex blundered through southern Ireland, and his one major engagement, the Battle of Curlew Pass, was a disaster. Rather than engage the enemy, as he was ordered to do, Essex in November 1599 agreed to a truce, the terms of which were heavily criticized by Elizabeth's new secretary, Robert Cecil.

Elizabeth was angry at Essex's actions and was even more so when the earl unexpectedly returned to England to confront Cecil. Essex arrived at Nonsuch

Palace in Surrey and burst into the queen's bedchamber while she was wearing nightclothes and before her makeup had been applied, which constituted a major breach of royal protocol. Elizabeth charged Essex with abandoning his post and placed him under house arrest. A subsequent tribunal stripped Essex of most of his offices and the queen refused to renew his monopolies, leaving him heavily in debt. Disgraced and impoverished, Essex then attempted a peculiar coup d'état. In February 1601, messengers were sent to Essex House to bring the earl before the Star Chamber. Instead of complying, Essex took the queen's messengers hostage, gathered 200 followers, and marched through London demanding the downfall of his enemy Cecil and an audience with the queen. His actions were declared treasonous, most of his supporters abandoned him, and he returned briefly to Essex House before crown forces besieged his home and forced his surrender. After a trial, Essex was convicted of treason and beheaded at the Tower.

Meanwhile, Elizabeth sent Charles Blount, baron Mountjoy, to Ireland to bring Tyrone and his followers to heel. By 1602, he had managed to complete his mandate, subduing Ulster (which enabled the formal plantation of Ulster by Scottish subjects beginning in 1609), repelling a Spanish invasion of Ireland, and accepting Tyrone's surrender in April 1603. The surrender occurred about a month after Elizabeth's death on March 24. The medical reasons for Elizabeth's death are unclear, but most speculate that it was caused by melancholy and depression after the recent deaths of many of her friends. She never officially declared James as heir, but she knew this was the probable outcome and, in fact, Cecil had spent the previous two years preparing James for his accession.

* * *

Discussion Question 4.4: How important were speeches such as the Tilbury Speech and the Golden Speech, and Elizabeth's choice to portray herself as the "virgin queen," in her efforts to present herself as a good queen to her people? How does she use her gender to her advantage?

VOICES OF THE PAST
THE EXECUTION OF MARY, QUEEN OF SCOTS

Mary, Queen of Scots, had been involved in several plots against Elizabeth, although it was not until the Babington Plot of 1586 that actual proof was discovered. Elizabeth was forced to sign her cousin's death warrant, but she ordered one of her secretaries of state, William Davison, not to carry out the warrant. The council defied her and ordered Mary to be beheaded in February 1587 (see Figure 4.4). The following extract records the events from Elizabeth's signing of the warrant until Mary's execution.

* * *

[The queen] delivered a writing to Davison … signed with her own hand, that a warrant under the great seal of England should be made for her execution, which should be in readiness if any danger should grow in that fearful time, and commanded him to acquaint no man therewith. But the next day … her mind changed and she commanded Davison … that the warrant should not be drawn. Davison came presently to the queen, and told her that it was drawn and under seal already. She being somewhat moved, blamed him for such haste. He notwithstanding acquainted the council both with the warrant and the whole matter, and easily persuaded them … that the queen had commanded it should be executed. Presently without all delay, was [order sent] … to see her executed according to the law....

Figure 4.4 *The execution of Mary, Queen of Scots.*

Credit: Science History Images/Alamy Stock Photo.

The fatal day now appearing, being the 8 of February, [Mary] dressed herself gorgeously and curiously, as she was wont to do upon festival days, and calling her servants together, commanded her [last will and] testament to be read, prayed them to take their legacies in good part.... Then fixing her mind wholly upon God, in her oratory ... with signs, groans, and prayers she craved His divine favor, till Thomas Andrews, sheriff of the county, signified unto her that she must now come forth. And forth she came with stature, countenance and presence composed unto majesty, a cheerful look, matron-like, and very modest habit, her head covered with a linen veil, and that hanging down, her prayer beads hanging at her girdle, and carrying a crucifix of ivory in her hands. In the gallery she was received [by one of her servants] ... pouring forth tears, bewailed his hap [situation], that he was to carry into Scotland the woeful news of the unhappy fate of his lady and mistress.

She comforted him, saying "Lament not, but rather rejoice, thou shalt by and by see Mary Stuart freed from all cares. Tell them that I die constant in my religion, and firm in my fidelity towards Scotland and France. God forgive them which have thirsted for my blood as harts [male deer] do after the fountain. Thou God, which art truth itself, and thoroughly and truly understandest the inward thoughts of my heart, knowest how greatly I have desired that the kingdoms of England and Scotland might be united in one. Commend me to my son, and certify him that I have done nothing which may prejudice the kingdom of Scotland; warn him to hold amity with the queen of England; and see thou do him faithful service."

... Which when she had said, and turned herself away, it was merited that her servants whom she would name, should be present.... So the gentlewomen, two earls, and the sheriff of the shire going before her, she came to the scaffold, which was erected at the upper end of the hall, on which was set a chair, a cushion, a block, all covered with black cloth. As soon as she was set, and silence proclaimed, Beale [clerk of the council]

read the warrant, she heard it attentively.... Then [the] dean of Peterborough began a long speech unto her touching the condition of her life past, present, and to come. She interrupted him once or twice as he was speaking, prayed him "not to trouble her, protesting that she was firm and resolute in the ancient Catholic Roman religion, and for that was ready to shed her blood."

... Then ... she falling down upon her knees, and holding the crucifix before her in her hands, prayed in Latin with her servants.... After the dean had made an end of prayer, she in English commended the church, her son, and Queen Elizabeth to God, beseeching him to turn away his wrath from this Island, and professing that she reposed her hope of salvation in the blood of Christ (lifting up the cross). She called upon the celestial choir of saints to make intercession for her, she forgave all her enemies, and kissing the crucifix, and signing herself with the cross, she said, "As thy arms, O Christ, were spread upon the cross, so receive me with the stretched-out arms of thy mercy, and remit my sins."

Then the executioners asked her forgiveness, which she granted them. And when the women-servants ... had taken off her outer garments, wailing and lamenting her case, she kissed them and signed them with the cross, with a cheerful countenance bade them forbear their womanish lamentations, for now she should rest from her sorrows, ... in like manner turning to her men-servants who wept with her.... And now having covered her face with a linen handkerchief, and lying down at the block, she recited the Psalm, "In thee, O Lord, do I trust, let me never be confounded." Then stretching forth her body, and repeating many times, "Into thy hands, Lord, I commend my spirit," her head was stricken off at two blows, the dean crying out "So let Queen Elizabeth's enemies perish," the earl of Kent answering, "Amen."

... As soon as a rumor was brought to Queen Elizabeth's ears, who little thought it, that the queen of Scots was put to death, she heard it with great indignation, her countenance and her words failed her, and with excessive sorry she was in a manner astonished, insomuch as she gave herself over to grief, putting herself into mourning weeds [garments], and shedding abundance of tears. Her council she sharply rebuked, and commanded them out of her sight, subjecting them to examination.

Source: William Camden, *Annales, or the Historie of the Most Renowned and Victorious Princess, Elizabeth, Late Queen of England* (London, 1635), 340–5.

* * *

Discussion Question 4.5: If Mary of Scots was guilty of treason and showed so many outward signs of her Catholicism on the day of her death, why do you think Camden's description of her death is so sympathetic?

PART TWO
THE STUARTS, 1603–1690

The seventeenth century was one of England's most disorderly. In the first half of the century, the early Stuart monarchs (see **Genealogy 3**), James I and Charles I, practiced a form of absolutism that alienated them from the main instruments of government, especially parliament but also the church. Their actions brought on the execution and assassination of several leading statesmen, and led to a lengthy and vicious civil war that pitted English subjects against one another and resulted in both regicide and England's only, and unsuccessful, experiment with republican government.

The restoration of the monarchy under Charles II saw many of the gains achieved in the previous two decades reversed, and older religious and constitutional issues returned, resulting in the state-authorized murder of hundreds of traitors and heretics. Fears of a return to absolutism and Catholicism under James II brought on another, speedier and more peaceful, revolution that resulted in enduring changes to England's political and criminal justice system by 1690. Although England in the seventeenth century might not have been, in the words of Christopher Hill, a "world turned upside down," there was plenty of death and disorder.

CHAPTER FIVE

EARLY STUART ABSOLUTISM, 1603–1642

DEATH AND DISORDER: THE GUNPOWDER PLOT

Early in the reign of James I, England came close to experiencing what would surely have been the most disorderly event in its history: an attempt to blow up parliament when the king, nobles, judges, and members of the Commons assembled for its opening. When James came to the throne, English Catholics expected that the son of Mary, Queen of Scots, would be tolerant toward their religion and ease the severity of the penal laws that had been passed under Elizabeth. James proved unwilling to do so, in part because of his belief in erastianism, which encouraged Catholics to turn once again to Spain, with whom England was still at war, for assistance with their cause.

One of the leaders of this effort was Guy Fawkes (1570–1606), a gentleman from York who had converted to Catholicism in the early 1580s. By James's accession, Fawkes had become an experienced mercenary soldier fighting for Spain against Protestants in the Netherlands. By 1603, Fawkes was in Spain seeking support for another military venture that could return a Catholic to the throne. His hopes at help from Spain were dashed with the signing of the Anglo-Spanish Treaty of

London in 1604, which said nothing about Catholic worship or toleration. If Fawkes and his fellow English Catholics wanted relief from persecution, they would have to take matters into their own hands.

In 1604, several conspirators – including Fawkes and the mastermind of the plot, Robert Catesby – hatched a plan to destroy parliament at a time when both houses, the king, senior members of the royal family, the law judges, and the Anglican bishops were together during the king's speech that traditionally opened parliament. The conspirators also planned to kidnap Princess Elizabeth, James's daughter, and install her as the new queen. As Elizabeth was a child and a female, Catesby planned to vest authority to rule the country in an unnamed Catholic peer, depending on who was still alive when the dust settled. After extensive planning, the conspirators leased an undercroft, or cellar, beneath the chamber used by the House of Lords, where the state opening of parliament would occur. In July 1605, they moved in thirty-six barrels of gunpowder and loads of firewood.

Figure 5.1 *The execution of the Gunpowder Plot conspirators, etching by Claes Visscher.*

Due to outbreaks of plague, the opening date of parliament kept changing, but eventually it was set for November 5. Fawkes was tasked with waiting in the undercroft, lighting the fuse, and then escaping on a ship anchored in the Thames, which would take him to the Continent. But Catesby had made a fatal error. Partly because of the need for money to mount the plot, he brought in a number of conspirators whose loyalty was suspect. One of these men anonymously warned a member of parliament, William Parker, lord Monteagle, not to attend the state opening. Monteagle promptly gave the letter to Robert Cecil, who passed it along to the king. The king ordered a search of the buildings surrounding parliament.

On November 4, the search party made their way into the undercroft, where they discovered Fawkes, the gunpowder and firewood, and several slow-burning matches to light the fuse. Fawkes was arrested and the undercroft was cleared out. Many of the conspirators took flight while Fawkes, who had given the name "John Johnson," claimed that he acted alone. "Johnson" was brought to the Tower of London where, after two days of torture that included being broken on the rack, he confessed the entire conspiracy. On November 8, Catesby and several other conspirators were

discovered at a house in Staffordshire and a company of 200 men under the command of the sheriff of Worcester besieged the home. Catesby and several others were killed during the siege, while the survivors were taken into custody and interrogated.

In January 1606, a trial held by a special commission of leading members of the judiciary and privy council, led by the attorney general, Sir Edward Coke, resulted in the conviction of the conspirators for high treason. Each was to be punished by being hanged, drawn, and quartered, the usual punishment for their crime. This involved the accused being dragged to the place of execution, hanged until nearly dead, cut down, and laid on the quartering block. Then his genitals and bowels were removed and burned before his eyes, his heart cut out and also burned, followed by decapitation and the quartering of the body. The quarters were to be displayed at some public place until the king authorized their removal, by which time the pieces were usually consumed by birds and insects. This method of execution was considered to be the worst possible form of death, because of the contemporary belief that the body needed to be buried in the ground whole in order to achieve the afterlife.

Eight conspirators suffered this fate (see Figure 5.1). Fawkes, knowing what awaited him, managed to leap from the gallows and break his own neck, freeing him from the excruciating pain of having his genitals and bowels removed and burned. Catesby was exhumed from his grave and decapitated, his head placed on a spike beside the parliament building. The discovery of the Gunpowder Plot and the punishment of its conspirators served to strengthen the Church of England and initiated further anti-Catholic sentiment in early Stuart England. Beginning in 1606, English people celebrated "Guy Fawkes Night" on November 5, and the custom continues to the present day. Fireworks are set off and effigies of Fawkes are burned on a bonfire. Although Fawkes was not neither the initiator nor the leader of the Gunpowder Plot, his name is most closely associated with it.

* * *

Discussion Question 5.1: What does the futile and perhaps foolish attempt of the Gunpowder Plot conspirators say about the state of Catholicism in early seventeenth-century England?

James, Absolutism, and Religion

When James VI of Scotland became James I of England in 1603, he was thirty-seven years old and had already ruled his northern kingdom with reasonable success for two decades (see Figure 5.2). Like Henry VII in England a century earlier, James had managed to strengthen a monarchy and government weakened by a succession of poor kings and powerful lords with strong clan affiliations. James was tall and thin, wore odd clothing that was foreign and even comical to the English eye, and spoke with a thick accent that was made all the more difficult to understand by a pronounced lisp. To many observers in early seventeenth-century England, these distinctly unkingly characteristics disguised the fact that James was highly intelligent and in writing had shown himself to be something of a scholar-king. Between 1580 and 1610, James produced a wide range of literature, including poetry and an academic treatise about its production, meditations about religion, a learned work about the dangers of smoking tobacco, and a work of demonology that covered topics as diverse as black magic, witches, werewolves, and vampires, which was possibly a source for Shakespeare's *Macbeth* (1606).

A few years before he came to the English throne, James had also produced two treatises about the nature of kingship, *Trew Law of Free Monarchies* (1598) and *Basilikon Doron* (1599), both of which were reissued in England upon his accession in 1603. In *Trew Law*, James espoused the European notion of divine-right, absolute monarchy, largely in response to ongoing Scottish and Continental debates about the king's contractual relationship with his subjects and legislative assemblies. Consistent with the ideas developed by Machiavelli and the French jurist and political philosopher Jean Bodin, James argued that kings were above the law and answered only to God and could, therefore, rule by royal prerogative rights. While James acknowledged that kings needed to respect customs and consult with parliament, he left little room for doubt that the king alone possessed absolute sovereignty. Even "wicked kings" were sent by God "for a curse to his people" and could not be overthrown.

James wrote *Basilikon Doron* as an instruction manual for his son and heir, Prince Henry. In a passage that foreshadowed his later difficulties with the English House of Commons, James reminded his son that a king was "a little God to sit on the throne, and rule over other men" and advised him to "hold no parliament, but for the necessity of new laws, which would be but seldom." These ideas were, in fact, little different in sentiment than those espoused by Henry VIII and Elizabeth, both of whom ruled regularly by proclamation and called parliaments

Figure 5.2 *James I, circa 1606, by John De Critz the Elder.*

Credit: GL Archive/Alamy Stock Photo.

only when they were absolutely necessary. Perhaps wisely, however, the Tudor monarchs put these beliefs into action instead of committing them to writing.

One area in which James's belief in absolute monarchy was demonstrated was his support for the royal supremacy of the church. Since the 1560s, Scotland had increasingly developed as a Calvinist Presbyterian nation, and James had experienced considerable challenges from the Scottish kirk, or church, over the issue of supremacy and hierarchy within the church. Nonetheless, James was nominally Presbyterian, a fact that did not escape the Puritans in England who had been frequently persecuted and frustrated in the aftermath of the Elizabethan settlement of religion. As James traveled south to assume to assume his crown in 1603, he was presented with the Millenary Petition, a document signed by 1,000 ministers that sought what they had been denied under Elizabeth, namely greater reform of the church, especially regarding the royal supremacy, the contentious ornaments rubric of the uniformity act, and the use of the term *priest*.

James responded to the petition by calling the Hampton Court Conference in 1604, a meeting that included the king, Anglican bishops, and Puritans. During this conference, James made it clear that he accepted the fundamentals of Anglicanism as established under Elizabeth. Its adoption of Calvinist theology, with which James was well familiar, combined with royal supremacy and clerical hierarchy, naturally appealed to the author of the *Trew Law* and to a man who had fought for precisely this combination in Scotland for decades. If God created kings, it was natural that kings would govern churches, and a church without bishops invited people to envision a society without a king. During the conference, James declared his position succinctly with the phrase "no bishop, no king." This was followed by his appointment of Richard Bancroft as archbishop of Canterbury in 1604, a conservative who, like Whitgift before him, strongly supported Anglicanism.

The conference was also a victory for the Puritans, in that James authorized the production of what, in 1611, became the English-language and highly readable *King James Bible*, which is still widely in use and is considered among the best works in early modern English literature. James also tended to be more lenient toward Puritans than had Elizabeth, provided that they did not foment rebellion and outwardly conformed to the most basic tenets of the Anglican faith. Even in the aftermath of events such as the Gunpowder Plot, James showed similar toleration for Catholicism, electing not to put the penal laws against Catholics in full force. The official response of the king was toleration for religious extremists, provided they were peaceful and accepted James's right to govern the church.

The Commons and the Ancient Constitution

If James had managed early on to develop a tolerant, if clearly erastian, attitude toward religion, his beliefs about absolute monarchy could not allow him to be so conciliatory toward parliament, especially the elected House of Commons. As we have seen, by the end of Elizabeth's reign, the frequency of parliaments had turned the Commons into a more powerful, semi-professional body that was more self-aware and combative than its medieval and earlier Tudor counterparts. Although Elizabeth generally accepted the right of that body, while in session, to discuss matters of relevance to the state, and although she showed a willingness to compromise on issues of religion for political expediency, nonetheless she often suppressed excessive displays of parliamentary independence through veto, rebukes, imprisonment, and dismissal. Whatever gains the Commons allegedly acquired under Elizabeth were theoretical at best.

Unfortunately, James entered this political climate with several disadvantages. Although he was an experienced king, he was not well informed about the workings of the English parliament – which functioned quite differently than the more amenable Scottish parliament, which sat as a single house – nor about the perceived changes that had occurred under Elizabeth. In addition, when James's first parliament met in March 1604, it had not sat since 1601 and several issues from earlier sessions, such as monopolies and the continued use of fiscal feudalism in the form of wardship and purveyance,[1] had not been resolved to parliament's satisfaction. James's reissue of his absolutist writings in 1603 also meant that, as members of parliament gathered in Westminster, many were concerned about a ruler who had publicly professed – and had advised his heir – that a king was a "little God" and that sittings of parliament should be "seldom" and should only occur to produce "new laws" rather than, for example, debate contemporary issues or utter grievances against the king or his ministers.

The Commons was little assuaged when, at the opening of the session, the king involved himself in a dispute regarding the election of Sir Francis Goodwin. As Goodwin was deemed an outlaw due to an unpaid debt, the Court of Chancery had determined that he could not take his seat, but this decision was overturned by the Commons on the historical grounds that it was responsible to determine its own composition. James stepped in to defend the authority of his courts and claimed that all privileges held by parliament were granted by the king alone. Also during that session, James attempted to bring about a union of England and Scotland into a single kingdom of "Great Britain," to be governed by a single parliament and set of laws. "What God hath conjoined," James told his parliament, "let no man separate." He did not want to be, in his words, "a polygamist and husband to two wives," England and Scotland. Instead, he wanted to be styled "King of Great Britain." Unsurprisingly, the Commons greeted this plan with little enthusiasm. England, it was argued, was a realm governed by its

---

1 Purveyance was the right of the crown to purchase goods for the military and royal household at below market rates, a system that had become rife with corruption by the end of the Tudor age.

ancient, national laws, created by English monarchs in concert with the English parliament.[2] Bringing about a union of the two kingdoms mostly for the sake of convenience was, to say the least, an unpopular and complicated solution, although parliament ultimately did agree to appoint a commission to consider the issue.

James's perceived abuse of parliament by involving himself in the election and pressing the union agenda was met with concerns that the foreign king was ignorant of English parliamentary history, practices, and privileges. In June, the Commons appointed a committee that produced a document known as the *Form of Apology and Satisfaction*, which was intended to be presented to the king. In the document, the Commons took the opportunity to instruct the king about the "misinformation" he had uttered about the privileges of parliament:

> [O]ur privileges and liberties are our right and due inheritance no less than our very lands and goods…. [T]hey cannot be withheld from us, denied, or impaired, but with apparent wrong to the whole state of the realm…. [A]lthough it may be true that in the latter times of Queen Elizabeth some one privilege now and then were … acted against …, in regard to her sex and age which we had great cause to be tender, and … those actions were then passed over.

The Commons' claim that it was "tender" toward Elizabeth's abuses of parliament because of her sex and age was as fictitious as its claim for ancient "privileges and liberties," which had little basis in history and law.

However inaccurate the claims in the *Apology* were, they reflected a position that had developed under Elizabeth about the extent to which parliament, and its relationship with the king, was founded on an "ancient constitution" that had its origins in Anglo-Saxon laws since before the Norman Conquest of 1066, as well as later developments, such as Magna Carta (1215) and the English common law as it had been practiced in courts and parliament since the thirteenth century. The rise of this concept was part of the "legal humanism" movement beginning in the 1570s, when antiquarians such as William Lambarde and William Camden began collecting and publishing treatises about medieval history and law.

The champion of the ancient constitution was Sir Edward Coke, who had served as speaker of the house in 1592, attorney general in 1594, and then chief justice of the Court of Common Pleas (1606), a position that enabled him to become the true defender of this relatively new idea. Coke and others supported the notion that parliament was an independent body that, when in session,

---

2   The Scottish parliament, for its part, also opposed the union, primarily on the grounds that Scotland would become much the lesser partner in the new relationship.

functioned as "King-in-Parliament," a superior source of sovereign authority whose actions, therefore, had greater legal power than the king operating alone. In essence, this was a claim that parliament could both limit the actions of the king and issue legislation that was superior to, or could supersede, royal proclamations. Although these ideas were only nascent in their expression in 1604, and would become much more developed over the ensuing two decades, they are reflected in the tone and context of the *Apology*. The *Apology* was never given to the king, but he knew its contents, which occasioned his prorogation of parliament. Rather than thanking parliament for its work, as was traditional, James instead stated: "I will not thank where I feel no thanks due.… I am not of such a stock as to praise fools."

At the end of the year, James issued a royal proclamation in which he assumed the title "King of Great Britain," devised the coat of arms to reflect a union between England and Scotland, and ordered that union currency be created, including a twenty-shilling piece to be called the "unite." He later ordered the use of a new British flag, the "Union Jack,"[3] to be flown on all ships employing English and Scottish crews. Two further sittings of parliament met in 1605 (which was dominated by the Gunpowder Plot) and 1606. In the latter, the union commissioners had completed their report, which commanded debate during the session. By the end of that session, the issue of the union was moribund; James's proclamation was ignored by nearly everyone, and even the king came to realize the futility of any further efforts at a legal union. Ultimately, the only concessions James got were recognition that Scottish subjects born after 1603 were naturalized English subjects, meaning they could inherit land in England and make suit in English courts, and that free trade should occur between the two kingdoms. More than anything, James's three parliamentary sessions in his first three years had shown him the value of calling as few parliaments as possible during his reign.

Crown Finances

When James came to the throne, England had been at war with Spain and in Ireland for nearly two decades, which left the English state with debt exceeding £300,000. Elizabeth's councillors had attempted to offset some of this debt by selling off crown land and other assets, which reduced annual royal revenues, but in fact it was primarily parliament that was relied upon for subsidies to cover the costs of war and the royal court. Under Elizabeth, one of the most important

---

3   A jack was a flag flown at the bow of ships to distinguish the nation to which the ship owed allegiance. In this case, it is also possible that the term Jack was intended as a short from for Jacobus, Latin for James.

sources of crown revenue, customs duties, had also decreased significantly, as a result of war, inflation, and the failure of Burghley, as treasurer, to update the customs rates, which remained stagnant for half a century. Burghley had also failed to increase the rental rates for crown land to keep up with inflation, in part because the beneficiaries of the current system were landlords like Burghley himself.

In addition, Elizabeth had been a single woman who did not, therefore, need to manage several royal households and who had become more frugal as she aged. By contrast, James was a man in his mid-thirties and needed to fund not only his own household but also that of his wife, Anne of Denmark, and his three children, of whom the households of Henry (until his death in 1612) and then Charles, as heirs, needed to be nearly as kingly as James's. Coming from a poor kingdom with a small population, James saw in England a much wealthier nation, and his spending was, without doubt, excessive. From the beginning of his reign, James and Anne lived lavish lifestyles, wore expensive clothing, partook of pricey entertainments, and hired England's best architect, Inigo Jones, to build several extravagant buildings in London and Greenwich. Unlike Elizabeth, James also spent considerable amounts of money on his courtiers, bestowing large annual pensions to both English and Scottish subjects. By about 1610, the royal expenses had increased more than 50 per cent from Elizabeth's last years, and the royal debt stood at over £600,000.

As it was unlikely for the king to reduce his spending, the only alternative was to increase royal revenues, which could occur only in two ways: improving the ordinary income of the crown through the traditional revenue-gathering sources, or securing extraordinary income in the form of parliamentary subsidies, which would also place the king in the position of becoming more reliant on parliament. Naturally, by 1606, with parliament already antagonistic toward the king, James and his ministers preferred the first option. The responsibility of increasing ordinary revenues fell primarily to Robert Cecil, whom James promoted to earl of Salisbury in 1605 and to lord treasurer in 1608. Salisbury's first task as treasurer was to update the *Book of Rates*, which regulated customs duties. He arranged for the duties to be collected by "farmers" who contracted with the crown to pay an annual fixed sum in exchange for the right to collect duties and retain whatever profits they brought in.

The farmers were also required to collect and remit to the crown impositions, an additional duty on hundreds of items. Although impositions had existed in much more limited form under Elizabeth, they were enlarged as a result of Bates's Case. In 1606, John Bates had brought suit against the government for its imposition on foreign currants, arguing that this was a new tax collected without parliamentary approval. The Court of Exchequer ruled that the king had the prerogative authority to regulate all manner of foreign trade, which enabled Salisbury to increase this revenue source in 1608. The collection of impositions proved administratively challenging and ripe for corruption, and it brought in only about £70,000 per year. This was a significant sum, but not nearly enough to make up for the crown's shortfall. Politically, impositions were also extremely unpopular, because they signaled the ability and willingness of the king to increase revenues through extra-parliamentary means.

By 1610, the failure of ordinary revenue sources to provide for the crown's expenses encouraged Salisbury to propose the "Great Contract" to a newly elected parliament. The proposal involved parliament granting the king a one-time sum of £600,000 to pay off his debt, plus an annual grant of £200,000 per year. In exchange, the king would give up most aspects of fiscal feudalism, including the rights of wardship and purveyance. However, both parliament and the king had reason to doubt the contract. From parliament's perspective, because the grant exceeded the amount currently collected from feudal dues, it had the potential of making the king even more independent of parliament. In addition, because the proposal was brought by a crown desperate for funds, the Commons used this leverage to air grievances about the king's excessive spending, encouraged James to be more frugal, and returned to several sore spots: the rights of freedom of speech and to set limits on the royal prerogative, especially as it was employed for impositions and monopolies.

The combination of a stern rebuke by the Commons and the infringement of prerogative was altogether too much for an absolutist such as James. In his closing speech to parliament, which put a decisive end to the contract, he reminded its members:

> The estate of monarchy is the supremest thing upon earth; for kings are not only God's lieutenants on earth … but even by God himself they are called gods.… [T]o dispute what God may do is blasphemy … so it is sedition in subjects to dispute what a king may do.… I will not be content that my power be disputed upon.… [D]o not meddle with the main points of government; that is my craft. I am now an old king.… I must not be taught my office.… I would not have you meddle with such ancient rights of mine as I have received them from my predecessors.

Mirroring closely the language of the *Trew Law*, James made it clear to parliament that his prerogatives were not subject to debate in the Commons, and that the legislature and indeed the law served at the pleasure of the king. This was largely a position that was also advocated by legal figures such as Sir Thomas Egerton and Sir Francis Bacon, both of whom would later serve as lord chancellor and who would, in this position, make enemies of Coke and other supporters of the ancient constitution.

With the Great Contract in ruins, James continued to rely on Salisbury, until his death in 1612, and then on Egerton to assist with finding new methods of funding the crown. By far the most controversial of these was the introduction of a new rank in the English aristocracy, that of baronet. Baronets were placed into the hierarchy between baron and knight and, uniquely, although they did not have the right to sit in the House of Lords, their title could be inherited by male descendants. James invited substantial gentleman to purchase these largely honorary titles for the sum of £1,095. These creations, which were based on wealth rather than service to the crown or realm, were despised by the traditional nobility and gentry, as the sudden influx of so many new members of questionable honor and lineage diluted and tainted the aristocracy. The crown also continued to issue monopolies on hundreds of items and levied forced loans, which were felt most severely by the type of men who sat in the houses of parliament. The "Addled Parliament" that met in 1614 aired grievances about these measures but was dissolved after six weeks having failed to produce any legislation.

* * *

Discussion Question 5.2: In what ways did James I inherit his problems from the Tudors, and in what ways did he create his own problems?

The King's Favorites

Another contentious issue in James's reign, especially after the death of the fiscally responsible Cecil, was the wealth and power he lavished on his court favorites. That monarchs had certain courtiers who curried greater favor than others was certainly nothing new; Ralegh, Leicester, and Essex had all thrived under Elizabeth. But James's choice to bestow pensions, positions, and titles on men of limited talent who provided no valuable service to the state was something that many of England's elite could not tolerate. Perhaps more troubling, in the eyes of certain officials, James had demonstrated that his choice of favorites were handsome young men, to whom the king was seemingly sexually attracted. Although there is little evidence that James acted out physically on these desires, nor that his favorites – who, like the king, were married and had children of their own – were bisexual, James's outward displays of affection by kissing them and keeping in close physical contact, including sharing a bed on more than one occasion, was regularly noticed by courtiers and government officials. Possibly, these ambitious young men simply came to understand the king's proclivities and played into them to gain preferment.

Two favorites, in particular, came to prominence. The first was Robert Carr, who came to the king's attention when he broke his leg during a jousting match. After helping to nurse the young man back to health, James granted the handsome

Carr a knighthood and awarded him a manor house in Dorset. By 1613, Carr had been created viscount Rochester and was a prominent privy councillor. Scandal soon erupted. Rochester began an illicit affair with the married Frances Howard, countess of Essex, a relationship supported by the powerful Howard family because it offered the possibility of greater influence at court. Thomas Overbury, Rochester's friend and mentor, strongly objected to the affair. In response, the Howards spread rumors that Overbury had disparaged the queen, which caused James – who had long resented Overbury's sway over his favorite – to offer him an ambassadorial assignment that would remove him from court. Overbury refused and the king, infuriated by his subject's insolence, had him thrown into the Tower of London, where he died in September 1613. Frances secured an annulment from her husband on grounds of impotence and married Rochester two weeks after Overbury's death. By 1615 – with Rochester now earl of Somerset and the king's lord chamberlain – rumors began to spread that Overbury had been poisoned to death with sulfuric acid to allow the annulment and marriage to proceed more smoothly. At trial, Somerset, Frances, and four conspirators were found guilty of murder. Although the king pardoned Somerset and the countess (the other four were hanged), the scandal further tarnished the image of the royal court and Somerset fell from favor.

Just before the Overbury scandal burst, James's second great favorite arrived at court. George Villiers, aged twenty-two, was the son of minor gentry and a polished courtier from time spent in France. James was instantly entranced by the handsome youth who possessed grace, refined manners, and skills at dancing, music, and other courtly entertainments. By 1615, Villiers had become a gentleman of the king's bedchamber and a knight with an annual pension. After Somerset's fall, Villiers rose with remarkable speed to become master of the horse, a baron and viscount in 1616, earl of Buckingham in 1617, marquess of Buckingham in 1618, lord high admiral in 1619, and finally duke of Buckingham in 1623. These appointments and creations quickly made Buckingham among the wealthiest and most powerful men in the country. His lands and properties, ability to control patronage, and work for James as his agent for the sale of titles, offices, and monopolies brought in an annual income exceeding £20,000 per year at a time when most nobles were earning less than one third of that figure.

In his position as lord high admiral, Buckingham also advocated for England's entrance into the Thirty Years' War (1618–48) in support of the Protestant forces of Frederick V of the Palatinate – James's son-in-law through his daughter Elizabeth – who had suffered a major defeat in 1620. Although James had, throughout his reign, shown himself to be a pacifist, it was difficult for him to stand idly by as his daughter's husband was forbidden from entering his homeland, which was under the occupation of Spanish forces. Entrance into war to restore Frederick to the Palatinate, however, required a subsidy from parliament, which had not met in seven years and which James had planned never to call again after the disastrous sitting in 1614. The parliament of 1621, therefore, met in a combative mood and demanded a price for its subsidy: the impeachment of Lord Chancellor Francis Bacon after evidence was offered that he had taken bribes; the toppling of Buckingham from favor; the abolition of monopolies and impositions; a full-scale war against Spain; and the termination of ongoing negotiations to marry Charles, the prince of Wales and heir to the throne, to Maria, the Spanish crown princess.

Although parliament managed to secure Bacon's removal, the king rejected the other issues on the grounds that they interfered with his prerogatives regarding the appointment of councillors, trade, foreign affairs, and royal marriages. Parliament responded in kind, asserting its privilege to discuss "arduous and urgent affairs concerning the king, state, and defense of the realm," a protestation that was written into the Commons' parliamentary journal. Predictably, James dissolved parliament, but not before ripping the protest from the journal and imprisoning several parliamentary leaders responsible for it, including Edward Coke. Coke's presence in parliament was caused by his removal, at Bacon's suggestion, as chief justice of the Court of Common Pleas (1613) and Court of King's Bench (1616) because of his continuing efforts, in court decisions and reports, to advocate for the ancient constitution, supremacy of the common law over royal innovation, and the authority of parliamentary sovereignty. In parliament, Coke became the chief voice of criticism against the king, heading a "Committee of Grievances" that sought to abolish monopolies and challenge the planned marriage. Coke was released from the Tower of London after nine months' imprisonment.

Plans for the "Spanish match" continued, with Charles and Buckingham setting out for Madrid in 1623, disguised and under assumed names, to bring the negotiations to a conclusion. After half a year of negotiations, however, the match failed to materialize. The Spanish demanded Catholic toleration in England and refused to agree to the reinstatement of Frederick, and Charles and Buckingham – who became fast friends as a result of this escapade – returned to London. Now that nothing stood in the way of declaring war with Spain in order to assist Frederick and the Protestants, James called parliament in 1624. Ultimately, this was James's most successful parliament, because both sides agreed on the central premise that war was necessary and that money was needed to prosecute it, although nobody on the parliamentary side believed that Buckingham was the man to do so.

As the Commons got on with its business, Buckingham initiated negotiations with Louis XIII of France to wed his sister, Henrietta Maria, to Charles. Though a Catholic nation, France was concerned about the encroachment of the vast Holy Roman Empire, which shared a long border with France, if the Catholics won the Thirty Years' War. This made France an unlikely ally of Frederick and the Protestant cause, making an Anglo-French marriage somewhat more tolerable than an Anglo-Spanish one. The plans were still underway when James died of malaria and dysentery in March 1625.

Charles and Parliament

Unlike his father, an arrogant pedant who never hesitated to speak his mind, Charles I was more taciturn and reserved and disliked public speaking because of a pronounced stammer (see Figure 5.3). These characteristics, combined with the king's general unwillingness to take advice, and his tendency to make hasty decisions without proper deliberation, gave the impression that he was too secretive and perhaps lacked the capacity to rule. Shortly after his accession, Charles married Henrietta Maria. By the standards of the time, the marriage was a happy one; Charles proved to be a faithful husband and loving father to his children, in contrast to James's less savory reputation in these areas. But his wife's Catholicism quickly became an issue. The queen worshipped in a private Catholic chapel, and in a secret agreement Charles agreed to educate his children as Catholics until age twelve and not to persecute Catholics within his realm. Fears for the return of

Figure 5.3 *Charles I, 1635, by Anthony van Dyck.*

"popery" at court, and murmured though incorrect claims that the king himself might be a closet Catholic, caused a rocky start to the reign.

When the king's first parliament met in 1625, therefore, it was already in a restive mood. It did not help that Charles had already shown his intention to continue using Buckingham as his chief advisor, a man who was reviled for his modest origins and quick ascent, for arranging the Catholic marriage, and for the incompetence he brought to the powerful position of lord high admiral. At the outset, parliament refused to grant the king "tunnage and poundage" for life. Since the mid-fourteenth century, the first parliament of a new reign had granted the king the right to collect customs duties, which were technically a parliamentary subsidy, as part of his ordinary income. However, James's and Salisbury's alleged abuse of that system encouraged parliament to grant the right for only one year, pending a parliamentary review of the customs revenue, which would have forced Charles to call another parliament the following year. Charles argued that the parliamentary granting of tunnage and poundage was mere courtesy, and he collected it throughout his reign, which was perceived by parliament as illegally gathered revenue. Parliament also refused to adequately fund the war effort. Charles and Buckingham had expected a subsidy of more than £1,000,000 to restore the Palatinate to the king's brother-in-law and contribute to the European war effort against Spain, but parliament only approved a paltry £140,000. This was far less than was needed, and it was less even than the usual subsidy index of £200,000.

Despite inadequate funding, Buckingham organized a naval expedition against Spain, the Cádiz expedition, that turned out to be an unmitigated disaster. Bad weather, poor naval commanders, modern fortifications in Cádiz, and the foolish decision to allow English soldiers to become drunk just before the Spanish army arrived resulted in the loss of 1,000 men and an embarrassing return to England with nothing to show for the adventure except an expense sheet of £250,000. When parliament met in 1626, it blamed the disaster on Buckingham's incompetence and initiated impeachment proceedings against him. Charles responded by accepting the blame himself – an unwise move for a monarch who styled himself as absolutist – and dismissed parliament to save his friend, but not before ordering the imprisonment of the leaders in the campaign against Buckingham. Mirroring the language and actions of his father, and presaging the future, Charles threatened the existence of subsequent parliamentary sittings: "Parliaments are altogether in my power for the calling, sitting, and continuance of them. Therefore, as I find the fruits either good or evil, they are for to continue or not to be." That is, parliament would only sit if it met the king's demands.

Desperately short of funds, Charles turned to the ancient feudal device of the forced loan. When numerous gentleman refused to pay the loan, which they argued was an illegal tax, Charles had seventy-six of them, of whom more than twenty were members of parliament, imprisoned. Five of the prisoners sued for a writ of habeas corpus, which was a document issued by King's Bench requiring captors (in this case, the king) to show cause for detainment. In the ensuing "Five Knights' Case," the judges found in favor of the king because, as a common law court, it had no jurisdiction over the exercise of the king's prerogatives, which included imprisonment on the "special command of the king." Though correct in law, this decision was not popular, and provoked concerns about the extent to which the king might employ his royal prerogatives against the fundamental historical rights of liberty and property. Meanwhile, the funds from the forced loan were used by Buckingham to lead a military force to La Rochelle, France, to aid the Huguenot rebels, who were Protestants being persecuted by the French government. Here, again, the expedition was a disaster, and this time Buckingham was directly involved as its commander, rather than distantly involved as lord high admiral.

When parliament met again in 1628, it had amassed a great deal of ammunition against Charles and Buckingham. To secure his subsidy, Charles allowed parliament to prepare a bill that rehearsed traditional arguments about arbitrary taxation and imprisonment, which the king could then sign into an act and, thereby, indicate his acceptance of its contents. Ultimately, the Commons responded with the Petition of Right, a document written by Coke consisting of four major claims. First, no man could be required to pay a non-parliamentary tax, a clear reference to the forced loan and the king's collection of customs despite parliament's refusal to make this a life grant. Second, no man could be imprisoned without charges being laid. Third, no military personnel could be billeted in private homes without consent, and fourth, no civilian could be subjected to martial law. The last two issues reflected serious grievances ongoing since 1625 in port towns, where soldiers and sailors resided until deployed.

Charles agreed to the terms of the petition to get his subsidy, but parliament made the dismissal of Buckingham a condition for the tunnage and poundage grant, which angered the king enough to prorogue parliament in June. Two months later, Buckingham was assassinated by a disgruntled naval officer whose motivations for killing the duke are still not entirely clear. Although the murderer was executed in short order, many people in England, including the membership of the Commons, celebrated the duke's death (see *Voices of the Past*: **The Assassination of the Duke of Buckingham**).

Charles recalled parliament in 1629 but immediately the old issues returned, including the king's collection of customs and his arrest of merchants for refusing to pay it. Puritan members of Commons, whose numbers had grown over the past few sessions, also took the opportunity to complain about a perceived pseudo-Catholic movement taking place in the Church of England and at court. Specifically, beginning under James a group of Arminians had emerged, who followed the teachings of the Dutch theologian Jacobus Arminius. In essence, Arminians believed that the Calvinist doctrine of predestination was incorrect, and that only ceremonies presided over by a sanctified priesthood and episcopacy could bring salvation. This position was contrary to the Thirty-Nine Articles of Religion and, to Puritans, seemed very much like the Catholic doctrine of faith and good works for salvation.

In March, as Puritan Member of Parliament John Eliot began reading out various resolutions in the Commons – that Catholics and Arminians were "capital enemies" of the realm, that royal advisors who supported the king's collection of customs would be impeached by parliament, and that anyone who paid these customs betrayed English liberties – Charles ordered the adjournment of parliament, pending its dissolution. As the speaker of the house, Sir John Finch, rose to end the session, several of Eliot's friends forcibly held him in his chair until the resolutions were read out in full. This act of defiance was a clear infringement of the king's prerogative to dismiss parliament, and Charles ordered Eliot and eight other radicals placed in the Tower of London, where Eliot died in 1632.

The Personal Rule

After the failure of the 1629 parliament, Charles, as had his father in 1614, resolved to rule for the remainder of his life without calling the legislature. Charles's first step toward his "personal rule" was to arrange a peace with France and Spain, to avoid the excessive costs of war that could not possibly be achieved without parliamentary subsidies. Early in the personal rule, princes Charles and James were born, each to become regnant monarchs in due course. Now that Buckingham was dead, Charles increasingly relied on several leading councillors – Richard Weston, Francis Cottington, and especially Thomas Wentworth (later earl of Strafford) and William Laud, the archbishop of Canterbury – to help support his efforts.

These men instituted a policy known as "Thorough," which involved introducing efficiency in government by eliminating offices that had become redundant (known as sinecures), replacing the fee-based system with fixed salaries, commissioning lords lieutenant to oversee the provinces, and bringing about uniformity and conformity in matters of faith. Many of these practices modeled those developed by Wentworth as lord deputy of Ireland. In addition, Charles took an active interest in daily administration, frequenting meetings of the privy council more than his predecessors, organizing its members into committees so that they could be more focused and productive, hearing petitions from subjects, and improving his knowledge of policy and the affairs of government.

Even with a more streamlined and less expensive administration, the most pressing issue for Charles was, of course, money, the collection of which was also engineered by his "Thorough" advisors. In general, this was accomplished through the continuation of the fiscal feudal policies that had been used since the time of Henry VII, plus additional ones that had fallen into desuetude. The king increased customs duties and impositions, issued monopolies, and farmed out other rights in exchange for a steady income, continued the practices of purveyance and wardship, collected recusancy fines from Catholics and Protestant dissenters, and recovered feudal dues associated with the use (and abuse) of royal forests. Charles also restored the "distraint of knighthood," which had not been used in more than a century. This old statute required men of certain financial standing to present themselves at the king's coronation to be knighted. The failure of hundreds of men to do so in 1626 meant that they were retroactively ordered to remit a fine, which brought £175,000 into the royal coffers. Naturally, though in theory legal, many of these revenue-gathering schemes were unpopular and threatened the fundamental constitutional right to the protection of personal property from confiscation by the state.

The most controversial financial device used was known as "ship money." Historically, coastal towns and communities that were threatened with possible invasion during times of war were required to pay a fee that would enable the navy to staff and fortify these regions. However, not only was England not at war but the king demanded the payment of ship money from the entire nation, including inland communities in which there was no possible threat of invasion, on the grounds that England was in a state of national emergency. Because the right to determine this state was part of the royal prerogative, the king technically operated within the letter of the law, if not its spirit. When John Hampden, a wealthy landowner, refused to pay on the grounds that ship money was an illegal tax, the government brought suit. A panel of twelve judges decided, by a single-vote majority, that the king had the prerogative right to determine a state of emergency and to collect ship money. The slim victory sent a clear message not only to the king but also to others who refused to pay that there was a constitutional crisis brewing. Nonetheless, the combined efforts of especially Weston and Wentworth brought in significant revenue for the crown and enabled it to operate without parliament for more than a decade, until many of these revenue streams began to dry up.

The second major issue for Charles during the personal rule involved religion. During his reign, Charles had promoted several supporters of Arminianism to high church positions, in large part because of their support for royal supremacy of the church. Charles's Arminian archbishop of Canterbury, William Laud, introduced a series of reforms to bring about orthodoxy and discipline, suppress Puritan demands for Presbyterianism, and introduce renewed efforts at ritual that looked, to many, like Catholic forms of ceremony. For instance, communion tables were returned to their "altarwise" positions, and priests were ordered to wear ornate vestments. To persecute those who rebuffed these reforms, Laud made extensive use of the Court of High Commission, used since Whitgift's time to punish Puritans, and the Court of Star Chamber. The best-known of these persecutions involved William Prynne, John Bastwick, and Henry Burton, who were tried at the Court of Star Chamber in 1637 for producing anti-episcopal pamphlets. Although the Star Chamber did not have the power over life and death, these three men were pilloried, whipped, mutilated by ear cropping, and imprisoned indefinitely. Their highly publicized punishment essentially turned them into martyrs for the cause of Puritanism and free speech.

Even mainstream Anglicans had difficulty accepting many of Laud's reforms, but ultimately the downfall of the personal rule was caused by Laud's attempt to introduce his reforms into the Scottish kirk. Laud ordered the kirk to implement a new prayer book modeled closely on the *Book of Common Prayer* and to embrace his other reforms. The kirk responded in 1638 by signing the National Covenant, whereby they formally opposed Laud's innovations; claimed that only the Scottish parliament and the kirk, and not the king, could determine religious policy; and later abolished the Scottish episcopacy. Charles viewed the actions of the covenanters as rebellious and raised an army of 30,000 men in 1639, to march on Scotland, initiating a series of conflicts known as the Bishops' Wars. Charles expected a swift campaign, but he misjudged the conviction of his northern subjects and the size of the army, equal in strength to the king's, that the Scots managed to assemble. If the king was going to succeed in a long campaign, he needed more money, and only parliament could provide enough of it.

* * *

Discussion Question 5.3: Historians sometimes refer to the personal rule of Charles I as either the "King's Peace" or the "King's Tyranny." Based on the early Stuarts' struggles with parliament, how accurate are these terms?

The Long Parliament and the Coming of War

When Charles's first parliament in eleven years was called early in 1640, many of its members, led by John Pym, were part of a radical faction that had seen men such as Eliot severely punished for their belief in the sovereignty of parliament. Consequently, in the Commons the discussions involved a long list of complaints about the king's perceived abuses in matters of church, state, and finances. Although Charles initially agreed to abandon the collection of ship money in exchange for a large lump-sum payment, the Commons prevaricated on accepting this offer – possibly because the sum would have been enough for Charles to see no further need for that session of parliament – and the king angrily dissolved what has come to be known as the "Short Parliament," which lasted a mere few weeks. Charles then made a tactical error by sending additional forces to Scotland even though he had no money to pay them. By August 1640 the king knew that he had to call parliament again. The body that met, composed largely of the same men who sat earlier that year, is known in history as the "Long Parliament" because it existed, in theory, for twenty years.

By the time parliament met in November, Charles was desperately in need of money and the threat from the Scots was serious. This threat provided the radical and Puritan-leaning leaders of the Commons – Pym, Oliver St. John, Denzil Hollis, John Hampden, and others – with a great deal of leverage with which to gain major concessions from the king. One of its earliest actions was to pass a bill stating that parliament could not be prorogued or dissolved without its consent. Although this significantly impinged on the royal prerogative, Charles agreed, which limited his ability to stop the events that followed. Unusually, this bill was enacted before the end of the parliamentary session, which was traditionally when all the business of parliament gained royal assent. With its newfound liberties, parliament quickly brought about the arrest of Laud and Strafford on the grounds that they had provided the king with advice and service during the personal rule that amounted to treason. There was little Charles could do to save his chief ministers, so he bowed to the will of parliament as it voted on bills of attainder. Strafford was beheaded in May 1641, while Laud was imprisoned for four years and not executed until 1645.

Strengthened by the fact that the king could not dissolve parliament, a series of bills were introduced and passed in the first half of 1641. The Triennial Act required that parliament meet for a minimum of fifty days once every three years. Various acts abolished the contentious courts of Star Chamber, High Commission, Requests, and other pseudo-legal bodies of the privy council. The Ship Money Act ended the collection of that revenue source, and others regulated or eliminated tunnage and poundage, impositions, monopolies, distraint of knighthood, and forestry laws – in sum, all the financial mechanisms that had enabled the king to rule independently. To all these bills, Charles was forced to give his assent because of his need for money.

When considering the wide-ranging assault on the royal prerogative caused by these bills, and also taking into account the early Stuarts' stalwart defense of absolute monarchy and their belief that parliament was supposed to be a transitory body meeting at the king's pleasure, these acts collectively represent by far the greatest constitutional developments in English history since the thirteenth century. Parliament was on the road to becoming a permanent, indeed necessary, instrument of English government, and the concept of parliamentary sovereignty, which had slowly emerged since the 1580s, was essentially achieved.

Had the Commons stopped at this point, when it had dismantled the mechanisms that enabled absolute monarchy and personal rule, the future would likely have unfolded very differently. But radicals led by Pym were not yet satisfied with the level of reform and introduced several measures in the fall and winter of 1641–2 sure to inflame the king. By far the most significant of these was the

Grand Remonstrance, introduced in November 1641 largely as a response to a recent uprising in Ireland that saw Catholic rebels murder thousands of English Protestants. This document listed more than 200 grievances against the king and called for major reform of the church and a purge of royal officials, with parliament having veto power over future royal appointments. The petitioners were careful not to implicate the king in many of these issues; instead, they blamed Catholics, the Laudian bishops, and the king's chief ministers during the personal rule. Although Pym had a large network of supporters, many in the Commons felt that the Remonstrance went too far, and a vote to determine whether it should be passed to the king was 159 for and 148 against, an extremely close margin that signaled a clear divide between the Puritan and royalist factions within parliament. With the Remonstrance, the radicals revealed a desire to go far beyond the restoration of the ancient constitution.

The Remonstrance was delivered to Charles in December, and he spent three weeks – assisted by members of parliament who now sided with the royalist cause – preparing a response. The king refused to abolish the episcopacy or remove the offending bishops and insisted that none of his ministers were so ineffectual as to merit their removal. By that time, however, parliament had also introduced the Militia Bill, wherein the army was to be placed under the command of parliament rather than the king. This measure was principally to enable parliament to deal decisively with Catholic rebels in Ireland without concern about the king's (or his wife's) perceived sympathy for papists. In practice, however, the bill would also have given parliament the ability to assemble an army against the king, which in fact is what happened. Compared to the earlier concessions, which largely involved royal revenue and restoring historical liberties of the person under the common law, these radical measures would have seen the derogation of royal prerogatives that had always been outside the purview of parliament.

Charles's next action, on January 4, 1642, was probably the greatest misstep of his rule. Perceiving all of his problems with parliament to have stemmed from the Puritan faction headed by Pym, Charles led armed guards into the Commons chamber to effect the arrest of five members plus one lord for high treason, on the grounds that they had incited the Scots to invade England and were fomenting open rebellion in London, which had become a Puritan stronghold. The five members had received advanced warning of the king's plans and were not in the chamber, forcing Charles to leave empty-handed and embarrassed. As the king and his guard left, members repeatedly shouted the word "privilege," as a reminder that parliament was supposed to be allowed to legislate without undue coercion from the crown. A speech the next day at Guildhall in London proved that the city had turned against the king, and to protect himself, his Catholic queen, and his children, Charles retreated to the countryside the following week.

Over the next six months, Charles engaged in a proclamation-, declaration-, and pamphlet-writing campaign, explaining his actions and his concerns that parliament was perverting and upending the historical constitution between the king and his people. Almost half of the Commons sided with the king and joined his cause, while the radicals who remained turned the Militia Bill into an ordinance[4] and began assembling troops. To prevent war, parliament sent the king its Nineteen Propositions, requiring him to apply the penal laws against Catholics; allow parliament to approve councillors, judges, and officers of state and determine how the king's children would be educated and to whom they should be married; give parliament command of the army; and issue a general pardon to all of parliament, including the five members. In essence, the propositions sought to give parliament control over all aspects of the English state, leaving the king little more than a figurehead – at best, a puppet. Naturally, Charles refused the propositions, stating "*Nolumus leges Angliae mutari*" ("We are unwilling to change the laws of England"). Charles assembled his own army using a device known as the Commission of Array and, at Nottingham in August 1642, openly declared hostilities and went to war with his own subjects.

* * *

Discussion Question 5.4: If, by May 1641, the Long Parliament had already achieved so much, do you think the radicals went too far with the Grand Remonstrance and the Militia Bill?

---

4   An ordinance enabled a bill that had received parliamentary majority but had not yet received royal assent to become law. It was normally used as an emergency measure, because bills only became acts at the end of a parliamentary session.

VOICES OF THE PAST
THE ASSASSINATION OF THE DUKE OF BUCKINGHAM

George Villiers, duke of Buckingham, was the early Stuarts' most trusted, and England's most hated, royal councillor. He proved to be an incompetent administrator and military leader, and parliament had twice attempted to impeach the duke. Both times, Charles I ended parliament to prevent this, which only made the public despise the duke more. In August 1628, John Felton assassinated Buckingham at the Greyhound Pub in Portsmouth, Hampshire. Felton was arrested, tried for high treason, and executed in November. The following note was discovered in Felton's hat: "That man is cowardly, base, and deserveth not the name of a gentleman or soldier, that is not willing to sacrifice his life for the honor of his God, his king, and his country. Let no man commend me for doing of it, but rather discommend themselves as the cause of it, for if God had not taken away our hearts for our sins, he would not have gone so long unpunished. JOHN FELTON." The following extract describe Felton's motivations and the duke's final moments.

* * *

There was a younger brother of mean fortunes, born in the County of Suffolk, by name John Felton, by nature of a deep, melancholy, silent and gloomy constitution, but bred in the active way of a soldier, and thereby raised to the place of lieutenant, to a foot company, in the regiment of Sir James Ramsey. This was the man that closely within himself had conceived the duke's death. But what may have been the immediate or greatest motive of that felonious conception, is even yet in the clouds.

It was said at first, that he had been stung with the denial of his captain's place, who died in England; whereof thus much indeed is true, that the duke, before he would invest him in the said place, advising first (as his manner was) with his colonel, he found him to interpose for one Powel, his own lieutenant, a gentleman of extraordinary valour, and according to military custom, … the lieutenant of the colonel's company might well pretend to the next vacant captainship under the same regiment. Which Felton acknowledged to be in itself very usual and equitable…. So the aforesaid conceit of some rancor harbored upon this denial had no true ground….

[T]he truth is, that either to [make] honest a deed after it was done, or to slumber his conscience in the doing, he studied other incentives, alleging not three hours before his execution, to Sir Richard Gresham, two inducements thereof. The first … was a certain libelous book … which made the duke one of the foulest monsters upon the Earth; and indeed, unworthy not only of life in a Christian court, and under so virtuous a king, but of any room within the bounds of humanity…. The second was the remonstrance of the lower house of parliament, against him, which perchance he thought the fairest cover, so he put in the second place. Whatsoever were the true motive, which I think none can determine but the prince of darkness itself, he did thus prosecute the effect.

In a cutler's shop on Tower Hill, he bought a ten-penny knife (so cheap was the instrument of this great attempt) and the sheath thereof he sewed to the lining of his pocket, that he might at any moment draw forth the blade alone with one hand, for he had maimed the other…. At Portsmouth on Saturday, being the 23 of August of that current year, he pressed without any suspicion in such a time of so many pretenders to employment, into an inward chamber, where the duke was at breakfast (the last of his repasts in this world), accompanied with men of quality and action.... And there a little before the duke's rising from the table, [Felton] went and stood expecting till he should pass....

[W]hile the duke came near with Sir Thomas Fryer close to his ear, in the very moment as the said knight withdrew himself from the duke, this assassin gave him with a back blow a deep wound into his left side, leaving the knife in his body. Which the duke himself pulling out, on a sudden effusion of spirits, he sunk down under the table in the next room, and immediately expired.... Thus died this great peer, in the 36 year of his age complete, and three days over, in a time of great recourse unto him, and dependence upon him, the house, and town full of servants and suitors, his duchess in an upper room, scarce yet out of her bed, and the court at that time not above six or nine miles from him, which had been the stage of his greatness.

Source: Henry Wotton, *Reliquiae Wottonianae* (London, 1654), 110–15.

✳ ✳ ✳

Discussion Question 5.5: Recalling Henry VIII's willingness to lose his three Thomases – Wolsey, More, and Cromwell – why do you think Charles I fought so hard to keep Buckingham out of harm's way?

CHAPTER SIX

WAR AND INTERREGNUM, 1642–1660

DEATH AND DISORDER:
THE BATTLE OF EDGEHILL

In the early modern period, wars were fought in a series of "pitched battles," in which opposing forces met each other at scheduled locations and times. After several minor skirmishes, the first such battle of the English Civil War occurred on October 23, 1642, at Edgehill, Warwickshire, when the king's army, on the march to London, met parliamentary forces under the command of Robert Devereux, earl of Essex. Using the Commission of Array, Charles I had managed to assemble a force of about 12,000 troops, made up of 2,500 mounted cavalry, 800 mounted infantry (dragoons), 9,000 foot soldiers, and 16 artillery guns. The parliamentary army, assembled with the authority of the Militia Ordinance, possessed 15,000 men, comprising 2,300 cavalry, 700 dragoons, 12,000 soldiers, and 7 guns.

The battle of Edgehill began at around three o'clock in the afternoon – an uncommonly late start – when Prince Rupert, Charles's nephew by his sister Elizabeth, gave the order to attack. His cavalry and dragoons quickly overran the parliamentary left flank, while Sir Henry Wilmot similarly routed the parliamentary right flank. Both royalist cavalries then made the tactical error of riding in pursuit of the fleeing enemy cavalry, rather than returning

to the field of battle and supporting their foot soldiers. Meanwhile, the royalist infantry under the command of Lieutenant General Patrick Ruthven and Sergeant Major General Jacob Astley advanced down the center and scattered the parliamentary foot soldiers, who had begun fleeing as their cavalry disappeared. The infantry on both sides were divided into pikemen, who held 12- to 18-foot-long pointed sticks used in close quarters to stab and unhorse their enemy, and musketeers, who were armed with matchlock arquebuses and were protected by the pikemen during reloading.

Initially, it appeared as if the royalist army had the clear path to victory, but its commanders had not anticipated that two parliamentary cavalry regiments, under the command of Sir William Balfour and Sir Philip Stapleton, had remained behind. They rode through gaps in the ranks of their foot soldiers to charge the royalist infantry, who had little defense against mounted riders and were forced into retreat. The king had also made a tactical error during this battle. Instead of keeping his own mounted guard – the "Lifeguard of Horse" – to protect him at the rear, Charles had allowed them to join Rupert's men, leaving him unprotected. Some of Balfour's men very nearly managed to take custody of the king and his sons, Charles and James, which, if he had been successful, might have made a quick end of the English Civil War. However, Balfour's men were forced into retreat by the royalist artillery.

As the royalist forces fell back amid the advance of the parliamentary foot supported by the two horse regiments, one of the leading infantry commanders, Robert Bertie, earl of Lindsey, and the royal standard bearer, Sir Edmund Verney, were killed. Verney's flag, the symbol of the royalist cause, was captured by a parliamentary ensign, Arthur Young. Just as the flag was being carried to the parliament's rear guard as a trophy of war and a sign that the battle had been won, the royalist cavalry finally returned and changed the balance of the battle so sufficiently that it managed to recapture the king's standard. Although the battle was not over, darkness began to descend on the field of combat, forcing both armies, after a final melee, to bring a natural close to the hostilities.

The Battle of Edgehill ended in a draw, although the king claimed it as a victory and issued a declaration to be published in all churches and chapels shortly after its conclusion:

> We must wholly attribute the preservation of us and our children in the late bloody battle with the rebels to the mercy and goodness of Almighty God, who best knowing the justice of our cause, and the uprightness of our heart, to his service, and to the good and welfare of

> our people, would not suffer us and the whole kingdom to be made a prey to those desperate persons, so we hold it our duty still to use all possible means to remove that jealousy and misunderstanding from our good subjects.[1]

The king also took the opportunity to remind his people that he did not favor "popery," that he would not have used an army to rise against parliament, and that the radicals he sought to arrest in parliament had committed treason, three of the reasons that the war began in the first place.

The casualty report for this impotent start to the English Civil War is not known but has been estimated at about 1,000 dead and 3,000 wounded, divided equally between royalist and parliamentary forces. As the war wore on, the casualty list rose considerably. Historians have arrived at the figure of 180,000 to 200,000 dead from battlefield killings and other causes directly related to the war between 1642 and 1651. This represented a loss of 3.5 per cent to 4 per cent of the English population, the vast majority of whom were men. By way of comparison, these figures are more than twice the percentage lost among all involved nations in World War I, which has been estimated at 1.6 per cent to 1.9 per cent, and rival the average percentage lost in World War II, estimated at 3 per cent to 3.7 per cent. For a "war without an enemy," as parliamentarian William Waller called it in 1643, the English Civil War was, nonetheless, a bloody conflict that claimed its fair share of fathers and sons.

* * *

Discussion Question 6.1: Why was it important for the king to claim the Battle of Edgehill as a royalist victory, despite it ending in a draw?

---

1   Charles I, *His Majesties Declaration to All His Loving Subjects* (Oxford, 1642), sig. A1.

Preparing for War

The English Civil War – also known as the English Revolution, Puritan Rebellion, and Wars of the Three Kingdoms – took place between 1642 and 1651 and was fought between royalists (or cavaliers) and parliamentarians (or roundheads).[2] Those who rallied to the king included about 30 per cent of the membership of the Long Parliament, who began meeting in 1643 in the "Oxford Parliament." These men had supported the early parliamentary reforms and agreed that Charles's absolutism, especially during the personal rule, had been abusive, but also that Pym and his fellow radicals had gone too far with the Grand Remonstrance and their demands regarding religion and the king's prerogatives. Charles also had the support of a large percentage of the countryside and the peerage, especially in the north and west of England, places that were far removed from national politics and where the traditional nobility, gentry, and yeomanry feared what might happen to their liberty and property if parliament was successful in upending the English constitution and the orderly nature of English society. Charles also enjoyed the support of the national clergy, particularly those who favored the liturgy and ceremony of High Anglicanism, the brand of religion that developed from Laud's Arminian reforms, or who preferred episcopalism over Presbyterianism. Catholics, so much as they were willing to get involved at all, also preferred Charles. This enabled the king, in 1643, to come to an arrangement with Catholic rebels in Ireland, offering toleration for their religion in exchange for troops to fight for the royalist cause.

On the parliamentary side, support came, first and foremost, from the members of the Long Parliament who remained in London, who were by no means a homogenous group when it came to the goals for war. They were joined by those who sought Puritan and Presbyterian reforms, but also by Anglicans who disapproved of the toleration that had been shown to Catholics. The industrial centers and ports, and the more populated regions of the south and east of England, also sided with parliament, largely because the merchants and proto-industrial capitalists who resided in these areas had suffered from the abuse of monopolies, customs, and impositions under Elizabeth and the early Stuarts. These supporters provided parliament with some advantages over the royalists. Parliamentary control of London and the ports prevented Charles from receiving foreign aid from those sympathetic to absolute monarchy, such as his French in-laws. The larger population in the south and east provided more tax revenue, greater ease of its collection, and better ability to mobilize military forces. However, parliament's method of funding the war through military impressment, the sequestering of royalist property, local assessments, and an excise tax on non-essential commodities – methods that looked much like Charles's and Strafford's means of funding the personal rule – were met with resistance and were considered by some to be illegal.

---

2   Cavalier and roundhead were both pejorative terms. Cavalier derived from *caballero*, a Spanish gentleman on horseback who fought at the king's side. Roundhead referred to London Puritans who wore their hair short, as opposed to most men who wore their hair to their shoulders.

Ultimately, whatever else the Civil War was about – securing principles of the ancient constitution and parliamentary sovereignty, limiting absolutism and royal prerogatives, protecting or reforming the church, enabling economic growth in a free market, solving local grievances around land use and illegal taxation, and protecting the fundamental rights of every freeborn Englishman to life, liberty, property, and freedom from oppression – it was not about class conflict or clearly delineated groupings within society. Each side had support from the peerage and gentry, from groups within the church, and from people of all ranks, vocations, and genders. In many cases, loyalty to either side was based on one's geographical location, whomever their social superiors told them to support, or whoever could offer the best incentive to join the conflict. Moreover, in various parts of the country, vigilante bands known as Clubmen formed to protect their local interests against both sides. Armed with cudgels and scythes, these men prevented forced conscription, confiscation of their crops, and assault by itinerant soldiers.

Nor was the Civil War initially about regicide, revolution, or republicanism. Very few people believed that the king should be deposed, let along executed, and even fewer would have entertained the idea of England without a king at its head, which would have been an extremely radical idea not only in England but throughout Europe. For this reason, there was a great deal of ambivalence within the parliamentary side early in the war. As Edward Montagu, earl of Manchester and a major general of the parliamentary forces, stated in 1644, "if we beat the king ninety-nine times yet he is king still, … but if the king beat us once we shall all be hanged." It was difficult for parliament to construct a genuine revolutionary mentality, when loyalty to God and king, according to the great chain of being, went hand in hand, while the alternative was disorder and anarchy. Whatever gains were to be made during the war, almost nobody questioned Charles's right to rule or that he would return to his throne at war's end. This was, like many before it, a rebellion about the restoration of rights that had allegedly been lost, not a revolution designed to bring about a radical new constitution.

Fighting the War

It is partly because of this ambivalence among parliament's military leaders that early battles, such as Edgehill, ended as either stalemates or royalist victories. Owing to its lack of success, by the fall of 1643 it was evident that the round-heads required additional support, which led, with parliament's reluctance, to the Solemn League and Covenant signed with Scotland. The Covenant promised that, in exchange for providing military support to parliament, Scotland would receive a large monthly stipend and would see both England and Ireland become Presbyterian nations.

Although this Covenant caused some parliamentarians to turn away from their cause, the Scottish army marched into England in July 1644 and, together with parliamentary forces, gained their first major victory of the war, at the battle of Marston Moor. The true standout in this battle was General Oliver Cromwell (see Figure 6.1), whose creative tactics saw the routing of Rupert's forces and the death of 4,000 royalist troops. Following the battle, Cromwell – who was also a member of parliament – criticized his superior, Manchester, for his indecisiveness. A few months later, parliament passed the Self-Denying Ordinance, which required members of the Lords or Commons to resign their military commissions. Through this measure, weak leaders such as Essex and Manchester were removed from their commands, although a strong leader such as Cromwell was allowed to retain his.

Another scheme involved the creation of the New Model Army, which broke with earlier traditions of wars being fought by militia bands assembled and

Figure 6.1 *Oliver Cromwell, by Edmund Lodge.*

funded by localities. Instead, command of the entire parliamentary force would be vested in a single person, in this case, Sir Thomas Fairfax, with Cromwell in charge of the cavalry, and the army would be a paid, professional, trained force. In addition, the army was to be commanded not by nobles, whose military skills were evidently not always up to the task, but by experienced and capable commanders regardless of their birthright. Promotion was to be based on good service rather than the old model of wealth, title, and patronage. The army was ideologically supported by *The Souldiers Catechism*, a godly pamphlet written to emphasize that soldiers fought "for the preservation of our Parliament, in the being whereof (under God) consists the glory and welfare of the Kingdom." Soldiers committed "to rescue the King out of the hands of his and the Kingdom's enemies, and to maintain his honour and just prerogatives" while also seeking to recover "the laws and liberties of [their] country." This was precisely the type of rhetoric needed to help parliament through its final stages of ambivalence about fighting the king and his army.

The new parliamentary army met the king's forces at the battle of Naseby in June 1645. Cromwell and his son-in-law, Henry Ireton, commanded the cavalry on the flanks, while Fairfax commanded the infantry in the center. Largely thanks to Cromwell, the battle ended in a decisive parliamentary victory, with about 1,000 dead royalists, including many of Charles's most experienced officers, and almost 5,000 captured. Another battle at Langport effectively destroyed the king's army, and Charles retreated to Oxford, bringing an end to the first phase of the Civil War. The next year, he surrendered himself to the Scots, but his unwillingness to abandon the episcopacy there prompted the Scots to hand Charles over to parliament in 1647, and he was imprisoned, in exchange for a large financial settlement. While parliament was deciding how to negotiate with the king, a crisis brewed. The army was no longer needed, but parliament was millions of pounds in arrears on military salaries and the army declared that it would not disband until it was paid, and, to protect its members from future prosecution, until it was indemnified for acts that occurred during the war. When parliament prevaricated, the army took matters into its own hands, sending a junior officer, Coronet Joyce, to secure the king's person and bring him to army headquarters so that they could negotiate directly with Charles.

In June 1647, Cromwell, Ireton, and Major General John Lambert presented to the king the army's Heads of the Proposals. The plan called for the king to allow freedom of worship for all Protestants, a reduction in the authority of bishops, biennial parliaments to sit for a minimum of 120 and a maximum of 240 days, and parliamentary control over the appointment of royal ministers and military officers for a period of ten years. None of these proposals was particularly radical and, in fact, the Heads was much less aggressive than the Grand Remonstrance or the Nineteen Propositions. This lack of radicalism, however, soon led to division within the army and parliament. A group of activists who came to be known as Levellers wanted further reforms, which were declared in the Agreement of the People and aired at the Putney Debates.

The Agreement was a manifesto that called for major constitutional changes to the franchise in England, including near universal manhood suffrage, freedom of religion, equality of all people under the law (with respect to "tenure, estate, charter, degree, birth, or place"), annual parliaments with new representation each time, and a constitutional monarchy with "supreme authority" vested in the elected representatives. Cromwell and Ireton maintained that the Agreement, especially in its support for the radical notion of democracy, was tantamount to anarchy, while colonels John Lilburne and Thomas Rainborough argued in favor of its demands. Ultimately, all these efforts were in vain. The king fled in the dark of night to the Isle of Wight, and although he was quickly recaptured, the army determined in early 1648 that it would no longer attempt to negotiate with the king, giving rise to an entirely new outlook on the future of the English monarchy.

Trial, Death, and Legacy

Charles's brief escape from captivity was accompanied by a secret "Engagement" with the Scots, by which, in exchange for military support and restoration to his throne, the king would establish Presbyterianism in England for a period of three years. Under these terms, war resumed for a short time in 1648, although the New Model Army under Cromwell and Lambert had little difficulty defeating the Scots at the battle of Preston in August. Fewer than 100 parliamentary soldiers were lost, in contrast to 2,000 royalists dead and 9,000 forced to surrender. Despite this decisive victory, parliament – which had been at odds with the military for some time – determined that it would attempt to reopen negotiations with the king, while the army had by this time begun thinking of Charles as a war criminal. In its Remonstrance of November, the army demanded "exemplary justice" upon the king, expecting, at the very least, that Charles would be forced to abdicate in favor of one of his children. To force the issue, Colonel Thomas Pride arrested or refused entry to the Commons to those members who wanted to negotiate, an event known in history as "Pride's Purge." By the end of December 1648, only about 200 members of the original Long Parliament remained, and only about half that number regularly attended, giving cause for that body to be referred to as the Rump Parliament.

It was this rump that decided, in early January 1649, to establish a High Court of Justice that would try Charles Stuart for high treason against his people. Remarkably, neither the chief justices of the law courts nor the House of Lords agreed that it was lawful to try the king by these means, prompting the Commons to declare itself independent of these bodies and capable of legislating alone and without royal assent, which was a significant constitutional aberration. The ordinance named 135 commissioners of the court, among whom were Fairfax, Cromwell, and Ireton, although only half of the commissioners heard the case against the king. When the court first met on January 20, the charge cited the king's "wicked design to erect and uphold in himself an unlimited and tyrannical power to rule according to his will, and to overthrow the rights and liberties of the people." Charles, for his part, several times refused to accept the authority of the court, questioning, "by what power I am called hither?" He continued: "Remember, I am your king, your lawful king.... Therefore let me know by what lawful authority I am seated here.... I have a trust committed to me by God, by old and lawful descent. I will not betray it to answer to a new unlawful authority." Nonetheless, the court sat for several days, often without the king being present, and heard from dozens of witnesses before declaring Charles guilty. On January 27, fifty-nine of the commissioners – scarcely 40 per cent of those named to the commission – signed the king's death warrant.

Three days later, Charles was beheaded outside his Banqueting House at Whitehall Palace (see *Voices of the Past*: **The Execution of Charles I**). Although this was not the first regicide in English history – as we have seen, several regnant monarchs were killed in secret or in battle during the Wars of the Roses – this was the first judicial killing of a king, purportedly by his parliament, acting on behalf of the English people, for infringement of the ancient constitution. In fact, however, this act was committed by a small, highly radicalized group. It is worth remembering that the original membership of the Long Parliament stood at more than 500 and that royalists, judges, peers, and those who preferred to negotiate with the king were all purged from parliament and the High Court before it sat in judgment. As well, many of the commissioners who heard the case, such as Ireton, were not members of parliament. In total, fewer than 10 per cent of the Long Parliament convicted Charles Stuart of treason, a group that represented neither the original grievances of 1640 nor the kingdom as a whole.

Largely because the regicides represented such a small, radical faction within parliament, Charles was not forgotten and, indeed, soon entered a degree of martyrdom. This was caused mainly by the publication of the *Eikon Basilike* ("Royal Portrait") a mere ten days after the execution. The book was allegedly written by Charles himself and described his various tribulations in a manner that made the king appear steadfast in the face of adversity, devoutly religious, caring of his subjects, and remorseful that he had allowed Strafford to be executed, a sin for which he believed he deserved to pay with his throne and his life. Whomever was the author, the *Eikon* was a masterly final stroke of royalist propaganda whose text and frontispiece encouraged parallels between Charles and the sacrifice of Christ. After the *Eikon* appeared in dozens of editions in multiple languages and gained a wide readership, parliament commissioned John Milton to write a response. His *Eikonoklastes* ("Icon Breaker," a clever play on the original title), published in October 1649, claimed the *Eikon* built up a false idol, but this did little to change the public's favorable opinion of Charles. Like his contemporaries, historians have developed rather polarized opinions about Charles I. To some, he was an incompetent tyrant; to others, a reticent man upon whom divine-right kingship was thrust and therefore worthy of sympathy. January 30 remained "king and martyr" day in the Anglican calendar for two centuries, in part because of Charles's refusal to abolish the episcopacy, even though it could very well have saved his life.

Milton's response to the *Eikon* was not surprising given that he had published, within weeks of the king's execution, his *Tenure of Kings and Magistrates*. In this work, Milton served as an apologist for the regicides and rebutted those who condemned the act, by claiming that all individuals, including kings, are born free and equal and that, therefore, parliament had the right to commit "tyrannicide" on the grounds that "the power of kings and magistrates is … derivative, transferred and committed to them in trust from the people, to the common good of them all, in whom the power yet remains fundamentally, and cannot be taken from them, without a violation of their natural birthright." When a monarch violated that trust, natural law required subjects then to rebel, and who better to do so than their elected representatives? In essence, this was a denial of the notion of divine right of kings, a very controversial idea at the time but one that was essential to proving his argument for the legitimacy of regicide. Milton also argued that a state – or a republican commonwealth – could exist without a monarch, provided that it was governed by men of goodwill who had the best interests of people at heart and who retained the trust of the governed.

Other writers, however, denied Milton's claims and argued, like Machiavelli and Bodin before them, that monarchs were absolute sovereigns regardless of their actions. Robert Filmer circulated these ideas as early as the 1620s, although his *Patriarcha* was not published until 1680. The most famous English defender of absolute monarchy was Thomas Hobbes, in *Leviathan*, written in the 1640s and published in 1651. Comparing the king to an all-powerful biblical sea creature, Hobbes argued that in the absence of such an individual in society, man would revert to an atavistic nature, become greedy and self-interested, live in a state of constant war and violence, making, in his famous phrase, "the life of man solitary, poor, nasty, brutish, and short." Although it is true, Hobbes argued, that subjects lived in a "covenant" (contract) with the king, once they vested that power in the king, it could not be taken away regardless of the sovereign's actions and, therefore, the king cannot justly be put to death. Yet, like Milton, Hobbes was also not a proponent of the divine right of kings; his monarch was secular and could be godless, ideas that were decried as atheistic. Over the next decade,

England would experiment with variations of Milton's and Hobbes's models of government, ultimately without much success in either case.

* * *

Discussion Question 6.2: If you had to defend Charles at his trial, what arguments would you have used?

Commonwealth England

After the king's execution in 1649, the rump moved swiftly to dismantle the old English constitution, in essence moving toward Milton's ideal commonwealth, to be run by men of goodwill who could serve the people. In March, the monarchy was declared to be "unnecessary, burdensome and dangerous," and was abolished, along with the House of Lords, while the episcopacy was heavily suppressed. The tripartite model of English government – king, lords, and commons – had been reduced to a single assembly, still consisting primarily of the rump, and a Council of State was created to replace the king's privy council. The new council consisted of three judges, three military officers, five peers, and thirty members of parliament, a total of forty-one members who represented the legal, martial, and legislative branches. Through these measures, England began its first experiment with republicanism in the form of a new Commonwealth government. Barely a month after *Tenure* was published, the republican government appointed Milton as Secretary of Foreign Tongues. Although officially the job involved composing official correspondence in Latin for foreign audiences, in practice he was responsible for producing propaganda on behalf of the regime. In this role, he produced his rebuttal to the *Eikon Basilike* and, in 1651, wrote the *Defense of the People of England*, in which he argued in support of the new model of government.

In the aftermath of the radical fervor that had brought about the execution of the king, the largest problem that the new government faced was its need to revert to a more conservative position and slow the tide of further revolution. Given the degree of radicalization that had occurred over the past decade, and its acceleration after 1647, this proved to be no easy task. The Levellers, for example, under the leadership of Lilburne, who had been in the Tower of London since the Putney Debates, and his supporters in the New Model Army continued to press for their agenda from the Agreement of the People, using freedom of the press to agitate for greater democracy, religious toleration, and legal reform. When, in May 1649, 400 Leveller soldiers mutinied on the grounds that their pay was heavily in arrears, Cromwell launched an attack at Burford, Oxfordshire, which resulted in the death of several of the mutineers and the summary execution of three leaders in a churchyard. This was the last of three Leveller mutinies in the army in that year, and the strong measures used to deal with the "Banbury rebels" destroyed the final Leveller power base and brought a measure of stability to the army.

The Commonwealth government also had to deal with religious extremism, which was caused by the absence of press censorship. Milton, in fact, had argued against censorship in his *Areopagitica* (1644), on the grounds that the best government was one that encouraged constructive criticism as fundamental to the concept of civil liberty. Using the press as their key medium, various sects emerged that challenged traditional interpretations of the Bible and the order of society. These groups – Anabaptists, Diggers, Fifth Monarchists, Millenarians, Muggletonians, Quakers, Ranters, and Seekers – sought to separate from the Church of England in preference for independent movements that sought liberty of conscience and truth from scripture. In 1649, for example, the Diggers, under the leadership of Gerrard Winstanley, declared that scripture did not allow private property. They therefore claimed various formerly common lands in several counties, removed the signs of enclosure (fences and hedges), and began cultivating the earth on communes, a movement that had to be suppressed by armed bands employed by local landlords. Many, like the Quakers, also declared themselves outside of the control of social superiors, the state, and courts, and practiced forms of worship that, to the increasingly conservative members of parliament, were deemed blasphemous. In 1656, parliament ordered one Quaker, James Nayler, to be pilloried, whipped, mutilated, branded, and imprisoned with hard labor to punish a particularly outrageous display of blasphemy that involved reenacting the arrival of Christ into Jerusalem on Palm Sunday. Although most of these movements failed to gain momentum because there was considerable disagreement between and among the various sects, parliament was criticized by Presbyterians and Anglicans for being too lenient on these extremist groups, and resorted to censorship to limit the spread of their ideas.

Another crisis facing the new government was uprisings in Ireland and Scotland, which became a continuation of the Civil War. In Ireland, Charles's arrangement of 1643 had brought about an alliance between the royalist commander, James Butler, marquess of Ormond, and the Catholic rebels, which meant that royalists were still control of Ireland. In May 1649, Cromwell was appointed lord lieutenant of Ireland (after Fairfax declined), giving him command of a large military force to regain control of the island. He was also tasked with eliminating the threat posed by the Irish support of Charles's eldest son, who was now styled in Ireland as Charles II, and with confiscating land from those involved in the Irish rebellion since 1641, so that these lands could be redistributed to those who had invested in military enterprises on parliament's behalf during the war.

With a well-trained and experienced New Model Army at his back, Cromwell swiftly and brutally achieved these aims. Between August 1649 and May 1650, he managed to reclaim twenty-five fortified towns and castles, and his sack of the towns of Drogheda and Wexford claimed the lives of at least 5,000 royalist supporters, Catholic clergy, and civilians. The royalist commander at Drogheda, Sir Arthur Aston, was clubbed to death while 300 of his soldiers, who had surrendered to Cromwell, were summarily massacred. A settlement was eventually achieved by 1652, but not before two-thirds of Irish land had been confiscated and given to investors and Cromwellian soldiers, leaving tens of thousands of landlords homeless and causing hundreds of thousands more to die of starvation because of their loss of livelihood and the army's practice of burning crops as it moved.

After the Irish campaign, parliament recalled Cromwell so that he could subdue the Scots, who had also declared Charles II as their rightful king and continued to seek the terms of the Solemn League and Covenant that would bring Presbyterianism to England. By September, Cromwell had managed to defeat the Scottish Covenanter army, under the command of David Leslie, which saw the death of 3,000 and the capture of 10,000 at Dunbar. Cromwell continued to move throughout the country, gaining military support from Ireland as troops were no longer needed there, and was eventually forced to put an end to an attempted Scottish invasion of England. The Scottish forces under the command of Charles met Cromwell's numerically superior army at Worcester on September 3, 1651, and the result was a decisive victory for Cromwell. Following the battle, Charles hid in an oak tree to avoid being captured, and possibly killed, by Cromwell's forces. Charles's survival by these means later gave rise to the celebration of Royal Oak Day, on May 29. After six weeks taking shelter with loyal supporters, Charles left England in disguise and remained on the Continent for a decade. Meanwhile, the subduer of Ireland and Scotland, Cromwell, returned to London in mid-September as a conquering hero.

Cromwell's exceptional successes, strong support of the army, and presence in London also enabled him to become more involved in parliament than he could in the preceding two years. One of his major goals, now that there was no longer a royalist threat, was to bring an end to the rump by finding a mechanism whereby it would dissolve itself and arrange for new elections that would return the Commons to its former size and balanced composition. However, in November 1651, the Commons had decided only that it would sit for not longer than another three years, which was far longer than Cromwell had expected. Milton's government of goodwill was quickly becoming an oligarchy. Cromwell also became concerned about the increasingly erratic decisions being made by the rump. His desire to bring about reconciliation with royalists, Ireland, and Scotland, for example, was routinely thwarted, as the rump and council pushed to have royalist lands confiscated to pay off debts, forced an unwelcome union on Scotland, and imposed the extremely oppressive Act of Settlement on Ireland. Likewise, Cromwell and a Committee for the Propagation of the Gospel had desired clear statements on religious liberty and toleration operating within the bounds of a national church guided by core beliefs. Despite the rump's passage of various harsh laws against adultery, blasphemy, and swearing, it had failed to deal adequately with religious extremism and did not work hard enough to promote Presbyterianism. There was also a concern that the rump was so dominated by lawyers that it became an institution prone to endless debate but, in fact, accomplished very little law reform.

By April 1653, Cromwell had had enough and demanded that the rump vest all responsibility for government in a smaller assembly made up of themselves and the army, and then dissolve itself, pending new elections. When the rump refused, Cromwell led a company of musketeers into the chamber, uttered the words "I say you are no Parliament; I will put an end to your sitting," and forcibly cleared the members at musketpoint. The doors of the chamber were sealed and somebody posted the sign "This house to let: now unfurnished." To replace this body, at least temporarily, Cromwell and officers within the army nominated a legislature known as the "Assembly of Saints." The assembly soon came into disrepute. Although godly men such as Cromwell initially welcomed its "saintly" composition, they soon came to realize that many of its members were religious extremists. The member for London, Praise-God Barebone, was a Fifth Monarchist, giving rise to the assembly quickly being hailed as "Barebone's Parliament." Barebone and others pushed for the reform of the legal system to be entirely consistent with scripture and argued for the abolition of the common law, ideas that reflected the inexperience of the members and their inability to legislate for the nation. This caused moderate members of the assembly to appeal to Cromwell for its dissolution, which was also accomplished, in December 1653, by military support.

* * *

Discussion Question 6.3: Given that its composition was not representative of historical parliaments nor of the "ancient constitution" in England over which the Civil War was fought, why do you think the rump refused to dissolve itself?

The Protectorate and Restoration

By the end of 1653, Hobbes's unpopular predictions about a leaderless commonwealth turning into a self-interested oligarchy had been proven correct. New leadership vested in a single individual was required, and it was to come from Oliver Cromwell as the new lord protector – and sovereign in all but name – of England. In some ways, Cromwell was perfect for such a role. He was a highly successful military commander, had the loyalty of the army despite its internal dissension, had shown himself (in the Heads of the Proposals) to be a moderate revolutionary, and had twice proven his ability to deal with incompetent, radicalized parliaments. Cromwell came from a lower-gentry family, descended from a sister of Henry VIII's minister Thomas Cromwell, and grew up in Huntington in county Cambridge, where independent Puritanism had grown strong. Although he was hardly the secular sovereign that Hobbes had in mind, Cromwell's modest upbringing, lack of extremism, and parliamentary experience in many ways made him the ideal candidate to assume the mantle of leadership.

Cromwell's new title and government was defined in Major General John Lambert's Instrument of Government, which was based on the earlier Heads of the Proposals and is sometimes considered England's first written constitution.[3] The Instrument recommended a tripartite government composed of a non-hereditary lord protector for life (Cromwell) to govern the "Commonwealth of England, Scotland, and Ireland and the dominions thereto belonging," a council of state of thirteen to twenty-one members chosen by the protector, and a parliament that had to sit for at least five consecutive months every three years. The latter provision allowed the protector to call, prorogue, and dissolve parliament, and was designed to ensure that parliament did not sit in perpetuity or refuse to dissolve itself, as had the rump. Cromwell was given the power of veto but was limited in its use by parliament's ability to vote again and enact the bill after twenty days had passed. He could command the military by consent of parliament when it was sitting and by majority agreement of the council when it was not. In the issuing of ordinances and commissions, the ordering of foreign affairs, and the declaring of war and peace, Cromwell had wide prerogative powers, provided he consulted with his council. Former royalists were incapable of voting or being elected for three successive parliaments and Catholics were disenfranchised. Freedom of Christian worship was allowed, except for Catholicism and sects that disturbed the public peace.

Cromwell became lord protector in December 1653 and his first parliament began sitting the following September. In the meantime, he and the council had issued nearly 200 ordinances and had arranged a peace with the Dutch, with whom England had been at war since 1652. In matters of religion, Cromwell was committed to the idea of liberty of conscience but his experience with extremism had taught him that certain boundaries of behavior were necessary. To this end, Cromwell created a "Commission of Triers" to assess the suitability of future parish ministers, while a "Commission of Ejectors" was responsible to dismiss ministers and schoolmasters who operated on the religious extremes, including

---

3   Up to this point, England had always relied on an unwritten constitution that had developed since the time of Edward the Confessor (reigned 1042–66). Though "recorded" for the benefit of future generations, the constitution was not "codified" in the way most are today.

die-hard Laudians and Arminians. Owing, perhaps, to this extensive, early use of the prerogative powers and the fact that he was now routinely referred to as "your highness," parliament devoted most of its first sitting to attempting to revise the constitutional arrangements of the Instrument, by limiting the powers of the council, increasing the powers of parliament, and removing Cromwell's ability to veto religious bills. To ensure the constitutional bill – which he would have certainly vetoed – was not passed to him, Cromwell dissolved parliament without warning in January 1655. This was a few days short of the five-month minimum, which Cromwell justified on the grounds that the Instrument had meant five lunar months (which average 29.53 days) rather than five calendar months (which average 30.44 days).

Eighteen months passed before another parliament was called, during which time Cromwell gained control of the counties by giving oversight to twelve major generals ("godly governors"), who were responsible for law and order and ensuring loyalty to the protectorate. He also went to war with Spain and, in the process, enabled the "Western Design," a largely unsuccessful effort to gain control of the Caribbean that, nonetheless, resulted in the conquest of Jamaica. The war with Spain, plus the high cost of administering the realm, required Cromwell to call a new parliament in September 1656. This parliament was dominated by another plan to revise the constitution, but one that was considerably more favorable to Cromwell. In the Humble Petition and Advice (1657), Cromwell's supporters suggested that he accept the crown and become king with the power to appoint his successor. They also suggested that Cromwell nominate an upper house of parliament. Although Cromwell declined the title of king (the powers of which he already possessed), he agreed that a second house was necessary. However, when parliament reconvened in January 1658, Cromwell's nominated upper chamber immediately came into conflict with the lower house, forcing Cromwell to dissolve parliament when it came to an impasse. Unfortunately, Cromwell died before he could call another parliament, in September 1658, and although he had not named a successor, the title passed to his son, Richard.

Unlike his father, Richard had poor leadership skills and no military command experience, which meant that he was not able to control feisty parliaments or retain the loyalty of the army, a body that had consistently proven essential to Oliver's success. During his first parliament, the issue of the existence and membership of the upper house returned, but the main issue of that session involved parliament's relationship with the army. Parliament sought to make significant cuts to the military budget and, following the army's petition to the lord protector, issued resolutions in the Commons making meetings of army officers illegal without the permission of parliament and requiring officers to swear an oath that they would not use force to subvert parliament. The army responded with a demand that Cromwell dissolve parliament and assembled troops to help bring this about, forcing the reluctant protector to capitulate. In May 1659, the army accepted Cromwell's resignation as protector and reinstated the Rump Parliament, with the intent that England be again governed as a commonwealth without a king or house of lords. This was essentially a return to the April 1653 situation despite how unsuccessful that model had been. The restored seventy-eight-member rump was, once again, woefully ineffective and sought to exert control over the army. By October it had been refused entry to the chamber, and Lambert and General Charles Fleetwood created a Committee of Safety to govern the country in place of the rump, which proved equally ineffective.

In February 1660, General George Monck entered London at the head of an armed force and, supported by the long-retired Fairfax, ordered the return of the Long Parliament – the rump plus all the members who had previously been excluded on the grounds of their royalist support or during the purge – on the condition that the body finally, after twenty years, dissolve itself so that new elections could be called. The new, moderate, and royalist-leaning parliament came to be known as the "Convention Parliament," because it had not been called by royal writ. Meanwhile, Charles II, who had been kept informed about England's affairs by Monck, issued the Declaration of Breda. In return for his restoration to the English throne, Charles promised full amnesty to all belligerents in the war (although there was a contingency for exceptions, principally the men who had signed his father's death warrant), freedom of worship provided it did not upset the peace of the kingdom, payment of arrears to the army, and that all land grants and purchases during the war and interregnum be subject to parliamentary oversight. Given the composition of the Convention Parliament – roughly balanced between royalists and Presbyterians, with few radicals – these terms were deemed more than acceptable, and Charles arrived to take his place as king on May 29, 1660. His entrance into London, on his thirtieth birthday, was triumphal and order returned to England: the restoration of king, lords, and commons, in – to quote the Declaration – a more "perfect union," had come to pass.

* * *

Discussion Question 6.4: If, by 1657, Oliver Cromwell was king in all but name, why do you think he refused the crown when it was offered?

An English Revolution?

The two decades of Civil War and interregnum were undoubtedly among England's most turbulent, but in the end, they were far from revolutionary. Almost none of the changes to the English constitution that had occurred during these years remained by 1660. The king's restoration was unconditional and the majority of traditional prerogative rights were retained. Neither the Declaration nor the Convention Parliament made any mention of the king's power over trade and foreign affairs, control of the military, selection of ministers, the right to call and dismiss parliament, the ability to suspend or dispense with laws, or any other prerogatives that had come under fire under the early Stuart monarchs.

This meant that the restoration was to take place under terms that had been achieved in the early months of the Long Parliament in 1641, before the radical ideas of Pym and his supporters emerged. In theory, England was more tolerant religiously than it had been before the war, but as we shall see this toleration went only so far. Parliament, dominated by the gentry in the Commons, had also proven that, when pushed, it could take matters into its own hands, although here, again, future events would show that without royal assent, it still lacked the authority to carry out its will. This is not to say that the tremendous loss of life of hundreds of thousands of English, Scottish, and Irish subjects were in vain, as the memory of the fate of his father helped to guide Charles II in his actions over the next two comparatively peaceful decades.

VOICES OF THE PAST
THE EXECUTION OF CHARLES I

Following the Civil War, Charles I was tried by a High Court of Justice and found guilty of being "a tyrant, traitor, murderer, and a public enemy." On January 30, 1649, Charles stepped out onto a temporary scaffold that was erected at his Banqueting House at Whitehall Palace (see Figure 6.2). The following extract contains the court's death warrant and the king's final moments.

* * *

Whereas Charles Stuart, King of England, is and standeth convicted, attainted, and condemned of high treason and other high crimes, and sentence upon Saturday last was pronounced against him by this court, to be put to death by the severing of his head from his body, of which sentence, execution yet remaineth to be done. These are therefore to will and require you to see the said sentence executed in the open street before Whitehall, upon the morrow, being the Thirtieth day of … January, between the hours of ten in the morning and five in the afternoon.… And for so doing, this shall be your sufficient warrant. And these are to require all officers, soldiers and others, the good people of this nation of England, to be assisting unto you in this service.…

Tuesday, the Thirtieth of January, the fatal day being come, … before his majesty was brought thence, the Bishop of London … read divine service in his presence.… Which ended about ten o'clock, his majesty was brought from St. James's to Whitehall by a regiment of foot, with colors flying and drums beating, part marching before and part behind, with a private guard of partisans about him, the bishop on the one hand, and Col. Tomlinson (who had the charge of him) on the other, both bare-headed, his

Figure 6.2 *The execution of Charles I, from a contemporary woodcut.*

majesty walking very fast, and bidding them go faster, added, that he now went before them to strive for a heavenly crown, with less solicitude than he had often encouraged his soldiers to fight for an earthly diadem.

Being come to the end of the park, he went up the stairs leading to the Long Gallery in Whitehall and so into the Cabinet Chamber, where he used formerly to lodge. There finding an unexpected delay in being brought upon the scaffold, which they had not as then fitted, he passed the time, at convenient distances, in prayer.

About twelve o'clock, his majesty refusing to dine, only ate a bit of bread and drank a glass of claret. And about an hour later, Col. Hacker, with other officers and soldiers, brought him, with the bishop and Col. Tomlinson, through the Banqueting House to the scaffold, to which a passage was made through a window.

Divers companies of foot and troops of horse were placed on each side of the street, which hindered the approach of the very numerous spectators, and the king from speaking what he had premeditated and prepared for them to hear.

Whereupon, his majesty finding himself disappointed, omitted much of his intended matter, and for what he meant to speak, directed himself chiefly to Col. Tomlinson....

"I think it is my duty, to God first, and to my country, for to clear myself both as an honest man, a good king, and a good Christian. I shall begin first with my innocence. In truth, I think it not very needful for me to insist long upon this, for all the world knows that I never did begin a war first with the two Houses of Parliament, and I call God to witness, to whom I must shortly make an account, that I never did intend for to encroach upon their privileges.... I do believe that ill instruments between them and me have been the chief cause of all this bloodshed.... I will only say this, that an unjust sentence [the execution of the earl of Strafford] that I suffered to take effect, is now punished by an unjust sentence upon me.... Sirs, ... I had a good cause, and I have a gracious God, I will say no more."

Then to Col. Hacker, he said, "Take care that they do not put me to pain. And, Sir, this, and it may please you – "

But a gentleman coming near the axe, the king said, "Take heed of the axe, pray take heed of the axe."

And to the executioner he said, "I shall say but very short prayers, and when I thrust out my hands – "

Then he called to the bishop for his cap, and having put it on asked the executioner, "Does my hair trouble you?"

Who desired him to put it all under his cap, which as he was doing, ... said, "I have a good cause, and a gracious God on my side.... I go from a corruptible to an incorruptible crown, where no disturbance can be, no disturbance in the world...."

Then the king asked the executioner, "Is my hair well?"

And taking off his cloak and George [the insignia of the order of the garter], he delivered his George to the bishop, saying, "Remember."

Then putting off his doublet, and being in his waistcoat, he put on his cloak again, and looking upon the block said to the executioner, "You must set it fast."

Executioner:	"It is fast, Sir."
King:	"It might have been a little higher."
Executioner:	"It can be no higher, Sir."
King:	"When I put out my hands this way, then – "

Then having said a few words to himself, as he stood, with hands and eyes lift up, immediately stooping down, he laid his neck upon the block, and the executioner again putting his hair under his cap, his majesty thinking he had been going to strike, bade him, "Stay for the sign."

Executioner:	"Yes I will and it please your majesty."

After a very short pause, his majesty stretching forth his hands, the executioner severed his head from his body: Which being held up and showed to the people, was with his body put into a coffin covered with velvet, and carried into his lodging.

His blood was taken up by divers persons for different ends: By some as trophies of their villainy, by others as relics of a martyr; and in some has had the same effect by the blessing of God, which was often found in his sacred touch when living.[4]

Source: J[ames] Nalson, *A True Copy of the Journal of the High Court of Justice, for the Tryal of K. Charles I* (London, 1683), 109, 112–14, 116–18.

* * *

Discussion Question 6.5: Ultimately, Charles I was convicted by less than 45 per cent of the commissioners named to the High Court of Justice. What does this tell you about the trial and Charles's refusal to accept the court's legitimacy?

---

4   It was believed that the "king's touch" could cure diseases, especially scrofula (tuberculosis of the lymph nodes). Despite the rise of Protestantism, which questioned the practice, Tudor and Stuart monarchs regularly performed the ritual because of high public demand.

CHAPTER SEVEN

RESTORATION AND REVOLUTION, 1660–1690

DEATH AND DISORDER: THE BLOODY ASSIZES

As we have seen in earlier chapters, early modern England took disorderly events such as rebellions very seriously, and the effort to restore order was often very violent. Soon after becoming king in 1685, James II faced a rebellion led by his nephew, James Scott, duke of Monmouth, who was his brother Charles II's eldest illegitimate son. Monmouth landed in Dorset in the West Country on June 11, 1685, and gathered a rebel force of artisans and farmers to fight for his claim to the throne. The well-trained royalist army proved far too strong an opponent, and the Monmouth Rebellion was decisively ended at the Battle of Sedgemoor on July 6. More than 1,300 were killed in battle and another 1,300 or so were taken into custody. Monmouth was executed for treason nine days later.

The deaths had just begun. A series of trials, or assizes, began in August to try the rebels who had been captured during the rebellion and awaited punishment. This, in itself, was a bit unusual. Although it was common for the leaders and organizers of rebellions to be executed, the rank and file were usually indemnified, or pardoned, and allowed to live as a sign of the monarch's mercy.

In this case, however, James dispatched the lord chief justice of England, "hanging judge" George Jeffreys, to the West Country to deal with the prisoners. Together with four other judges, Jeffreys traveled to Winchester, Salisbury, Dorchester, Taunton, and Wells, presiding over more than a thousand treason trials in just one month. The first casualty of these assizes was Alice Lyle, an elderly woman who had harbored fugitives after the defeat at Sedgemoor. Many, including members of the jury that convicted her of treason, had expected the sentence to be remitted by the king, but they were disappointed. Initially sentenced to being burned at the stake, the sentence was commuted to beheading, which was carried out in Winchester on September 2.

By the end of September, nearly 300 other rebels were sentenced to be hanged, drawn, and quartered. In the Taunton Assize, 500 prisoners were tried in two days, with 140 hanged in the aftermath. Their remains were displayed on pikes through the West Country as a warning to those who still considered rebellion against their king. Another 800 men and women were sentenced to be transported into the English colonies in the Caribbean. Although this might appear merciful, many considered transportation worse than death. They lived as indentured servants enduring extremely harsh conditions, never seeing England again, and more often than not dying before their term of indenture was over. Still others remained imprisoned awaiting trial, where they succumbed to gaol fever (typhus) because of the poor diet and sanitary conditions of early modern English prisons.

For good reason, these trials in the West Country have come to be known as the "Bloody Assizes." Even at a time when public executions for various felony offenses were relatively common, this number of deaths at the hands of the state in such a short space of time was extraordinary. When Jeffreys returned to London, the king, far from rebuking the judge for his severity, promoted him to lord chancellor and made him a baron. This act surely did little to engender love or loyalty for the Catholic monarch. When James II was forced to abandon his throne in 1688, Jeffreys was imprisoned in the Tower of London, where he died in 1689.

Numerous pamphlets were published after his death, including *A New Martyrology, or, The Bloody Assizes* (1693), which styled itself a sequel to Foxe's *Book of Martyrs*. The author ended the book with an elegy:

> He [Jeffreys] with commission rid the land about,
> But still he aim'd to keep fair justice out,
> With angry look he brow-beat rightful cause,

> And his bold hand did *sacrifice* the laws,
> Tore 'um or trampled on 'um with his paws....
> *Inquisitor* like *Spain* in *England* sate,
> And at their pleasure steer'd the helm of fate,
> He rid the *Western* Circuit all around,
> But where he came no justice to be found;
> He improv'd his talents *martyrs* to condemn,
> Hang draw and quarter was his daily theme.
> He bid 'em to confess, if ever they hope
> To be repriev'd from the fatal rope,
> This seem'd a favor, but he'd none forgive,
> The favor was, a day or two to live;
> Which those had not that troubled him with trial,
> *His business blood*, and would have no denial.[1]

Another author wrote satirically that Jeffreys "had such respect to the souls of men, that he scarce hanged any but those that were innocent."[2]

Historians often cite the "Bloody Assizes" as the cause of defense lawyers entering the criminal courtroom. The Treason Act of 1696 granted those accused of high treason access to counsel, the right to compel witness attendance, and a copy of the charges against them, all of which defendants had previously been denied. Although the "Bloody Assizes" were, perhaps, the most severe judicial killings in English history, they helped to bring about modernity in the criminal justice system that, over the next century, saw a dramatic decrease in the number of executions in England.

* * *

Discussion Question 7.1: Why do you think James II promoted Jeffreys to the position of lord chancellor despite likely knowing this would be an unpopular decision given Jeffreys's actions during the Bloody Assizes?

---

1   Thomas Pitt, *A New Martyrology, or, The Bloody Assizes* (London, 1693), 68.
2   Anonymous, *The Merciful Assizes: Or, a Panegyric on the Late Lord Jeffreys* (London, 1701).

The Merry Monarch

Like most of the Tudor and Stuart monarchs, Charles II was bright, well educated, and multilingual (see Figure 7.1). He was also the most popular Stuart monarch, in part because of his affable nature and because he showed himself to be tolerant, tactful, moderate, and compromising, all in contrast to his father. One example of this is his stance toward the regicides, the radical rump, and the supporters of the protectorate. In the Act of Indemnity and Oblivion, all persons associated with the parliamentary side were pardoned, with the exception of about one hundred people, half of whom were punished with property confiscation, imprisonment, and bans from public office. The other half were found guilty of high treason, but many had already died or fled the country. In October 1660, ten regicides were hanged, drawn, and quartered, and the bodies of Cromwell and Ireton were exhumed and hanged, with their heads placed on spikes at Westminster Hall, where the High Court of Justice had sat. To be sure, these were extreme acts of violence, but the list of exclusions from the act could have been much longer had Charles and the Convention wanted it that way. As a symbol of further reconciliation, other parliamentary supporters

Figure 7.1 *Charles II, after 1660, by Thomas Hawker.*

Credit: incamerastock/Alamy Stock Photo.

were not only pardoned but given titles and positions within the government. Many royalists, however, were less than impressed with this largesse; considering that the Declaration of Breda had implied that confiscated land would not be restored, these men often received less favor from the king than his father's former enemies.

It also did not hurt Charles's reputation that, during the Great Fire of London of 1666, he personally led the rescue efforts and was reportedly seen throwing buckets of water on the flames himself. Although hundreds of buildings and a huge portion of the historical City of London were lost, Charles's actions (and those of his brother James) were credited as having resulted in minimal loss of life. In the aftermath, the king arranged for food supplies to be brought to the city, issued a proclamation that required neighboring cities and towns to receive those who became homeless, and set up a court to resolve disputes between landlords and tenants. At Charles's encouragement, the "new City" was rebuilt with improved sanitation and fire safety, including buildings constructed of brick and stone rather than wood. Modern landmarks, such as St. Paul's Cathedral and the Monument, still prominent features in London today, were built by famous architects such as Christopher Wren. Perhaps most importantly, the fire seemed to coincide with purging the last major bout of bubonic plague from London, which had killed at least 75,000 people between 1665 and 1666, but which disappeared from the metropolis thereafter.

Charles's moderation toward his enemies and care for his subjects made up for some of his more obvious shortcomings, such as his preference for alcohol, dancing, entertainment, and sport rather than politics. The restoration court became a center of patronage for artists, musicians, authors, and scientists; early in his reign, Charles founded the Royal Observatory in Greenwich and the Royal Society of London, still one of the world's foremost learned societies. The theater, which had been heavily suppressed during the republic and protectorate, resurged. Charles's time in France resulted in him bringing to England modern fashions, such as the three-piece suit and wigs, and culinary delicacies, such as champagne.

Frequent subjects of gossip were Charles's dalliances with mistresses. Although his wife, the Portuguese princess Catherine of Braganza, bore him no living heirs, Charles openly consorted with various women who bore him no fewer than fourteen children, all of whom were illegitimate and therefore ineligible to inherit the crown. Because it was the responsibility of a father to provide for his children regardless of their legitimacy, Charles did so through titles (including making his eldest son duke of Monmouth, leader of the 1685 rebellion), lands, and offices, at great expense to the court and to the resentment of courtiers and councillors who feared, rightly or wrongly, that the king's women and bastard children exerted undue influence over his state decisions. It is small wonder that Charles was referred to as the "merry monarch."

The Cavalier Parliament

Like most English monarchs, Charles was perpetually in need of money but history had taught him that many of the revenue streams used by the late Tudor and early Stuart monarchs could not be revived. Impositions, monopolies, ship money, and the profits of fiscal feudalism – wardship, purveyance, forced loans, distraint of knighthood, and numerous other means – had become immensely unpopular. Accordingly, the Convention passed the Tenures Abolition Act, which brought an end to feudalism in England. To replace these sources of revenue, Charles was granted tunnage and poundage for life, an excise tax on alcohol and other beverages, and later a "hearth tax," which was collected based on the number of chimneys in a home and was, therefore, a graduated tax based on one's wealth. Various parcels of crown land that had been confiscated during the war were also returned. All together, these sources of revenue were expected to bring in £1,200,000 per year. This was more annual revenue than any previous English monarch had access to, and should, in theory, have been more than enough to fund the court.

In practice, the situation was far more complicated. In the first place, the amount of money these sources would bring in could only be estimated, rather than guaranteed, which meant that the court was never sure how much money would come into the royal treasury. All it took to reduce expected income was a depressed economy or the onset of Continental wars. In addition, parliament asserted its right to determine the levies described in the *Book of Rates*, which limited the government's ability to increase the customs duties to make for up for income shortages. Parliament had also authorized the collection of a poll tax in order to pay off the New Model Army, so that it could be disbanded. Together with the loss of traditional feudal revenues and the requirement to pay the hearth tax, the poll tax placed a heavy financial burden on the English gentry and citizenry throughout the country, who bore the greatest onus of parliamentary taxation. Furthermore, as discussed, Charles operated a very expensive court, filled with patronage, positions, and pensions, not to mention the extraordinary funding that would be needed during the Great Plague and Great Fire. Finally, collectively most of these sources of revenue were determined by parliament, which placed Charles in a highly dependent situation with a body that, in the past, had used the king's paucity as leverage in securing better constitutional terms.

This leverage was aided by the claim of Charles's first parliament – the so-called Cavalier Parliament, which sat intermittently from 1661 to 1679 – that statute took precedence over proclamations, a natural evolution of Charles's desire in the Declaration of Breda to work with a "free parliament." Charles had also, in the declaration, granted "liberty to tender consciences," provided they did not "disturb the peace of the kingdom," and promised to "consent to such an Act of parliament, upon mature deliberation ... for the full granting that indulgence."

This largely left it up to parliament to determine what nonconformist religion in England should look like and gave it the ability to legislate in ways not originally intended by the king. Had Charles intended to offer an "indulgence" to Catholics, who had offered him succor during his exile, and to the various puritanical sects that had emerged in the 1640s, or were these outlier religions disturbing to the peace of the realm? Whatever Charles thought or wanted, parliament, which was dominated by Anglicans (including the bishops in the restored House of Lords) and royalists, opted for persecution.

This decision resulted, between 1661 and 1665, in the passage of the "Clarendon Code," named after Edward Hyde, earl of Clarendon, Charles's first lord chancellor. In fact, the name was a misnomer, as Clarendon likely had little to do with the passage of the religious code and disagreed with much of it. Regardless, the Clarendon Code involved the passage of numerous pieces of legislation. The Corporation Act (1661) required town officials to swear an oath that they would accept Anglican communion, thus preventing Presbyterians and Puritans from holding public office. The Act of Uniformity (1662) ordered clergy and teachers to use the *Book of Common Prayer* and assent to its doctrine, by which about 1,750 ministers were removed from their parishes. In the same year, another act required Quakers to swear their allegiance to the king, even though their belief did not allow them to accept hierarchy or state authority, and the Licensing Act sought to suppress radical pamphleteering by, for example, Fifth Monarchists. The Conventicle Act (1664) made religious meetings of more than five nonconformists illegal, and the Five Mile Act (1665) forbade clergymen who had been expelled to live close to their former parish or of living near any town unless they swore allegiance to the king and the prayer book. At this stage, no attempts were made to persecute Catholics, for the simple reason that penal laws already existed and could be applied as needed. In sum, despite Charles's promises for religious liberty, the hegemony of the Church of England was strengthened, while all dissenting faiths were suppressed.

* * *

Discussion Question 7.2: Why do you think Charles II gave royal assent to the Clarendon Code, despite it being at odds with the Declaration of Breda and with Clarendon's own position?

War, Politics, and Religion

By the time the Clarendon Code was passed in its entirety, Charles and parliament faced pressing foreign affairs issues. The most significant of these was the resumption of war with the Dutch. The cause of the war was the passage, in 1660, of the Navigation Act, a revised version of one passed by the rump in 1651, and the Staple Act (1663). Together, these acts forbade English colonies (to be discussed in the next chapter) from trading with other countries, including the Netherlands, France, and Spain; required goods to be transported in "British bottoms" (British owned and crewed ships); and ordered that certain goods shipped to or from the colonies first pass through an English port. There were good reasons for these measures, such as ensuring that England's store of bullion (gold and silver) remained in the country and that customs duties could be collected from recalcitrant colonial merchants, but it also had the impact of damaging international shipping, which up to this point had been dominated by the Dutch. Anglo-Dutch competition and belligerence in the Americas and Africa eventually led to a declaration of war, supported by a large parliamentary grant to build up the navy.

The war initially went well for England. The English managed to take New Netherland (later renamed New York) from the Dutch in America, and Charles's brother, James, duke of York and lord high admiral, and cousin Prince Rupert claimed several victories over the Dutch fleet. However, by 1666, France had entered the war as an ally to the Dutch, and the devastation of domestic events – plague and fire – encouraged the king to make overtures of peace. In the meantime, Charles began secret negotiations with France, which led the Dutch (who were aware of the king's general intentions) to undertake the Battle on the Medway. In June 1667, the Dutch navy made its way into the Thames and up River Medway in Kent, where the unmanned and unarmed English naval battleships were anchored. The English lost fifteen ships and were forced sign the Treaty of Breda under generally unfavorable terms; the English kept New York but lost several islands in Indonesia that were valuable in the spice trade, and they were forced to revise the Navigation Act to make it friendlier to the Dutch. In the end, the war was disastrously expensive, dramatically increased the national debt, and led to a trade depression that further reduced income to the royal treasury.

The loss of the Anglo-Dutch War was blamed primarily on Clarendon, who was dismissed from his office and went into exile following an impeachment hearing. Clarendon's departure gave rise to a ministerial coalition known as the "Cabal." The word had a double meaning. By definition, it referred to a secretive faction involved in political intrigue, but it also conveniently functioned as an acronym for the five members who belonged to it: (C) baron Clifford, (A) the earl of Arlington, (B) the duke of Buckingham, (A) lord Ashley, and (L) the duke of Lauderdale. There was, in fact, little that these five men agreed on and little evidence that their efforts were secretive and collusive, but in this case perception was more important than reality. Unlike the early Stuarts, who had tended to prefer a single favorite as advisor (especially Villiers, the duke of Buckingham), Charles's use and abuse of these men allowed him, in essence, to carry out his own desires while the Cabal fought among themselves in the privy council and parliament. The Cabal, which generally shared the opinion that royal power needed to be strengthened, also gave the impression that the king was moving the government back toward an absolutist stance.

Among Charles's and the Cabal's personal desires by the late 1660s and early 1670s was allowing greater freedom of religious worship, both to those being persecuted by the Clarendon Code and to Catholics who still suffered under harsh penal laws. Charles's mother, who died in 1669, was Catholic, as was his Portuguese wife, and he had close ties to the French court of Louis XIV, where he had spent time during his exile. Moreover, his brother and heir, the duke of York, had secretly converted to Catholicism in 1668 or 1669, and although he continued to attend Anglican services, his religious beliefs were becoming known. There was, naturally, also the question of Charles's own religious position, especially given the ambiguity of the Declaration of Breda about freedom of worship. A clue to the king's religious outlook may be found in the Treaty of Dover, signed between Charles and Louis in 1670. The public purport of the treaty involved an alliance against the Dutch in return for a stipend that would help relieve the king of his dependence on parliament. However, there was also a secret provision known only to the king and certain members of the Cabal, by which – in exchange for more money – Charles promised to convert to Catholicism at a convenient time in the future.

Coincidentally, in the same year parliament passed a second Conventicle Act, which renewed efforts to suppress nonconformity. The Cabal was against it and encouraged the king to use his prerogative powers to address the matter. Constitutionally, the king still had the right as fount of all justice to exercise what was known as "suspending and dispensing" powers, but the practice was extremely controversial because of the frequency with which the early Stuarts had resorted to it, and because the Cavalier Parliament had come to believe that such actions could not be used to overturn parliamentary legislation. Nonetheless, in 1672, Charles issued the Declaration of Indulgence, which suspended penal laws against nonconformists and relaxed those against Catholics. For the first time in more than a decade, Charles was at odds with his parliament, which had considerable leverage because money was needed to prosecute the third Anglo-Dutch war. In exchange for its subsidy, parliament revoked the declaration and responded by issuing the Test Act. The statute required all officeholders to accept a declaration against Catholicism and transubstantiation and take Anglican communion at least once a year. The duke of York refused to take this "test" and resigned as lord high admiral, an act that publicly outed the heir to the throne as a Catholic. Two additional consequences of these events were the collapse of the Cabal, which had engineered the alliance with France, and the Treaty of Westminster that brought an end to war.

Parties, Plots, and Rebellions

The revocation of the Declaration of Indulgence and the passage of the Test Act initiated another wave of anti-Catholic hysteria in England. This hysteria was piqued by James's marriage to Mary of Modena, a fellow Catholic, in 1673. By his late wife, James already had two daughters, Mary and Anne, both of whom had been raised as Anglicans and, it was expected, would marry Protestants.[3] As James at the time of his second marriage was already forty years old – only a few years younger than the king – there was every reason to believe that he might either predecease his brother and never accede to the throne or reign for a very short time. In either situation, the crown would go to his daughter Mary, and the Catholic threat that seemed to envelop the monarchy would dissipate. But James's new wife was only fifteen years old when they married and had every chance to bear him a son, who would be raised Catholic and would, by right of male primogeniture, automatically take precedence over his sisters. This was a situation that parliament took very seriously. Even the efforts of Charles's new chief minister, Thomas Osborne, earl of Danby, to ease these concerns by enforcing strict Anglican conformity and rigorously applying the Clarendon Code was not sufficient to allay these fears.

Together with a financial crisis associated with recovering from the Anglo-Dutch war, the Catholic threat was felt in parliament in another way: the division of its members between a "court" party loyal to Danby and a "country" party responsive to the earl of Shaftesbury, a former member of the Cabal (Ashley). Generally, the court party supported divine-right monarchy and the king's right to use his royal prerogatives (within limits), and it stood behind the Church of England and traditional Anglican worship – essentially the type of men who rallied to the royalist cause in 1642. Later, this party was derisively referred to by their opposition as "Tories," which referred to Irish cattle thieves, a reference to the inaccurate perception that they favored Catholicism and did not respect men's property. The members of the country party were the champions of parliamentary sovereignty and limited constitutional monarchy, and they wanted toleration for non-radical Protestant dissenters – the type of gentlemen who supported the parliamentary cause in 1642. Later, this group was referred to by their opposition as "Whigs," or Scottish cattle drivers, giving the perception that the country party preferred Presbyterianism and were of a lower social class. Neither party had a majority in parliament, nor was their initial association anything more than a loose understanding of basic principles, but their emergence represented fracturing within the Cavalier parliament that had, by 1678, been sitting for nearly two decades.

---

3   James's first wife, Anne Hyde, also produced several sons, although none survived more than a few years.

The crisis between the two parties was precipitated by the revelation of Titus Oates, a defrocked Anglican clergyman, that the queen's physician, Sir George Wakeman, and several other Catholics planned to employ Jesuits to poison the king, place James on the throne, and restore Catholicism to England (see *Voices of the Past*: **The Jesuit's Firing Plot**). Oates's claims, though entirely fabricated, stood up well under questioning from the privy council and parliament and were "confirmed" when a magistrate who had interrogated Oates ended up dead, allegedly at the hands of the papists. The plot played perfectly into fears of Catholic rebellion since the time of Elizabeth, and with growing concerns about pro-Catholic sentiment at the royal court and the king's secret dealings with France, Oates was believed despite the flimsy nature of his evidence. As the rumors grew and fear wracked the nation, many trials and arrests followed. Wakeman was tried and acquitted of the charges, but at least a dozen men were executed for their alleged role in the plot, some of whom were very high-profile, though largely apolitical, Catholics. Oates was eventually charged with sedition and perjury, fined, and sentenced to life imprisonment, although he was ultimately pardoned in 1689 by William and Mary.

The Commons also sought to impeach Danby after evidence was offered proving that he had been complicit in secret negotiations with Louis XIV, prompting the king, after nearly two decades, to dissolve the Cavalier parliament to protect his minister. The dissolution of parliament, however, turned out to be a significant error. Capitalizing on evidence of a Catholic plot and having the strong support of country gentlemen and town merchants, the Whigs came to dominate in the new parliament elected in 1679 and even the appointment of Shaftesbury as lord president of the privy council did nothing to slow the events that followed. Fully aware of parliament's position regarding the Catholicism of James, duke of York, the lord chancellor offered to set limitations on the power of any Catholic successor, but the Whig-dominated parliament instead introduced the Exclusion Bill. The bill sought to prevent James from taking the throne in favor of his daughter Mary, who had recently been wed to William of Orange, the Protestant head of state of the Dutch Republic and no friend of Louis XIV. The ousting of Danby had removed most Tory support from parliament, so the bill was almost certain to pass if it was put to a vote. To prevent this, Charles prorogued and then dissolved parliament. The new parliaments that met in 1680 and 1681 were little different in composition and continued to press for the exclusion, again prompting the king to dissolve these assemblies. It was during these parliaments that the "Abhorrers" came to be called the "Tories," while the "Petitioners" became the "Whigs." To support their respective positions, Robert Filmer's *Patriarcha*, written in the 1640s, was published in 1680 to promote the Tory cause, and John Locke began work on his *Two Treatises on Government*, to be discussed below, to advocate for the Whigs.

After the dissolution of parliament in 1681, Charles did not call another session during his lifetime, which was to last for another four years. Although the

Cavalier parliament had, in 1664, passed a new Triennial Act making meetings of parliament every three years recommended rather than required, the decision not to call a session in four years violated the spirit of the act and caused some in England to foresee the return of absolutism. This was not helped by the effective proscription of Whigs from government after 1681. Those who could be clearly identified as Whigs were removed from the king's council and the magistracy, and leadership of the local militia bands were remodeled to exclude supporters of the country party. For his role in the Exclusion Crisis, Shaftesbury was accused of treason, but as London was dominated by Whigs, it was hard to find a jury willing to convict him. When the Tories managed to gain control of London in 1682, Shaftesbury fled to the Netherlands to avoid new legal proceedings. Another consequence of Charles's decision to rule without parliament was his need to make up for the lost parliamentary subsidy. Along with finding some savings in the operation of the court, Charles was forced to strengthen the methods by which ordinary revenue was collected, efforts that reminded some of his father's fiscal policies during the personal rule half a century earlier.

The actions taken against the Whigs over the previous two years prompted several extremists to concoct the Rye House Plot in the spring of 1683. The ill-conceived plan involved assassinating the king and his brother James as they returned to London after a day at the horse races. The races were cancelled and the plans fell through. Two months later, news of the plot leaked, which resulted in several arrests and the execution of a dozen people by beheading or being hanged, drawn, and quartered. Another dozen men were imprisoned and fined, while ten – including Locke – fled to the Netherlands. Arthur Capell, the earl of Essex, committed suicide at the Tower of London to avoid the humiliation of public execution. The conspirators of the Rye House Plot expected that if they were successful the crown would have been claimed either by James's daughter and heir, Mary, or by the eldest son of Charles II, James Scott, duke of Monmouth. Although Monmouth was illegitimate and therefore had no claim to the throne, he was touted as a strong candidate by various supporters. After being identified as a conspirator in the Rye House Plot, Monmouth placed himself into exile to avoid prosecution. Charles II died in February 1685, but not before, on his deathbed, converting to Catholicism.

James II and the Return of Absolutism

Despite, as discussed in the opening of this chapter, the Monmouth Rebellion and the "Bloody Assizes" early in his reign, James II acceded to a relatively stable throne (see Figure 7.2). Over the previous few years, the national and local governments had been purged of Whigs and replaced with Tories who, despite their dislike of Catholicism, nonetheless believed in James's divine right to rule and had supported that position during the Exclusion Crisis. James, of course, was well aware of the various political and religious controversies that had enshrouded not only his brother's reign but also his father's. Therefore, he started his reign with every intention of supporting the constitutional developments that had emerged since 1660 and the supremacy of the Church of England as the national religion with the king at its head. Those who doubted James's intentions and despised his religion would only have to wait – it was hoped – a mere few years until the Protestant Mary and her French- and Catholic-hating –

Figure 7.2 *James II, as the duke of York, circa 1670, by Peter Lely.*

and constitutional-monarchy supporting – husband, William of Orange, took their rightful place on the English throne.

James's early relations with his Tory-dominated Loyal Parliament were good. The institution granted him the same generous revenue stream as his brother had received, which, owing to an increase in trade, placed him in a much better financial position than Charles. But that parliament also quickly came to learn that the king was very much his father's son; James was no puppet of his people and sought to rule, if not absolutely, at least independently, with his royal prerogatives intact. In November 1685, James announced his plans to keep the army, which had been assembled to deal with Monmouth's Rebellion and another uprising led by the Scottish earl of Argyll, intact. Beyond its expense, maintaining a standing army in peacetime was, with the exception of protectorate England in the late 1650s, against English tradition because it was seen to curtail fundamental liberties. The proximity of the army to the capital also raised concerns that the king might use the army to enforce his policies in London. Moreover, James indicated that he planned to allow Catholic officers to command regiments, which was in contravention of the Test Act. After parliament was prorogued, never to be called again during his reign, James used the same powers to place Catholics into government offices, welcomed a *papal nuncio* (ambassador) into his court, and employed a Jesuit confessor, whom he also admitted to the privy council. After carefully manipulating the judiciary through dismissals, James sought and won a legal decision on his right to use his suspending and dispensing prerogatives to obviate the Test Act.

The success of James's legal case empowered him to issue, in April 1687, a Declaration of Indulgence suspending the Clarendon Code and providing relief for both dissenters and Catholics. A series of questions posed by lords lieutenant to commissioners of the peace – justices, mayors, and aldermen – led to the purge of hundreds of Anglicans, many of whom were Tories. Similar steps were taken at the universities. Naturally, Catholics were frequently chosen as replacements, but as the number of prominent Catholics had dwindled considerably in England by this time, this also meant that many of these new officeholders were not necessarily up to the task. Quakers, Baptists, and Presbyterians were also appointed, to the dismay of the Anglican church. James also established an Ecclesiastical Commission – a body that in essence replaced the Court of High Commission that had been abolished by the Long Parliament – under the authority of Lord Chancellor Jeffreys, to oversee the Church of England and persecute individuals within the church who were deemed too intolerant of nonconformity. This body arrested seven bishops, including the archbishop of Canterbury, on charges of seditious libel, and had them imprisoned in the Tower for claiming in a petition that the Declaration was an abuse of the king's suspending powers. At trial, the bishops were acquitted, largely because their right to petition the king was guaranteed in the ancient constitution.

In sum, in the space of a mere two years, James had managed to alienate the one group in England who truly supported his claim to the throne, the Anglican-leaning Tories. In their minds, the king had demonstrated willful disregard for parliament, abused his prerogative powers of appointment and dismissal of officeholders and the judiciary, abused English legislation through the suspending and dispensing powers, weakened the Church of England through the Commission and the manipulation of the episcopacy, resorted to arbitrary imprisonment despite habeas corpus, and placed England into a virtual state of martial law.

Still, many people were willing to wait out the king's death, as by 1687 James was almost the same age as Charles II had been at his demise. The situation changed, however, when rumors began circulating that Queen Mary was pregnant. Both Tories and Whigs knew that if the child was a boy, he would eclipse the claims of his half-sisters to the throne and be baptized Catholic, plaguing England with a Catholic monarch for generations to come. In June 1688, Mary made this fear a reality when she gave birth to James Francis Edward.[4] The birth was witnessed by dozens of courtiers, which was unusual but not unheard of at the time. Important events such as the birth of a possible future king needed to be supported by eye-witness testimony to avoid later claims of illegitimacy. Later, the Protestant witnesses all stated that they had turned away from the queen at the time of the birth to respect her privacy. This enabled the king's enemies to claim either that the child was born still or that there never was a child, but that another baby was smuggled into the queen's bedchamber in a warming pan.

* * *

Discussion Question 7.3: To what extent were the problems that James II faced caused by the actions of his brother, Charles II?

The Revolution of 1688

Shortly after the birth, a group of seven men, led by Danby, comprising both Tory and Whig positions conspired together and wrote to William of Orange, inviting him to invade England for the purposes of protecting his wife's birthright and the Protestant faith. They wrote that "[t]he people are so generally dissatisfied with the present conduct of the government, in relation to their

---

4   Following the ousting of his father as king, James Francis Edward, who came to be known as the "Old Pretender," would attempt to regain the throne during the Jacobite rising of 1715. His son, Charles Edward, the "Young Pretender," would make a similar attempt in 1745. Both efforts failed miserably.

religion, liberties and properties (all which have been greatly invaded) … that your highness may be assured, there are nineteen parts of twenty of the people throughout the kingdom, who are desirous of a change." They also claimed that William would have the support of the vast majority of the nobility and gentry, and that the standing army would not present a challenge because there was so much division between the Catholic and Anglican officers and soldiers. In fact, William had already been planning an invasion, so this invitation merely solidified ongoing arrangements. By September, he had assembled his forces – more than 400 ships and 20,000 men – and issued a declaration assuring the English people of his plan to maintain Protestantism, ensure a free parliament, and investigate the legitimacy of the new prince.

The fleet departed the Netherlands on November 1 and arrived in England four days later, not without irony, on Gunpowder Day. Over the next few weeks, as William's men moved toward London, undertaking minor skirmishes along the way, James attempted to reverse some of his more controversial policies and dropped the writ for a new parliamentary election, but he refused to restore the Test Act. He also refused to accept assistance from France on the grounds that he would lose domestic support. In hindsight, this was certainly a mistake, as James soon discovered that most of his staunchest supporters had already rallied to William's cause, as had his daughter, Anne. In the face of nationwide anti-Catholic rioting, James sent his wife and baby across to France and attempted to escape himself, throwing the Great Seal of England into the Thames. Although he had disguised himself, James was captured by sailors as he attempted to flee and was returned to London on December 16. Through royal commissioners, William communicated to James that he needed to leave London, which he did, and William entered the capital on the 18th. Although James was under Dutch guard, he was allowed to escape, and he fled to France on December 23, never again to return to England.

Whether the revolution in 1688 was, as historians once commonly referred to it, "glorious" because so little blood was shed, it was certainly a critical moment in English history and is often seen to have inaugurated a new historical era in England.[5] At the end of December, William took over the government provisionally while a Convention Parliament was arranged. When that body met in late January 1689, it was well represented with both Tories and Whigs, including many who had been in one or more of Charles's exclusion parliaments. Given this composition, it is perhaps not surprising that lengthy debates took place about how to move forward. Everybody agreed that James could not return to England as king, but there was much dispute about what the future should look like. The Whigs simply preferred to name William as monarch, in effect claiming that the power

---

5   Historians often refer to the "long eighteenth century," from the revolution settlement of 1689 to the end of the French Revolution in 1815, as the next major period of English history.

of the crown came from the people of England. The Tories strongly supported the divine right of kings, which meant that James was the only rightful monarch until his death. They suggested that James retain the crown but that William (or William and Mary) become regent until James's death, at which point – assuming one accepted the warming pan controversy – Mary was the heir by divine right.

Another option, assuming that James's abandonment of England constituted an abdication of his throne, was to place the crown directly on Mary's head, with William as her consort. William, however, who had nearly as close a claim to the throne as Mary (they were first cousins, as William was the son of James II's

Figure 7.3 *William III, circa 1691, by Thomas Murray.*

sister), was unwilling to be his wife's "gentleman usher." In the end, after much deliberation by both houses of parliament, they agreed that James had abdicated his throne, which was now vacant and needed to be occupied. This led to the first time and only time in English history when two people – William III and Mary II – were joint regnant monarchs (see Figure 7.3 and Figure 7.4). They agreed that if Mary predeceased her husband (which she did, in 1694), William would continue to reign for the remainder of his life (he died in 1702) and then the crown would pass to their children. However, should Mary die childless (which she did), her sister Anne would claim her inheritance after William's death, thereby maintaining the notion of natural succession by divine right. In fact, Anne would go on to reign from 1702 to 1714. In effect, this resolution was a *via media* between the Whig and Tory positions; Mary ascended by divine right, whereas William was named by parliament as regnant rather than being, as had been Philip in the late 1550s, simply king by right of his wife.

Figure 7.4 *Mary II, as a princess, circa 1677, by Peter Lely.*

The New English Constitution

When William and Mary were officially crowned at Banqueting House – the same building where Charles I had met his end – they were also presented with a document, known as the Declaration of Rights. In many ways, the Declaration was a descendant of earlier petitions to the crown, such as the Petition of Right (1628) and the Grand Remonstrance (1642), a combination of complaints about James II and assertions of rights guaranteed by the ancient constitution. Among the complaints against the former king were abuse of the suspending and dispensing power, prosecution of the seven bishops, keeping a standing army during peacetime, violating the freedom of elections, arming and employing Catholics, and imposing sentences without due process of law. The Declaration, therefore, was mostly about redressing these grievances. The suspending and dispensing power could only be used with parliamentary consent, all taxes must be approved by parliament, all subjects had the right to petition the king, a standing army could not exist in peacetime without parliamentary approval, freedom of speech in parliament was a fundamental right, and "for the amending, strengthening and preserving of the laws, parliaments ought to be held frequently." These, the Declaration attested, were the "undoubted rights and liberties" of English subjects. As a result of the Declaration, which became the Bill of Rights later in the year, English parliaments have met annually since 1689 and have, as a result, achieved the style of a sovereign assembly that England's ruling classes had been seeking for a century.

It is important, however, to note that although England was now a constitutional monarchy in which sovereignty was vested in king-in-parliament, it would be wrong to think of the monarch as a mere figurehead or as a puppet of parliament. The king still retained numerous royal prerogatives, including the right to declare war and peace (which William did prodigiously), call and dismiss parliament, veto legislation, appoint councillors and judges, create peers and knights, determine foreign affairs and trade, assemble and command the army, and many others. That the king was now constitutionally required to seek the advice or consent of parliament in certain instances, and that he was now "contracted" to rule in the best interests of his people, did not mean that he lacked sovereign authority. Another major step in the revolution settlement was the production of a Toleration Act, which repealed most of the Clarendon Code and made nearly all forms of Protestant worship legal, while Anglicanism would still be the only national religion. Here, again, was a compromise between Whigs, who preferred broad toleration of Protestants and the ability of churches to govern themselves, and Tories, who preferred the supremacy of the Church of England. The act did not include toleration of Catholics, who would have to wait nearly another century and a half (1829) before they could worship openly, vote, and hold public office in England.

The new constitution that came into existence in 1689 was based heavily on the work of John Locke, especially his *Letters Concerning Toleration* (1689–92) and *Two Treatises on Government* (written circa 1678–80, published 1690). In the first of the *Two Treatises*, Locke offered a vigorous refutation of Filmer's *Patriarcha*, which argued for the divine right of kings. In the second, Locke claimed that all people had a natural right to defend their "life, health, liberty, [and] possessions" from being taken, even by the king. Although for the sake of living in civil society and the resolution of conflicts, man contracted with the king and legislators, their failure to live up to the terms of the contract could result in their removal and replacement. This "social contract theory of government" went beyond Hobbes's arguments in the *Leviathan* by allowing bad legislators to be replaced, if necessary by revolution:

> [W]henever the legislators endeavour to take away, and destroy the property of the people, or to reduce them to slavery under arbitrary power, they put themselves in a state of war with the people, who are thereupon absolved from any farther obedience, and are left to the common refuge, which God hath provided for all men, against force and violence. Whensoever therefore the legislative shall transgress this fundamental rule of society, and either by ambition, fear, folly or corruption, endeavour to grasp themselves, or put in the hands of any other absolute power over the lives, liberties, and estates of the people, by this breach of trust they forfeit the power, the people had put into their hands, for quite contrary ends, and it devolves to the people, who have a right to resume their original liberty.

Even in the immediate aftermath of the revolution of 1688, Locke's ideas were fairly radical, but they did help to explain how the events that led to the placement of William and Mary on the throne could have been allowed to occur. Locke also argued for the separation of powers in government, particularly an executive, embodied by the king and his council, and legislative branches, embodied by parliament and local assemblies, in order to provide checks and balances against the actions of each other for the public good.[6] Locke's writings were extremely influential in the eighteenth century, when revolutions were exported to America, France, and throughout the Atlantic world. For this reason, Locke is considered one of the founding fathers of the European Enlightenment and the American Constitution.

---

6   Locke's separation of powers is bifurcated; the third branch that would be added to this scheme, the judiciary, is absent from Locke's writings, although it can be inferred that he expected actions and laws to be tested by courts.

Although it occurred beyond the chronological scope of this book, one additional piece of legislation deserves to be mentioned, because it is considered to have completed the revolution settlement. This was the Act of Settlement (1701), which determined the issue of succession to the crown in the event that Queen Anne died childless. Between 1684 and 1700, Anne had been pregnant seventeen times, with all but one pregnancy ending in miscarriage, a stillborn child, or a child who lived for a matter of months. In July 1700, her only living son, Prince William, duke of Gloucester, died, leaving Anne without an heir. Although Anne was only thirty-six years old, years of pregnancy and miscarriage had demonstrated that she was unlikely to produce another child. In theory, the closest in line to succession was her younger brother, James Stuart (the warming pan baby), but the Bill of Rights had excluded all Catholics from the inheritance, which thereby passed over the majority of the Stuart line. The central purpose of the Act of Settlement was to name the closest Protestant by blood as heir to the throne, who at the time was Sophia, electress of Hanover, granddaughter of James I, or her children. Ultimately, her son George I would claim the throne in 1714.[7]

The act, which is still in effect in Britain, also contained several additional provisions that were designed to correct problems that had occurred during the seventeenth century. It required the monarch to "join in communion with the Church of England," that is, to be not only Protestant but also Anglican. It also forbade the monarch from leaving the dominions of England, Scotland, or Ireland, or from waging war against foreign countries in which England had no interest, without the consent of parliament. These provisions were designed to ensure that foreign-born kings spent the majority of their time in Britain and did not use English armies to fight wars on behalf of their other dominions. The act also excluded any foreigner from sitting in the privy council or parliament, or from holding high civilian or military office. This was so that foreign-born kings did not employ subjects from their other dominions instead of English subjects, as had James I and William III. In order to prevent the type of undue royal influence on parliamentary affairs that had pervaded the reigns of the Stuarts, another provision stated that crown officeholders could not also sit in parliament.[8] To promote judicial independence and prevent royal manipulation of the legal bench – recall that Edward Coke was twice removed from his judgeship and that James II manipulated the bench to strengthen his suspending

---

7   This provision was important in the creation of Great Britain in 1707; the union of the two crowns, first sought by James I, was secured to ensure Scottish acceptance of the Hanoverian succession over a potential Stuart claimant.

8   This provision is still used when members of parliament wish to give up their seats before a general election. Because members of parliament are not permitted to resign, they seek a minor crown office ("Crown Steward and Bailiff"), sometimes held for a matter of hours, thereby requiring their removal from parliament.

and dispensing powers – the act ensured that judges could only be removed by parliament, and only if it could be proven they were not "of good behavior." Finally, the act stated that the king could not issue a pardon to individuals who were under impeachment proceedings by parliament. In sum, the Act of Settlement resolved issues that earlier documents, such as the Bill of Rights and Act of Toleration had not addressed.

By the end of the seventeenth century, therefore, England had emerged as a mixed constitutional monarchy. It was headed by the executive branch – the monarch, privy council, and high officeholders – and dominated by an annual, bicameral parliament, of which the House of Commons was considered the senior partner and in which many members essentially became professional politicians who ascribed to a particular party ideology. These two branches of government, together with an independent judiciary, worked in concert to govern and legislate, but also had the ability to redress perceived abuses committed by the other branches. In addition, the Lockean contract theory of government allowed subjects to replace poor legislators, especially through the use of general elections that, at least in theory, could improve the composition of parliament and restore the social contract. Viewed from a modern mindset, of course, this system was hardly perfect; the franchise was still limited to landowning men of a certain financial status and members who sat in parliament were unpaid and were, therefore, usually a great deal wealthier than their constituents, issues that would not be resolved for another three centuries. Nor was this yet the "Westminster system," which included a first minister, cabinet, and governing and opposition parties. But it was the revolution settlement that put mechanisms in place that allowed for these aspects of modern government to develop in the future.

* * *

Discussion Question 7.4: Were there any abuses committed by the Stuart monarchs that the restoration and revolution settlement of 1689–1701 failed to address? Why do you think this was the case?

VOICES OF THE PAST
THE JESUIT'S FIRING PLOT

The following extract taps into two great fears among Londoners during the late Stuart period. First, as Frances Dolan has shown, many people believed that the Great Fire of London of 1666 had been deliberately set by Catholics, an event reminiscent of the failed Gunpowder Plot.[9] Second, at the height of the "popish plot" started by Titus Oates, Londoners feared that Jesuits were flooding into the country intent upon assassinating Charles II to make way for his Catholic brother, James. The story of Elizabeth Owen, an accused arsonist of a home in Central London, and a woman thought to be a Jesuit, was, therefore, a perfect tale for a pamphlet writer seeking to profit from these fears.

* * *

Though Rome has been so often baffled in her weak and shallow contrivances, yet her agents think it not convenient to give over ... to the abhorrence and detestation of all sober and civil persons. Nor can they prevail to work upon any but poor contemptible proselytes [converts], whom they, by the powerful charms of gain, do bring into snares, that so their work may be perfected, though to their utter ruin, as may be observed in the many firing plots the cunning Jesuits have of late contrived. In which for the most part they employ silly servant-maids, promising them after the pernicious work is done that they shall receive much wealth, which makes them go boldly on to perpetrate the horrid deed. But then being taken by the hand of justice, they are left in great confusion and amazement, not knowing where to find the man that did enjoin them their destructive task.

An instance of which may be plainly seen in a late unlucky mischief which happened to the house of Mr. Cooper, commonly known by the name of the Sussex House, near to Fetter Lane End in Fleet Street, the manner of which was as followeth. About a month since, Mr. Cooper, having an occasion for a servant-maid by reason of the departure of his former, was by a friend of his wished [recommended] to one Elizabeth Owen who had of late dwelt in Gracechurch Street. And upon his friend's recommendation he accordingly entertained her in his house in nature of his servant, she behaving herself seemingly well and never was observed to have anyone follow her, except one young man, whom she called cousin, pretending he was her uncle's son.

On Sunday last, being the seventh of November, her mistress and she had a small falling out about the dressing of a dinner and some words passed, but in no likelihood of such force as to prompt her on to such a desperate revenge, the feud being reasonably pacified.... About nine o'clock in the evening, she was observed to go upstairs, at which time ... she went into the garret [attic] [and] ... opened several trunks, in which were clothes which she took out and bundled up, putting several of her own amongst them. After that, with several candles (the tallow of which being found melted on the floor) she set the trunks on fire, placing them where she thought they soonest would take hold of the timber.

This being done, and she seeing them to begin to blaze, went downstairs and placed herself in the bar, this being between ten and eleven o'clock. When immediately the smoke came downstairs, of which ere [before] any besides those of the house smelt it she began to complain of, saying that there was an intolerable smoke which

---

9   Frances E. Dolan, *True Relations: Reading, Literature, and Evidence in Seventeenth-Century England* (Philadelphia: University of Pennsylvania Press, 2013), chapter 3.

almost put her eyes out. Whereupon her mistress answered she saw no such mighty smoke as she pretended, but if there was any, she believed that it proceeded from the burning of faggots in the chamber overhead, there having been some gentlemen of her acquaintance lately in the same. But the wench persisted that it could not come from thence, but that the house, she feared, was on fire, or words to that effect.

The smoke still increasing more and more, they were induced to believe some mischief indeed happened, or that some brand [ash] rolling out of the chimney might have taken hold of the hangings. So that running upstairs, they went into the room where the fire had been made but found all things in good order. When looking farther, they observed a smoke to come down the other pair of stairs that were yet higher, so that when they went up them they found the garret all on fire, being fired in several places, and that in one place it had burnt quite through the floor into the chamber underneath. Whereupon they immediately called for help, which was not long ere they had sufficient from their neighbors and through providence in a short time mastered that raging element which then began to blaze through the roof of the house. And Heaven knows, had it not been so stayed [stopped], it being amongst old buildings, what harm it might have done or where have ended.

After the fire was beaten down and the hurry was over, they began to search into the cause of it or how it should happen, which they long had not done before they found, as we have already mentioned, several parcels of grease, which come from the melted candles, and that the trunks being first opened were set on fire, which being

light and dry had fired the rest. Both the garrets being fired in several places, the trunks burnt to ashes, but the ashes of no woolen apparel found amongst the rest, which made them enquire what might become of the woolen that was in them.[10] And upon further search [they] found that it was thrown out at the window into a little paved yard and, as it is before-mentioned, many of Elizabeth Owen's own clothes packed up amongst them, which caused her master and mistress to suspect her as guilty of firing their house. And thereupon, by the advice of several neighbors, they caused her to be apprehended and for that night secured.

The next morning she was carried before the Right Worshipful Sir William Turner, alderman and justice of the peace for the City of London, who examined her strictly in all points but could not get nothing out of her, she being of a sullen dogged temper. Only she did declare to some persons of worth and credit that she did not design the fire should have begun so soon, but that it should have been much longer ere it had kindled so that it might have surprised her master and mistress, with all the rest of the family, herself only excepted, and have burnt them in their beds, so horrid and desperate was her hellish design. After a long examination she was committed to Newgate, where she now remains.[11] Not long after she was committed, her pretended cousin came to look for her, who, perhaps had he been taken and narrowly sifted [examined], might have proved the Jesuit or the Jesuit's agent that employed her to act this desperate exploit and horrid villainy.

Source: Anonymous, *The Jesuit's Firing-Plot Revived* (London, 1680).

* * *

Discussion Question 7.5: What specific language does the pamphlet author use to tap into late Stuart fears about fire and Catholics?

---

10 Clothing made of wool was then quite expensive, so Owen was planning on taking it with her.
11 In December 1680, Elizabeth Owen was tried and condemned for arson and theft ("The Tryals at the Sessions in the Old-Bailey," December 8, 1680, Old Bailey Proceedings Online, www.oldbaileyonline.org, reference number t16801208-8-1).

PART THREE
EMPIRE AND SOCIETY

The sixteenth and seventeenth centuries witnessed both continuity and change in many aspects of society. In social hierarchy, family structure and authority, and gender roles, English society was obsessed with order. Order was preserved using a variety of means, both informal and formal, the latter involving various officeholders and legal institutions that were mandated to preserve the peace and, when necessary, restore order at any cost. Often, this resulted in death.

This period also saw some significant changes. The economy experienced a series of crises beginning especially under Elizabeth but also saw the benefits of increased trade through the development of European trading networks and overseas colonies. These economic changes saw the creation of a new merchant elite and provided luxury goods to the wealthy who could afford to consume conspicuously. Intellectual thought also saw some major developments, largely because of the adoption of humanism and the scientific revolution in England. Older belief systems that relied on magic, superstition, and astrological phenomena gave way to scientific inquiry and speculations about the universe based on new methods of observation and experimentation. The extensive use of the printing press and rise in education and literacy saw other intellectual developments, such as a tremendous outpouring of literature in many genres.

CHAPTER EIGHT

EXPLORATION, TRADE, AND EMPIRE

DEATH AND DISORDER: THE MURDER OF PEMISAPAN

At first, relations between the English and North American Indigenous peoples were perfectly orderly, but they did not stay so for long. When Philip Amadas and Arthur Barlowe arrived in Ossomocomuck – the coastal region of modern North Carolina – in 1584 on a voyage of reconnaissance, they were greeted by an emissary of the Algonquian great weroance (king or chief), Wingina. Although the Englishmen and the emissary could not talk to each other, they used gestures to communicate. The newcomers invited the emissary to visit their two ships, fed him wine and meat, and gave him a hat and a shirt as gifts. The emissary reciprocated by spending half an hour fishing in the river, returning with enough food to feed the sailors on both ships.

The next day, the emissary returned with Wingina's brother and lesser weroance, Granganimeo, together with forty or fifty men, all "very handsome and goodly people, and in their behavior as mannerly and civil, as any in Europe." Through gesture and rituals, Granganimeo welcomed the newcomers and over the course of several days, the English and Algonquians visited each other and traded gifts. The Algonquians brought venison, rabbit, fish, melons, nuts, and root vegetables, food that was much-needed by the English,

while the English gave clothing, kettles, and musical instruments. When the English visited Granganimeo's territory, Roanoke Island, his wife and other women ensured that the filthy Englishmen, and their clothes, were thoroughly cleaned.

During these early encounters, it had become evident that Wingina's people were at war with other communities in Ossomocomuck, and they saw in English technology – hatchets, axes, armor, swords, and guns – a possible advantage against their foes. Thus, they were alarmed when their new friends indicated their intention to return to England. Two men were chosen to accompany them on their return, Manteo and Wanchese, so that they could learn more about their new friends. In London, they stayed at Walter Ralegh's home on the banks of the Thames and developed their language skills to serve as interpreters when they returned. In the meantime, Ralegh, who had been granted large, undefined parts of North America in 1584, went about preparing ships and assembling men for a colonizing expedition. Seven ships and 600 men departed Plymouth in April 1585, with Sir Richard Grenville in command of the fleet and Ralph Lane, an experienced officer from the Irish campaigns, to become governor once the colony was settled.

Shortly after their arrival in America, problems began. In the course of visiting several Native villages, the English accused the Aquascogocs of stealing a valuable silver cup. When their weroance could not produce the cup, Amadas and several men burned the town and spoiled the crops, a scorched-earth strike that forced the villagers to flee. It was at this point that the Natives learned that the English might not, in fact, be their friends. Word quickly spread to Wingina, who was at war with the Aquascogocs, prompting the weroance to seek a closer alliance with the powerful English soldiers. Accordingly, Granganimeo visited the English and offered them a parcel of land on the northern tip of Roanoke Island, to place them in Wingina's debt. Ultimately, only 108 colonists settled on the island because an accident with the flagship had resulted in the loss of most of the food supplies. Grenville had been forced to depart with most of the would-be colonists to resupply. Under the watchful eyes of Wingina and Granganimeo, Lane began constructing a fortification and several houses, while the Natives brought them food and other supplies.

As the Indigenous peoples spent more and more time with the English, however, they began to fall ill, probably of influenza, which their medicine could not cure. Wingina and his men even resorted to Christian prayer, which they believed was the reason that the Englishmen remained healthy. The death of Granganimeo from sickness finally caused Wingina to alter his attitude toward the newcomers. He changed his name to Pemisapan – for reasons we might never fully understand – and began orchestrating an uprising. Pemisapan informed Lane that several thousand warriors from Choanoac, one of his rivals, were amassing to kill the English colonists. This news prompted Lane to go on the offensive, setting off with dozens of men and several of Pemisapan's people as guides, to confront his alleged enemy. In March 1586 Lane arrived in the territory of Choanoac only to be told, through conversation with their weroance Menatonon, that Pemisapan had deceived him. Just in case

Menatonon was lying, Lane took his son, Skiko, as a hostage.

When the party returned to Roanoke Island, half-starved and infuriated by the deception, Pemisapan had already informed the remaining English settlers that Lane and the others were dead. Lane's arrival forced Pemisapan to change his plans. In the interests of restoring peace, he informed the English that his people would plant the earth and provide enough food for their needs. The peace was short-lived. Soon, Pemisapan and his followers destroyed the crops and departed the island, leaving Lane and his men to fend for themselves. Meanwhile, Pemisapan attempted to amass an army of 800 men, planned to have Lane killed in the middle of the night, and in the ensuing confusion would return to the island with his force and murder the rest of the English colonists.

When this plan was revealed to Lane, he ordered his men to gather up all the canoes on the island to prevent the Natives from warning Pemisapan of English plans to reciprocate, during which the English beheaded at least two Indigenous men. The next morning, Lane and twenty-five of his men rowed to the mainland where Pemisapan greeted them at his village of Dasemunkepeuc. In the presence of Pemisapan and a dozen or so of his highest-ranking advisors, Lane then loudly uttered a watchword – an invocation to fight, "Christ our victory!" – and the English opened fire. Amadas shot Pemisapan, but his wound was not fatal. As the English continued their massacre, Pemisapan ran into the woods. Edward Nugent, a soldier who had served with Lane in Ireland, ran in pursuit. Even wounded, Pemisapan proved a capable runner, but eventually Nugent caught up with him and soon emerged from the woods carrying Pemisapan's head.

One week later, Sir Francis Drake arrived at Roanoke and offered Lane and his men a lift home, which they gratefully accepted. They were nearly starving and feared Native reprisal for the murder of their leaders. England's first attempt at settlement in America was a failure bathed in blood.

* * *

Discussion Question 8.1: To what extent were the English newcomers and the Indigenous peoples responsible for the death of Pemisapan?

Trade in Europe

During the sixteenth and seventeenth centuries, England began numerous travel, trade, exploration, and settlement activities that led to the growth of Tudor and Stuart England from its insular origins and to the rise of a vast and powerful British Empire in the eighteenth and nineteenth centuries. This process began in the early sixteenth century, when young men traveled to Europe for sightseeing, experience with other cultures and languages, and educational opportunities – an event later known as the "grand tour of Europe" – and sometimes later returned for diplomatic, employment, and mercantile undertakings. Because of the delicate religious, political, and military relations in Europe at this time, travelers needed to be licensed by the monarch for travel, which involved offering proof that they were loyal to the crown, had good reasons for traveling abroad, and had sufficient financial resources to undertake the tour. Throughout the period 1520 to 1690, English men and women journeyed into Europe, learned new languages, customs, styles, religions, and intellectual developments, and brought these back to their home country, often publishing travel narratives on their experiences that even, at times, took to criticizing English traditions and cultures in comparison to those on the Continent. In these diaries, the "otherness" these cosmopolitan travelers encountered was often described using their own limited understanding of different cultures, resulting in as much misunderstanding as enlightenment about the wider world.

Although personal enlightenment during these global interactions was important, the first century of Tudor activities (to about 1585) outside of England was primarily about finding new trading routes and opportunities that allowed the nation to develop its economy without serious risk of competition from better-established traders in Continental Europe. When, for example, English subjects from Bristol who were fishing and trading near Iceland began to experience competition from Germany, they started looking farther west, into the Atlantic Ocean. It was within this context that John Cabot was granted a charter from Henry VII in 1496 to explore the North Atlantic. Cabot sailed across the ocean the following year, ultimately arriving in Newfoundland and Labrador and claiming the region for the English king. Later voyages by Cabot, his son Sebastian, and others, over the next two decades, enabled Bristol fishermen to undertake annual fishing expeditions to North America. Others sought the elusive Northwest Passage to Asia. However, the passage was not to be found, and by the middle years of Henry VIII's reign, Newfoundland was also being visited annually by French and Portuguese fishermen, who managed to dominate the region and eclipse English activities in the New World for another half century.

Interest in trade and exploration picked up again in the reign of Mary, this time with the intention of finding a Northeast Passage. Although this quest – and numerous others undertaken until the early seventeenth century – failed, voyages by Richard Chancellor resulted in the English making friendly relations with Ivan (the Terrible) IV of Muscovy (Russia). This was a fortunate situation for England, because by 1550 its principal trading commodity since the late fifteenth century, wool, had become increasingly less viable as a major export. Before this date, England, through its London-located Merchant Adventurers, had sent most of its unfinished wool to Antwerp, where it was finished and then distributed throughout Europe. Several events occurred beginning mid-century that severely weakened this trade, including a strained relationship with the Adventurers' main competitor, the Hanseatic League; various "wars of religion" in Europe, which limited trade opportunities; the Dutch fight for independence from Spain, which impacted the Antwerp nexus; and the oversaturation of English wool on the European market, which reduced demand and value. Meanwhile, English proto-industrial activities had led to the availability of new commodities (such as cheaper forms of cloth manufactured in England, the so-called new draperies) for export, and the nation's elite increasingly sought luxury goods available only in foreign markets, such as silk and spices.

The opening of trade with Russia, therefore, allowed England to forge new and essential trading relationships, which were first managed by the Muscovy Company, a joint-stock company chartered in 1555. The English traded their new draperies for a variety of products – furs, hides, tallow, wax, and especially cordage, or rope used on ships – as "privileged traders," meaning they had the right to operate in Russia without paying customs or other duties. Their special status deteriorated with the death of Ivan in 1584 and the challenge of navigating into the White Sea and the overland routes to Moscow prevented wide-scale English trade in the region. One of the leading Muscovy Company agents, Anthony Jenkinson, also traveled through Russia in 1562 and entered Persia (roughly modern-day Iran), delivering letters from the queen to the shah, resulting in the Company trading for silk, spices, and other luxury goods in the region through to 1580. Persia was of more interest to the English because it could be accessed via the Mediterranean Sea, a route far more preferable, if not safer, than the land route through Russia. Here again the trade proved difficult; English merchants found the overland route challenging and dangerous, and several agents were murdered in Persia and set upon by pirates, resulting in the loss of lives, goods, and ships.

Persia was also intermittently at war with the Ottoman Empire, centered in Constantinople (Istanbul) in modern-day Turkey. Consequently, when Persia and Turkey returned to a state of war in 1578, the English capitalized on this by forming agreeable terms with agents of the Ottoman Empire, who needed, in particular, steel, lead, and tin in order to cast artillery, all commodities that the English had in good supply as a result of their natural resources and new domestic industries. Elizabeth chartered the Turkey Company (1581) and Venice Company (1583) – together later known as the Levant Company (1593) – and under their auspices the English established various "factories" throughout the empire and sent a resident ambassador to maintain relations with the sultan. This was also a special trading relationship, because a papal ban on exports of weapons or their raw materials from Christian countries to Muslim Turkey – which was dutifully observed by France and Spain – was not something England cared much about, especially given its increasingly poor relations with European Catholic nations. The English were more than happy to send the habiliments of war to Turkey in exchange for luxury commodities. From the late 1570s, the English continued to move further into the Persian Gulf, trading with Iraq and Syria.

Although it was always at risk from temperamental rulers, pirates, and competition from the often better-established Dutch, French, Portuguese, and Spanish merchant networks, English trade in eastern Europe – and to a lesser extent, trade in the Iberian countries undertaken by the Spanish Company (1577) and in Scandinavia by the Eastland Company (1579) – generally thrived throughout the Elizabethan period. The English market was soon flooded with Persian silks, Turkish tapestries, oils, wines, teas, currants, aloes, and spices – pepper, cloves, nutmeg, cinnamon, and ginger. It was also during this time that the English crown began the process of issuing monopoly privileges for various commodities, initially as rewards for the individuals who opened up and then maintained trade in Europe. As discussed in Chapter Four, the issue of monopolies would soon become a major grievance of Elizabeth's later parliaments. Nonetheless, because of their monopolies and privileges, trading company subscribers and commodity distributors had become a proto-capitalist merchant elite, whose wealth easily rivaled that of the nation's gentry and nobility. These men later became leading voices in parliament, while the next generation became highly critical of the early Stuarts' efforts to control customs and impositions, which impacted them directly.

* * *

Discussion Question 8.2: In what ways did the expansion of trade into Europe break down England's historical insularity?

Travel and Trade in the East

In the late 1570s, the English made their way into India and Indonesia. This was facilitated, in part, by Sir Francis Drake's circumnavigation of the world between 1577 and 1580. Drake had initially planned to cross the Atlantic, sail down the coast of South America, enter the Strait of Magellan, sail north, make contact with Native peoples, trade commodities, distress Spanish colonies as far north as California, and return via the same route. The expedition did not work out quite as planned. Although Drake managed to get to California, renamed the region Nova Albion (New England), plundered and sacked Spanish settlements, and took numerous ships as prizes, at some point he decided to return by way of the Moluccas, the Spice Islands in the Banda Sea in Indonesia, where he arrived in November 1579. This was a region that had long been under the control of the Portuguese, so Drake's arrival provided the local Indigenous people the opportunity to develop new trading relationships.

Drake traded for a large quantity of cloves and, although he did not possess sufficient royal warrants to arrange a formal trading partnership, secured an informal agreement to trade in preference over the Portuguese. Drake touched upon a number of other Indonesian islands before eventually returning to England, via the Cape of Good Hope, in September 1580. The Spanish ambassador soon petitioned for reparations for Drake's acts of piracy, which prompted the queen, who had profited immensely from the enterprise, to knight the circumnavigator on the deck of his ship, the *Golden Hind*. As previously discussed, this was one of several events that served as a prelude to the Anglo-Spanish War (1585–1604).

Although Drake's activities led to various failed attempts to return to Indonesia over the next two decades, it was the arrival of the Dutch there that eventually prompted the English, who believed Drake had secured a trade agreement, to take greater action. This resulted in the chartering of another joint-stock enterprise largely owned by the Levant subscribers, the East India Company (1600). The charter granted the Company a monopoly on trading east of the Cape of Good Hope and throughout the Pacific Ocean basin. Over the next several years, James Lancaster, Henry Middleton, and others sailed to the east, with instructions to compete with the Dutch and Portuguese trade in the region and set up factories in locations such as south and west India, Java, and Amboyna (Ambon) in the Spice Islands.

Immediately, the English confronted numerous problems, including scurvy and illness caused by the long sea journey, difficulties with the Indigenous sabanders (island governors), and the dominance of the Portuguese and especially, by 1610, the Dutch. Various incursions between the English and Dutch resulted in an unofficial war that saw many deaths and the confiscation of cargo, and even an Anglo-Dutch treaty signed in 1619 – which granted both parties access to the pepper and spice trade in exchange for mutual defense of the area – was insufficient to quell the animosity. The situation became worse when the Dutch executed ten English merchants at Amboyna on the grounds of conspiracy, an event known as the "Amboyna massacre," causing the English to leave the Spice Islands and formally cede them to the Dutch in 1667. From the 1620s, until beyond the Stuart period, the East India Company focused its attention on India, particularly in the region of Gujarat.

Trade and Plunder in the Atlantic

While the Muscovy, Levant, and East India Companies were trading in eastern Europe and the Pacific, the English also began trading into the Portuguese-controlled region of West Africa. Of specific interest were the gold and pepper to be found in Guinea, a 2,000-mile coastal area also known as the Gold Coast. English voyages to this region began in 1553 and instantly involved clashes with Portuguese merchants, who had been actively trading in the region since the mid-fifteenth century. The situation between the English and Portuguese became so tense in 1554 that the English agreed to turn a teenaged Martin Frobisher over to their rivals as a surety of good behavior. Frobisher was allowed to return home in 1557, when Mary, now married to Philip of Spain, forbade English activities in Guinea. However, the voyages of Thomas Wyndham and William Towerson – which involved trading tin and cloth for gold and ivory – attracted further enmity by seizing Africans to bring back to England, plundering and burning the villages of those who refused to trade, and taking as prize Portuguese ships carrying valuable cargos.

In 1561, the Portuguese ambassador in London formally protested English activities in Africa. He complained of English seizure of ships and requested that the English be prohibited from trading in any regions "conquered" by the king of Portugal. Elizabeth replied that, while she would punish proven acts of piracy, she could not prevent her subjects from trading in any regions where the Indigenous peoples wanted English trade or where there was no clear evidence of European occupation. In this response, Elizabeth articulated a legal position that would later become critical to English expansion into the Americas: that the mere discovery of newfound lands, or presence of other Europeans in them, did not automatically confer sovereignty unless they had the "obedience, dominion, and tribute" of the Indigenous peoples and demonstrated clear physical presence through fortifications and other signs of possession. The queen suggested that if the king of Portugal had such authority, he could restrain his African subjects from trading with the English. If the Africans continued to trade, they did not recognize Portuguese dominion and were, therefore, free to trade with whomever they pleased. This was largely the same argument Elizabeth gave to the Spanish ambassador in 1580, after complaints about Francis Drake's activities during his circumnavigation.

Another trading activity involving Africa in the 1560s was England's first venture into the slave trade. Backed in part by the queen, the wealthy shipowner and merchant John Hawkins took part in four voyages between 1562 and 1569, with the intent to capture Africans from the west coast and sell them as slaves in the Spanish Caribbean, thereby mimicking Spanish slaving activities that had been ongoing since about 1520. Although non-Iberians selling slaves in the Spanish Americas was forbidden by a Spanish statute banning contraband trade in the region, success was anticipated because England and Spain were then generally on good terms and because the Spanish colonists were seeking additional labor on their profitable Caribbean plantations. During the first two voyages, Hawkins captured and plundered several Portuguese and Spanish vessels, gathered several hundred Africans from the Gold Coast, and sailed across the Atlantic to sell his cargo. The success of these two voyages, however, quickly soured when the third and fourth voyages both ended in failure. During the last trip, the largest of the slaving voyages, Hawkins set out with six ships including two royal warships, arrived in the Caribbean with more than 500 Africans in his holds, and touched upon many ports to sell his cargo before being forced by severe storms to San Juan de Ulúa, in Central America. There, Hawkins met considerable Spanish resistance when, coincidentally, a Spanish flotilla arrived. In the ensuing sea battle, Hawkins lost three-quarters of his men, his fleet was reduced to two ships, and he limped home to Plymouth after a financially disastrous expedition.

By the time Hawkins arrived home, Anglo-Spanish relations were already becoming rocky because of English support in the Netherlands. Within this political climate, the Caribbean policy swiftly changed from one of tacitly accepted trade to unofficial plunder. Though officially disavowed by the crown, the years between 1570 and 1577 saw at least a dozen plundering expeditions to the Caribbean, largely led by Drake, which led to his eventful circumnavigation toward the end of the decade. At the outset of the war in 1585, Drake was commissioned to return to the Caribbean in command of twenty-one ships and 1,800 men for official privateering, acts of licensed piracy designed to distress the queen's enemies during wartime. Drake and his fleet looted Santo Domingo, Cartegena, Cuba, and St. Augustine, Florida, before arriving at Walter Ralegh's new colony of Roanoke and bringing its demoralized colonists, fresh off the beheading of Pemisapan, back to England in July 1586. Drake's subsequent and highly successful Cádiz raid and role in the defeat of the Spanish Armada, as discussed previously, secured his legacy as, perhaps, England's greatest seadog.

The Anglo-Spanish War also led to renewed interest in trade along the Gold Coast, particularly for pepper, ivory, and timber, leading to the crown chartering the Senegal Adventurers (1588) and later the Guinea Company (1618). Although the former company undertook several successful ventures in the late sixteenth century, the latter was less successful. This was partly because of several failed attempts to find gold mines rather than relying on trade; partly because, as in Indonesia, the English were constantly in competition with the Dutch and Portuguese; and partly because of increasing criticism about monopolies and other crown policies during the reigns of the early Stuarts. After the restoration, the Royal Adventurers to Africa (1662) was chartered, under the direction of Prince Rupert of the Rhine. This led to the creation of the more successful and enduring Royal African Company (1672), under the patronage of James, duke of York, which had wide-ranging powers of trade and settlement throughout West Africa.

Under the auspices of this charter, the company set up forts and factories and, by 1690, with Dutch and Portuguese rivalry considerably reduced, had transported between 90,000 and 100,000 Africans across the Atlantic, primarily to English colonies in North America and the Caribbean. The company also traded for ivory and, especially, gold, which was sold to the English mint to produce coinage.[1]

Attempts at Colonization in the Sixteenth Century

English settlement in North America and the Caribbean began with a welter of projects that had their origins in the mid-1570s. The first of these was the plan, first encouraged by Humphrey Gilbert, to seek the Northwest Passage. This plan was taken up by Frobisher and Michael Lok under the auspices of the Muscovy Company. Gilbert's and Frobisher's belief in the existence of the Northwest Passage was inspired by the world maps of Gerard Mercator and Abraham Ortelius, produced between 1564 and 1570. These maps speculated on the existence of an easily navigable passage across the northern coast of North America, egressing at the Strait of Anian, which separated North America from Asia. For further assurance on this matter, Frobisher turned to John Dee, a respected mathematician who had advised Muscovy Company navigators. In the process of helping Frobisher, Dee also advocated for a "petty navy," which would be responsible for securing safe English travel in the northern seas and collecting duties from foreigners who traded there. Over the next few years, Dee produced several treatises that used a wealth of historical, geographical, and legal evidence to argue for state-funded English exploration not only into the North Atlantic but also of North America and other areas not currently occupied by the Spanish.

As Dee was striving to broaden the crown's interest in exploration, Frobisher was exploring the North Atlantic. He departed England in three small ships in June 1576, eventually arriving – with two ships – at Frobisher Bay (today it is Iqaluit in the Canadian territory of Nunavut) on Baffin Island, soon to be named Meta Incognita ("unknown place"). He soon came into conflict with the local Inuk, who took five of Frobisher's men prisoner while he managed to capture one of their men and bring him back to England in October. Frobisher also returned with a piece of black ore, which was believed to be gold. Consequently, Frobisher's second voyage, backed in part by Elizabeth, was a much larger undertaking expected to bring back cargo holds full of gold-rich ore. The fleet arrived in Frobisher Bay by July 1577, where Frobisher took formal possession in the queen's name. No efforts were made to penetrate further into the Northwest Passage. Instead, the expedition returned to England in September with tons of ore and three more

---

1 In 1668, the mint began producing the "guinea," a coin worth 21 shillings.

Inuk, who quickly died. On his third voyage, in 1578, Frobisher was instructed to plant a colony of one hundred men on the island of Kodlunarn (today's Countess of Warwick Island), which represented the first English plans to settle in North America. The colony was not planted, but Frobisher managed to press a bit further into the Northwest Passage. When, however, he returned to England with more than 1,300 tons of ore, his earlier cargoes had finally been adjudged mere rock, to the financial ruin of Frobisher and Lok. Elizabeth personally lost £4,000, a substantial sum even for a monarch, and was thereafter disinclined to invest in speculative exploratory ventures.[2]

As Frobisher's voyages were coming to an end, those of Gilbert were being reinvented. Fresh from his participation in the conquest of Ireland, Gilbert proposed distressing Spanish fishing in Newfoundland and shipping in the Caribbean by establishing a military base of operations at a strategic location in North America. Although he requested a charter of colonization from the queen, it is clear that Gilbert initially had little interest in planting a permanent colony. Instead, the charter was to be a "cloak" under which he could get ships across the Atlantic in the guise of an explorer rather than a pirate. With relations with Spain souring, Elizabeth granted Gilbert his charter in 1578, entitling him to discover and settle any lands in North America not presently under the possession of another Christian prince, phrasing that became a blueprint for colonizing charters throughout the early modern period. Without crown financial or naval support, Gilbert was not able to get underway until 1583, funded primarily by Catholic gentlemen who wished to travel to North America to escape the recusancy laws. In the intervening time, Gilbert sought advice from the two Richard Hakluyts – uncle and nephew – exploration enthusiasts who helped to change Gilbert's plan from one of piracy to a genuine desire to plant a colony. Dee also drew a map for Gilbert, which encouraged settlement in the area of Newfoundland.

Accordingly, when Gilbert arrived in Newfoundland, he declared the region to be an English possession. Within a few weeks, Gilbert's enterprise was endangered by sickness, desertion, and the destruction of his flagship. On his return voyage to England in a frigate, Gilbert went down with his ship in the region of the Azores, allegedly clutching a copy of Thomas More's *Utopia*. In 1584, the terms of Gilbert's charter passed to his half-brother, Walter Ralegh, although the new charter indicated a plan to settle further south, in the region of the Carolinas. Thus, Ralegh dispatched Amadas and Barlowe on a reconnaissance mission to seek out a viable location far enough north of Spanish-occupied Florida. As we have seen, they arrived in the North Carolina Outer Banks, made

2   Despite additional voyages by John Davis, Henry Hudson, and others into the early seventeenth century, the Northwest Passage was not discovered until the nineteenth century.

positive relations with the Algonquian, and returned home with two of them, who became translators between the two peoples. In their report, Amadas and Barlowe indicated that the region they reconnoitered could yield commodities consistent with a Mediterranean climate – including olives, grapes, and sugar – which would thereby relieve England of its reliance on Spanish and French goods (oil and wine). The Indigenous peoples were described as "gentle, loving, and faithful, void of all guile and treason."

Further support to settle in the region of "Virginia" (the name authorized by Elizabeth for the new land) came from the younger Hakluyt in an important manuscript known as the "Discourse of Western Planting" (1584). The treatise was commissioned by Ralegh in an effort to engender state funding, and in its twenty-one chapters Hakluyt developed a comprehensive protocol for colonization. An Anglican priest, Hakluyt argued that spreading religion and civility to "idolators" was a basic Christian responsibility. He expressed concern that English trade had become "beggarly," mostly because of the challenges encountered in Africa, Europe, and Asia. In addition, by the planting of a colony, the Northwest Passage to China could be more easily searched out. Several chapters were also devoted to concerns over Spanish power in the Caribbean, the tyranny that Spain had exercised in South America, and the danger of the king of Spain continuing to be enriched by gold from the New World. Although Hakluyt's treatise was not successful in gaining state funding, it did result in the knighting of Ralegh, permission to impress men from port towns to serve in his ships, the release of Ralph Lane from service in Ireland to govern the colony, and private investments from Francis Walsingham and other high-ranking men.

The first voyage departed in April 1585 with seven ships and 600 men. Ralegh was forbidden by the queen to travel to North America, leaving Grenville and Lane in overall command of the enterprise. Unfortunately, navigating the North Carolina Outer Banks proved more difficult than expected, resulting in damage to the largest vessel and the loss of most of the supplies. The plan to settle 600 men was quickly scuttled. Instead, Lane was to remain with just over 100 men while Grenville returned to England with the remaining would-be settlers to resupply. Meanwhile, as we have seen, with the permission of Wingina and Granganimeo, Lane supervised the building of a small fort on Roanoke Island. Over the course of the winter and spring, 1585–6, relations between the English and local inhabitants slowly deteriorated, leading to conspiracies and uprisings that, by the end of the summer, had resulted in the murder of Pemisapan and evacuation of the colonists. The evacuation occurred mere weeks before Grenville returned with supplies. Finding Roanoke desolate, Grenville made the peculiar decision to leave fifteen men behind with about a year's provisions – in order to maintain English presence in the region – and departed, unaware of the enmity between the English and the Indigenous peoples.

The most valuable fruits of this enterprise were the observations and images produced by Thomas Harriot and John White, respectively a scientist and artist, whose efforts were combined in *A Brief and True Report of the New Found Land of Virginia* (1588), an overly optimistic report about the Carolinas and its peoples that influenced English perceptions of the New World for half a century. White returned to Roanoke in 1587 for another attempt at settlement, this time on the mainland. He stopped at Roanoke Island to retrieve the fifteen men left behind by Grenville, but found the colony deserted. White was soon caught up in a series of near-mutinies that forced him to rebuild at Roanoke rather than proceed, as planned, to Chesapeake Bay.

By August, he was on his way back to England to resupply, leaving behind 115 people, including his daughter and son-in-law and their daughter, Virginia Dare, the first English child born in America. He was never to see them again. By November 1587, rumors of a Spanish armada forced the queen to order the stay of all English ships. By the time White could head up a recovery expedition in 1590, the rescuers found the colony abandoned, the word "CROATOAN" written on a post. White interpreted this as a sign that the colonists had relocated to a nearby island, but poor weather prevented him from following up on this clue. Instead, he returned to England, putting an end to Elizabethan attempts to settle North America. Ralegh did manage, eventually, to get to the Americas. In 1595, he led an expedition to the Orinoco River in the Amazon on an unsuccessful search for El Dorado, a town rumored to be laden with gold.[3]

* * *

Discussion Question 8.3: To what extent was Elizabeth's reluctance to provide support – financial and otherwise – for exploration and settlement in the Americas advantageous and detrimental to the rise of empire?

Settlement in the Seventeenth Century

Following the end of the Anglo-Spanish War in 1604, various metropolitan agents began to plan another attempt to settle North America. A trading company charter was issued in 1606 to the Virginia Company of London and Plymouth that authorized the settlement of two colonies in the regions of modern-day Virginia and New England. Although James I naturally asserted sovereignty over any regions settled

---

3   Ralegh returned to the region in 1617, this time attacking a Spanish settlement, a breach of international law that led to his execution the following year.

by his subjects, the colonies were otherwise to be self-administered by a company governor in London and colonial governors in North America, with overall – albeit lackadaisical – control held by the king and his privy council. Ultimately, only the London branch of the company managed to settle a colony, Jamestown, along the banks of the Chesapeake, in April 1607. The colony was immediately beset by numerous problems, largely related to poor instructions from London and quarrelling among the leadership in Jamestown, especially that involving Captain John Smith. The colonists were also unprepared for the harsh conditions they encountered. The optimistic reports of Barlow, Harriot, and others proved to be woefully inaccurate: the climate was marshy and infested with insects, and the earth needed a great deal more physical labor for the cultivation of crops than was initially expected. Moreover, the planters initially sought to grow much-desired Mediterranean commodities – olives, grapes, and sugar, the cultivation of which quickly proved futile – rather than grains and other crops that would help bring about self-sufficiency. One of the major supply ships, the *Sea Venture*, wrecked in Bermuda in 1609, and by the time two small ships could be constructed and sail to Virginia, the English population had been severely reduced due to starvation, disease, and general apathy. However, the discovery of Bermuda also led to a new charter which saw the settlement of that island group.

Even the issuance of two additional charters, in 1609 and 1612, and the production of a martial code for the colony, which demanded obedience and hard work and meted out severe punishments for infractions, did little to improve the situation. The colony's financial survival soon depended on the growth of tobacco, which did not help to improve Jamestown's self-sufficiency. Growing tobacco required a large amount of land, causing the colonists to move beyond the relative protection of Jamestown into the surrounding community, which was also shared by the Powhatan Native confederacy. After some initial skirmishes, English relations with the Powhatans improved as the result of John Rolfe's marriage to Powhatan's daughter, Pocahontas, in 1614, but her death in England in 1617, followed by her father's death a year later, renewed enmity between the newcomers and the Indigenous population. With the English increasingly encroaching on Native land and failing to protect themselves from possible attack, Powhatan's brother, Opechancanough, led an attack on the colonists in March 1622 that saw the death of about 350 English subjects. This attack resulted in a changed attitude toward the Powhatans, who were now perceived as disorderly enemies who needed to be violently conquered for the English to thrive and survive (see *Voices of the Past*: **The Jamestown Massacre**).

The Virginia massacre also exposed the main problems with the company's governance and organization, which had become torn by faction and was nearly bankrupt, having failed to pay any dividends to its investors. In 1624, the crown was forced to dissolve the company and revoke its charter, prompting Charles I in 1625 to proclaim Virginia as a royal colony, to be governed by the privy council and a resident governor named by the king. Meanwhile, in 1620, the

New England Company was created from the remnants of the Plymouth branch of the London Company. The colonists, many of whom were of a Puritanical religious disposition, arrived on the *Mayflower*, and by 1629 the Massachusetts Bay colonists, who dominated in the region, were chartered as the Massachusetts Bay Company, with (unusually) their main governing body residing in Boston rather than London. Soon, disputes within the colony led to the creation of Connecticut, Maine, New Hampshire, and Rhode Island as distinct entities.

By 1632, various complaints against the Massachusetts Bay leadership led to the creation of a committee of the privy council to investigate these alleged abuses. This resulted in the creation, in 1634, of the Committee for Foreign Plantations, a body that, in several guises, continued to exist beyond 1690. The creation of this committee, and one of its earliest recommendations – to dissolve the Massachusetts Bay Colony and turn New England into a royal colony – signaled a change in the relationship between the metropolitan center and colonial periphery. Although the colonies retained significant amounts of independence with regard to internal affairs and local legislation, the committee began more systematic review of colonial laws to ensure that they were broadly consistent with English sensibilities. It also investigated various complaints raised by individual colonists against their local administrators and adjudicated disputes between colonial entities.

The early problems with the Virginia Company, Massachusetts Bay Company, and the failed Newfoundland Company (1610) encouraged the crown, after 1625, to rely more heavily on the proprietary model. This involved granting territory to individual petitioners, usually high-ranking members of the aristocracy, with minimal crown oversight. Under this system, various islands in the Caribbean, including Barbados – which soon became the wealthiest and most important colony in the English overseas empire – were granted to the earls of Carlisle and Montgomery. Maryland was settled in 1632 by George Calvert, baron Baltimore, a former secretary of state, and his son, Cecil, as a haven for English Catholics. The creation of colonies halted during the Civil War and interregnum, although Cromwell worked hard to ensure the English overseas remained loyal to the Commonwealth, and Jamaica was claimed as an English colony after it was taken from the Spanish in 1655 as part of the "Western Design" to assert greater control in the Americas. After the restoration, several additional proprietaries were created: the Carolinas (1660), Delaware, New York, and New Jersey (all in 1664), and in 1681, Pennsylvania was created as a haven for Quakers.

The English Empire in the Americas

Despite its humble and rocky beginnings, the English empire in the Americas, by the end of the seventeenth century, boasted perhaps half a million inhabitants, or roughly one in ten English subjects, with another 100,000 Scottish and Irish settlers among them. People traveled across the Atlantic Ocean for a variety of reasons, including the scarcity of employment in England; the prospect of advancement, marriage, or land ownership they were otherwise denied in their home country; religious and political discontent during the first half of the seventeenth century; and for the chances of adventure and exploration that the Americas offered.

Many young men and some women indentured themselves, or voluntarily agreed to undertake arduous labor on plantations for a period of three to seven years, in exchange, eventually, for land and the ability to marry and raise a family. Certain convicted criminals, whose physical labor was desperately needed especially in the plantation colonies, were transported to Bermuda, the Caribbean, and the southern colonies and placed into indenture instead of being executed. Members of the clergy – Calvinists, Catholics, and Quakers – went to assist in converting Indigenous people and to build a better society than they had experienced in England. Increasingly after the 1620s, hundreds of thousands of Africans were sold as slaves to the southern and Caribbean colonies, enduring considerable hardship both on the "middle passage" across the Atlantic and under the harsh regimes of their English owners, despite the creation of various slave codes throughout the second half of the seventeenth century.

The geographical, religious, economic, and constitutional nature of the colonies also created a great deal of differentiation between and among them. The northern colonies – New England, Newfoundland, New York, Pennsylvania, and others – were more urban, industrial, and mercantile, and were populated by families and free laborers working in farms and proto-industrial factories. They traded primarily with England, exchanging raw materials and manufactured goods for fish, cod, rum, lumber, and fur, the latter of which was purchased from Indigenous traders. The southern and Caribbean colonies were plantation-based, in which large numbers of unfree laborers cleared land, drained swamps, and produced tobacco, indigo, and sugar. Naturally, the various commodities produced in the colonies also had considerable impact in England, whose population was the primary consumer of the colonies' luxury products. Especially after state monopolies died out by the middle of the seventeenth century, the transportation, distribution, and sale of these products also created a mercantile elite, men usually without title but with considerable wealth whose rise challenged the great chain of being.

These colonies also had different experiences with the Indigenous peoples, especially in the northern regions, where the Pequot War (1634–8), King Philip's War (1676–8), and Bacon's Rebellion (1676) ended poorly for the native populations. The actions taken against Indigenous peoples in the south after 1622 also reduced their population significantly, while the Caribbean colonies had few native populations to begin with, allowing those colonies to develop quite differently from those on the mainland. Sometimes Anglo-Indigenous relations were friendly, especially in areas where the peoples actively traded with one another for mutual benefit, but traces of enmity – fueled by fear, suspicion, racial tension, and the English colonists' insatiable quest for land acquired under traditional European notions of private property ownership – was a persistent feature in the English empire in America. Historians have demonstrated that the efforts of the English to turn the landscape into one of "houses, fields, and fences" contrasted sharply with Indigenous perceptions about land use. The various colonies were also sites of conflict between Europeans as secondary theaters of war during, for example, the Anglo-French War (1627–9), the Anglo-Spanish Wars (1625–9, 1655–60), and the Anglo-Dutch Wars (1652–74), which often resulted in treaty negotiations that also affected the future of the colonies by helping England gain international recognition for its overseas empire.

By 1690, especially with the production of various navigation acts between 1651 and 1663, which regulated trade across the English Atlantic world and relations between the mother country and its colonies, the English had the most powerful European empire in North America, and England benefited enormously – financially, structurally, and in terms of global authority – from its existence. The colonies remained largely self-administering and were governed through local "planter assemblies," although the expansion of the powers of the various committees for foreign trade and plantations after 1670 is sometimes seen as the "end of American independence" and the start of a process leading eventually to rebellion in the eighteenth century. An example indicating the seriousness with which the English state approached the idea of a unified empire emanating from Westminster may be found in the "Blathwayt Atlas," a collection of forty-eight manuscript and printed maps assembled by William Blathwayt, head of the privy council's plantations committee, in 1683. The collection was designed to provide the committee with a visual representation of the entire English empire, so that more informed decisions could be made about its future. There is little doubt that the creation of this empire brought early modern England out of its insular origins and gave it a global character.

* * *

Discussion Question 8.4: Historians have suggested that the emigration of certain subjects from England to the New World in the seventeenth century served as a "safety valve" – or a method of relieving built-up tensions – in early modern England. Based on knowledge gained in earlier chapters, how would you assess this argument? What problems existed in England between 1585 and 1690 that emigration could ease?

VOICES OF THE PAST
THE JAMESTOWN MASSACRE

By 1622, the Jamestown colony contained about 1,200 English subjects and had, throughout its fifteen-year existence, struggled with starvation, poor climate, apathy among the colonists, and troubles with the Algonquian peoples known as the Powhatan Confederacy. In this year, the chief weroance, Opechancanough, abandoned traditional diplomacy and determined to extirpate the English from the region. On March 22, 1622, the Powhatan entered several small English settlements in Jamestown and the surrounding area and murdered roughly one-quarter of the English colonists (see Figure 8.1). As described in the extract below, the English seized upon this massacre as a casus belli *and an excuse for conquest.*

* * *

An occasion was ministered of sending to Opechancanough the king of these savages, about the middle of March last, what time the messenger returned back with these words from him, that he held the peace concluded so firm, as the sky should sooner fall than it dissolve. Yea, such was the treacherous dissimulation of that people who then had contrived our destruction, that even days before the massacre, some of our men were guided through the woods by them in safety ... and many the like passages, rather increasing our former confidence, than any wise in the world ministering the least suspicion of the breach of the peace, or of what instantly ensued. Yea, they borrowed our own boats to convey themselves across the river (on the banks of both sides whereof all our plantations were) to consult of the devilish murder that ensued, and of our utter extirpation, which God of his mercy (by

Figure 8.1 *The Jamestown massacre of 1622, by Matthaeus Merian.*

Credit: FLHC 93/Alamy Stock Photo.

the means of some of themselves converted to Christianity[4]) prevented.

And as well to the Friday morning (the fatal day) the 22 of March, as also in the evening, as in other days before, they came unarmed into our houses, without bows or arrows, or other weapons, with deer, turkeys, fish, furs, and other provisions, to sell and truck [trade] with us, for glass, beads, and other trifles. Yes, in some places, [they] sat down at breakfast with our people at their tables, whom immediately with their own tools and weapons, either laid down, or standing in their houses, they basely and barbarously murdered, not sparing either age or sex, man, woman or child, so sudden in their cruel execution, that few or none discerned the weapon or blow that brought them to destruction. In which manner, they also slew many other people then at their several works and husbandries in the fields, and without their houses, some in planting corn and tobacco, some in gardening, some in making brick, building, sawing, and other kinds of husbandry, they well knowing in what places and quarters each of our men were, in regard of their daily familiarity, and resort to us for trading and other negotiations....

And by this means that fatal Friday morning, there fell under the bloody and barbarous hands of that perfidious and inhumane people, contrary to all laws of God and men, of nature and nations, 347 men, women, and children, most by their own weapons. And not being content with taking away life alone, they fell after again upon the dead, making as well as they could, a fresh murder, defacing, dragging, and mangling the dead carcasses into many pieces, and carrying some parts away in derision, with base and brutish triumph. Neither yet did these beasts spare those amongst the rest well known unto them, from whom they had daily received many benefits and favors, but spitefully also massacred them, without remorse or pity, being in this more fell [fierce] than lions and dragons, which (as histories record) have been so far from hurting, as they have both acknowledged, and gratefully required their benefactors. Such is the force of good deeds, though done to cruel beasts, as to make them put off the very nature of beasts, and to put on humanity upon them. But these miscreants, contrariwise in this kind, put not off only all humanity, but put on a worse and more than unnatural brutishness.... Yet were the hearts of the English ever stupid, and averted from believing anything that might weaken their hopes of speedy winning the savages to civility and religion, by kind usage and fair conversing amongst them....

Thus have you seen the particulars of this massacre, ... wherein treachery and cruelty have done their worst to us, or rather to themselves. For whose understanding is so shallow, as not to perceive that this must needs be for the good of the plantation after, and the loss of this blood to make the body more healthful, as by these reasons may be manifest. First, because betraying of innocency never rests unpunished.... Second, because our hands which before were tied with gentleness and fair usage, are now set at liberty by the treacherous violence of the savages.... So that we, who hitherto have had possession of no more ground than their waste, and our purchase at a valuable consideration to their own contentment gained, may now by right of war and the law of nations, invade the country and destroy them who sought to destroy us. Whereby we shall enjoy their cultivated places.... Now their cleared grounds in all their villages (which are situate in the fruitfulest places of the land) shall be inhabited by us, whereas heretofore the grubbing of woods was the greatest labor.

---

4   Some settlements were saved because converted Indigenous peoples informed the colonists about Opechancanough's plans.

Thirdly, because those commodities which the Indians enjoyed as much or rather more than we, shall now also be entirely possessed by us.... Fourthly, because the way of conquering them is much more easy than of civilizing them by fair means, for they are a rude, barbarous, and naked people, scattered in small countries, which are helps to victory, but hindrances to civility. Besides that, a conquest may be of many, and at once; but civility is in particular, and slow,

the effect of long time, and great industry.... By these and sundry other ways, as by driving them (when they fly) upon their enemies ... and by animating and abetting their enemies against them, may their ruin or subjection be soon effected.

Source: Edward Waterhouse, *A Declaration of the State of the Colony and Affairs in Virginia* (London, 1622), 13–24.

* * *

Discussion Question 8.5: Considering the violence committed by the English against the Indigenous peoples in 1585–6, what do you find surprising or suspicious about Waterhouse's account of the massacre of 1622?

CHAPTER NINE

ORDER, AUTHORITY, AND OBEDIENCE

DEATH AND DISORDER: THE MURDER OF THOMAS ARDEN

Among the most disorderly of crimes in early modern England was petty treason, the act of a social inferior murdering a social superior, such as a wife killing her husband or a servant killing his master. Such an act perverted the great chain of being, signaled disorder in a society that relied on order for stability, and, more fundamentally, upset the integrity of the family unit, which this society perceived to be the central instrument of authority in the state. Thus, it is perhaps no surprise that a great deal of the popular literature that emerged from humanism was devoted to describing this heinous act of disobedience. One of the first such tales to be printed – and frequently reprinted – was the murder of Thomas Arden.

In 1550, Thomas lived with his wife, Alice, and daughter, Margaret, at Faversham Abbey, Kent, which had been purchased by Thomas sometime after the dissolution of the monasteries. Thomas was a gentleman of good standing in the community, having at some point served as the town's mayor. Alice, whom all sources describe as young and beautiful, began an affair

with Richard Mosby, a handsome tailor who frequented the Arden house for business. Their sexual relationship was apparently no secret to Thomas, but he turned a blind eye because of the business opportunities that Alice's family afforded him. In time, Alice began to hate her husband and wished him dead, so that she could marry Mosby.

Alice's first attempt to murder Thomas involved purchasing a vial of poison from a painter and mixing it with milk, which she served to Thomas for his breakfast. The taste was off and Thomas refused to drink more than a sip. Alice became more aggressive in her attempts, involving three men – John Green, George Bradshaw, and Black Will – as confederates. Green was presently involved in a land dispute with Thomas and was happy to rid himself of his adversary. Bradshaw, a goldsmith, and Black Will, a highway robber "as murdering a villain as any in England," were veteran soldiers who were willing, for a fee, to commit murder. Thomas's manservant, Michael, was recruited to help so that he could be free to marry.

Several failed attempts to murder Thomas followed. One involved Michael leaving the doors of the house open so that Black Will could enter at night and murder Thomas in his sleep. The plan fell apart when Michael feared that the mercenary would murder him as well, so he locked the doors fast, later claiming that Thomas had risen from his bed and locked the doors himself. On the next attempt, Black Will was supposed to attack Thomas as he returned one night from London, but Thomas luckily came into the company of several friends and was not alone when he passed by his would-be murderer. The sources describe at least two more failed attempts.

Finally, on St. Valentine's Day, 1551, the group made its final attempt, although the facts over several sources are not entirely consistent. Black Will hid in a parlor closet while the Ardens, Mosby, and his sister Cicely sat down to supper. Afterward, while Arden and Mosby were playing a game of backgammon, Black Will emerged from the closet, placed a handkerchief over Thomas's head, and strangled him. Mosby struck Thomas on the skull with a pressing iron, drew a dagger, and cut Thomas's throat. Then Alice got into the act, stabbing her husband's body seven or eight times.

Thomas's corpse was carried to a meadow behind the house, where it was expected that the evening snow would cover all evidence. The perpetrators thought that Thomas's murder would be ascribed to a visitor attending the village's Valentine's celebrations. Black Will was paid the sum of £8 for his services, and the remainder of the party returned to the parlor to play games and music. To allay suspicion, they wanted the neighbors to believe that Thomas was alive and well that evening, and that his murder took place sometime after the party had ended.

The next morning, Alice raised the alarm to her neighbors that her husband was missing and a search party soon found Thomas's body. The snow, however, had subsided shortly after the body was deposited and instead of covering the body and evidence, it revealed several footprints and a blood trail leading back to the Arden house. Besides, Thomas was not dressed in a proper manner to have ventured out on a cold February night, leading the search party to believe he had been murdered indoors. Headed by the town's mayor and magistrate, the search party began its investigation, soon finding the victim's blood and hair, and the knife and handkerchief poorly hidden in the house. Under duress, Alice confessed, naming all her co-conspirators. Arrests followed: Alice, the domestic servants, Mosby, and Bradshaw, but not yet Green and Black Will, who had managed to escape.

At the next Faversham assizes, the conspirators were tried and convicted. Alice, because she was Thomas's wife and, therefore, his social inferior, was charged with petty treason. She was burned at the stake in Canterbury, the standard punishment for women convicted of treason. The domestic servants were also treated as traitors to their master. Michael was hanged in chains and Elizabeth, his fellow servant, was burned at the stake, both at Faversham. Mosby and his sister Cicely were hanged at Smithfield, in central London, and Bradshaw was hanged in chains at Canterbury. These punishments contrasted sharply with the usual method of execution for simple murder, which would have been hanging at the gallows followed by a Christian burial. After some years, Green was brought to justice for his role in the crime. Black Will was also eventually captured and hanged at the scaffold, but not for the murder of Thomas Arden. His work as a highwayman and criminal-for-hire had finally caught up with him.

The planning that went into the murder of Thomas Arden was unusual for the time. Although most homicides were committed against family members and people who knew each other, they usually happened on the spur of the moment as the result of a heated argument. The facts surrounding Arden's murder, with several co-conspirators and multiple failed attempts leading eventually to success, all serve to make this case more interesting than a typical Tudor homicide. Indeed, this 1551 case was so unusual that it was described in detail in *Holinshed's Chronicles*, a late-Tudor work, first published in 1577, that William Shakespeare often used as a source for his plays. A play, *Arden of Faversham*, followed in 1592. Its authorship is unknown, but has been attributed to such famous playwrights as Thomas Kyd and Christopher Marlowe. The story also appeared in the *Newgate Calendar* in 1780, a biographical collection of famous murders. The death of Thomas Arden, therefore, has become one of the best-known murder cases in Tudor history.

* * *

Discussion Question 9.1: Why do you think the murder of Thomas Arden was repeated so often in the history and literature of the early modern period?

Order and the State

Orderliness, obedience, and respect for authority were expected in all aspects and among all elements of society, from the structured way in which the various stages of life unfolded, to the rigid hierarchy of the great chain of being, to moderation in or abstinence from all forms of vice – including gambling, alcohol, swearing, sexual innuendo, and sexual impropriety – to the critical importance of maintaining control within the single most important unit within society, the family. Naturally, given the importance attached to order and obedience, and the dangers and chaos that ensued from disorderliness or disobedience, there were numerous instruments of authority within early modern English society.

The first instrument of authority was the central government, especially as embodied in the king, privy council, and parliament. We have already seen numerous examples of the state stepping in when riot or rebellion occurred in the Tudor period, such as the Pilgrimage of Grace, the Prayer Book Rebellion, Wyatt's Rebellion, and the Northern Rebellion, most of which were handled swiftly, often with deadly consequences for their participants. These national insurrections, and more minor local varieties, were sometimes handled by the lords lieutenant who represented each county, appointments that began in the 1540s. Always members of the peerage, the lieutenants were primarily responsible for maintaining and commanding local militia units during times of war or rebellion.

Beyond the ability to assemble temporary forces in times of emergency, however, the Tudor and Stuart state did not have access to the same coercive abilities to maintain order that would become common in later periods, such as standing armies and trained police forces. Historians have referred to this style of government as the "weak state" model, which was a deliberate effort on the part of the central government to remain bureaucratically small, which reduced strain on limited crown finances and offered minimal oversight of the English peripheries. Instead, the state expected that English subjects and the many lesser officeholders charged with controlling the parishes would respect its authority and follow various directives, instructions, and injunctions in the interests of cooperation and maintaining peaceful relations both with the central government and among communities and neighbors.

Order and disorder might, for example, be regulated through the use of royal proclamations and declarations issued by the monarch and privy council. One particularly well-known example is James I's *Book of Sports* (1617), which regulated which sports could be played on Sundays and other holy days. Archery and dancing (elite activities) were acceptable; bear- and bull-baiting (common activities) were not. Other centralized policies included, for example, who could and could not hunt in royal forests; the penalties associated with religious recusancy; temporary powers given to sheriffs and justices of the peace in times of crisis; the regulation of weights, measures, and food prices ("victualing laws"); and literally hundreds more designed to emphasize the authority of the state to maintain and restore order, as well as the privileges held by the crown, nobility, and gentry as the natural rulers of society. Proclamations and declarations were read aloud in church on Sundays and by town criers during market days, and they were posted on parish doors for the benefit of the small percentage of society who could read, in hopes that new orders and regulations would pass orally from the semi-literate to the illiterate in alehouses and other public venues. In their preambles and seals, these documents resounded with royal authority and emphasized the divine status of kings and queens, the majesty of kingship, and the power of the council as a delegated sovereign authority. This was especially true after the reforms of Thomas Cromwell and the increase in the authority of the council under Henry VIII.

Order was also enforced in laws passed by the English parliament, such as the Ale Houses Act (1551), which empowered justices of the peace to license alehouses throughout England to control "the abuses and disorders as are had and used in common ale-houses." The Elizabethan period, in particular – which was wracked by population increase, the beginnings of land enclosure, agricultural dearth, plague, inflation, and the decline of wages and employment opportunities – saw several pieces of legislation designed to maintain order throughout the country. A good example is the Act of Artificers (1563), which fixed prices on various commodities to protect consumers from unscrupulous sellers, placed a cap on wages to ensure that workers did not leave their positions to seek better-paying ones, required unemployed artisans and apprentices to accept work as laborers, and ensured that those working in artisanal trades had completed a full apprenticeship before practicing their trade, in order to protect guilds and skilled workers from unfair competition. One of the reasons for this act was the onslaught of Protestant immigrants and exiles from Catholic countries, who often had considerable trade experience but lacked guild accreditation and were willing to work for less pay, thereby denying opportunities for English apprentices and trained artificers.

As economic crises continued to mount during this period, Tudor parliaments also passed various poor laws, the most important of which were produced under Elizabeth (1597–1601). These acts created local "overseers of the poor," who collected a poor rate and determined who was entitled to relief in their parishes. Overseers were required to distinguish between the deserving and undeserving poor, the former being those who could not work (the "impotent poor") and those who wanted work but who could not find it (the "able-bodied poor"), and the latter being those who could work but chose not to (the "idle poor," vagrants and beggars). Depending on their individual situations, the impotent and able-bodied poor were given relief in the form of money, food, and clothing ("outdoor relief") or were placed into "houses of industry" ("indoor relief") to undertake work using materials provided by the overseer, with hopes that they would eventually enter an apprenticeship or service. The idle poor were denied poor relief and either returned to their home parishes or were placed into "houses of correction," known after 1555 as "bridewells."[1] Collectively, these acts sought to reduce the amount of civil disorder caused by plague, vagrancy, lack of employment, and other forms of economic, social, and agricultural strife.

* * *

Discussion Question 9.2: What do you think were the strengths and weaknesses of the preferred "weak state" system of government?

The Church and the Clergy

Despite some tumult during the early modern period, the church was also a place where order, authority, and obedience were taught and enforced. Emanating from the central authority of the archbishops and bishops, and filtering down to the parish level throughout the nation, adherence to the great chain of being and obedience to God's laws and secular authority were routinely preached from the pulpit; these messages were widely heard because of the legal requirement to attend church every Sunday. Priests reminded their congregations of social and moral expectations, and of the responsibility of children to respect – and pray for the health and well-being of – their parents, wives their husbands, youth their elders, commoners their lords and masters, and subjects their monarch.

---

1   The term derives from the first house of correction, Bridewell Palace, which was given to the City of London by Edward VI to house vagrant children and wayward women.

These descriptions of proper moral, sexual, gender, and rank boundaries of behavior were usually accompanied by reminders of the chaos that disorder caused. Priests emphasized disorder's consequences both in the short term – social outcasting, the inversion of God's and nature's laws, and the inexorableness of minor sins turning into major ones – and in the long term – mortal sin leading to criminal conviction, execution, and the sacrifice of everlasting salvation. The church's official responsibilities at key stages of life – birth, baptism, marriage, and death – also emphasized an orderly and natural progression through one's corporeal existence. Even the organization of seating with the church was based on orderliness: the rulers sat on cushioned pews at the front; the ruled sat on wooden benches at the back; men sat closer to the priest than their wives and children.

The clergy also, either openly, anonymously, or pseudonymously, produced a wide range of "conduct books" which emphasized the ideal codes of personal conduct expected of elites, commoners, women, children, parents, and spouses. They also produced various works that exhorted obedience to authority, such as the catechism of Alexander Nowell (1563–73), the many writings of the prolific William Perkins (1584–1604), and the tellingly titled homily *An Exhortation Concerning Good Order and Obedience to Rulers and Magistrates* (1547). These works, which were expounded in church, taught by schoolmasters, and expected to be part of a man's basic instructions to his wife and children, stressed the duty of Christians to honor their superiors and show faith in God's determination of the natural order. Resistance to authority was tantamount to the denial of God's commands and to open rebellion and treason against husbands, fathers, nobles, and the monarch. In some cases, lay individuals undertook the task of writing about ideal Christian lives, thereby reinforcing the church's teachings. Perhaps the best example is Phillip Stubbes's *A Crystal Glass for Christian Women* (1592), which was a biography of his recently deceased wife. In her short life, abbreviated by death at the age of 19, Katherine Stubbes had lived, according to her husband of four years, a perfectly orderly Christian life.

In addition to publishing conduct books, the clergy was also partly responsible, along with numerous other authors who generally preferred to remain anonymous, for publishing literally thousands of small pamphlets, sometimes known as "chapbooks," and ballads that were produced in London and sold in urban bookshops and rural villages throughout the countryside. In some ways the opposite of conduct books, the central theme of these pamphlets was the lives and acts of disorderly people, usually those who committed criminal or perverse acts that upset national and local orderliness. Many of these small books, which were typically four to twelve pages in length, opened with a biblical analogy before reciting an illustrative case of murder, rape, deception, or depravity, including the unnatural murder of one's parents or children and sexual impropriety such as homosexuality, pedophilia, and prostitution. The

Devil featured in nearly all these pamphlets as a providential agent who sought to corrupt mankind, and the religious theme of inexorable backsliding – the slippery slope that began with minor vices and led to fatal consequences – was commonly explored. Many of these types of works were produced, beginning in 1676, by the official minister (or "ordinary") at London's Newgate Prison, which held many prisoners destined to die at the gallows for their crimes. These accounts often ended with "last dying speeches," words allegedly uttered by the condemned just before execution, which were a combination of confession, support for the justice system headed by the king, and acknowledgment of the need for an orderly society.

* * *

Discussion Question 9.3: Why do you think clergymen and other pamphlet writers devoted so much of their efforts to describing disorderly or unwanted behavior in society, rather than focusing on examples of orderly or desired behavior?

Patriarchy, Neighborliness, and Community

Although the duty of commoners to obey their superiors and maintain orderly behavior was emphasized in conduct books and pamphlets, so too was the duty of superiors to act humanely, govern wisely, and model appropriate behavior through displays of gravity, dignity, and respectability in all things. Elites who acted outside of these expectations were perceived to have inverted the social order. It is partly for this reason, for example, that Mervyn Tuchet, earl of Castlehaven, was tried by his aristocratic peers in 1631. Castlehaven was accused of committing sodomy with his page, who confessed to the crime, and for assisting his servants in raping his wife, Anne, although there is also evidence that she manipulated the events to avoid suspicion of committing adultery with one of the servants. Ultimately, Castlehaven was convicted and beheaded for his crimes. Despite his high rank and the privileges that normally came with it, his opprobrious acts brought disrepute to the aristocracy, and only his death could restore order and faith in the hierarchy of man.

The occasional punishment of individuals such as Castlehaven stemmed largely from the widely held and taught notion of the patriarchal-deferential relationship (also known as paternalism and deference) in society. This was the notion that rulers, or social superiors, had a moral and legal responsibility to protect those they ruled, much as a husband and father protected his wife and children. Lords were expected to provide for their tenants especially during times of need, such as periods of agricultural strife or economic downturn, or when there were disputes between neighbors, landlords, and tenants. They were also expected to provide during holidays by opening up their homes and giving away food and sundries that would allow tenants and servants to celebrate, especially at Christmas. December 25 was also one of the four "quarter days," during which service and apprenticeship contracts expired and were renewed, making it another good time for patriarchy to take place. The historical origins of "Boxing Day," when employers gave gifts to their servants and awarded them with a day off to celebrate with their family and neighbors, dates to the seventeenth century.

In exchange for this protection and generosity, social inferiors were expected to show deference to their superiors. They were exhorted to obey and respect the king, landlords, and priests and show deference in the presence of their masters through bows, curtseys, doffing of hats, and stepping aside as the rulers of society strode or rode by. And they understood that the failure to do so could result in "legitimate" forms of violence that were relatively minor – perhaps a smack to the head or being struck on the back with the flat of a sword – but which reminded deferents of their obligations. Deference also involved duly paying rents and taxes and accepting the legal and moral judgment of superiors.

Although deferents were allowed, in certain circumstances, to protest the king or their lords when they felt their rights, or the patriarchal-deferential relationship, were being infringed, they were expected to do so peacefully, without resorting to violence and weapons. It is for this reason that "illegitimate" forms of violence, such as riot and rebellion, were – as we have seen throughout this book – dealt with so seriously. The main reason why the hierarchical system of early modern England worked and was generally accepted by all ranks of people is because, with the exception of the very lowly, nearly everybody in society was both a patriarch and a deferent, a master and a servant. Even the king was a servant to God, and even a poor laborer was a master to his wife and children, making this system more fluid than modern, class-based notions of "rich" and "poor" or "have" and "have not."

Codes of conduct and boundaries of behavior were also enforced by those within kinship networks and neighborhoods, among people who – unlike those in the reciprocal patriarchal and deferential relationship – were of more or less equal status. Extended families and neighbors were expected to care for and protect each other during times of want and need, not so much out of a paternalistic social obligation as out of a mutual understanding that everybody, at certain times, required this type of assistance. This aid could extend to the lending of money (without interest); giving charity, such as food or clothing; helping with building a barn, seeding a field, or shearing sheep; watching another's children; offering advice and assistance during pregnancy or child-birth; mourning and empathizing over one's loss; mediating petty disputes; offering the hand of unconditional friendship; and generally being a "good neighbor." Indeed, the appellations "goodman" and "goodwife" (or simply "goody") were often used to describe neighbors who contributed positively to the local community.

Neighbors and the wider community were also expected to regulate the behavior of one another, to relieve the limited resources of the state and church from these responsibilities. Sometimes, the community was required to step in when minor codes of conduct were breached. Men of poor character – drunks, blasphemers, and wife beaters – and women of "lewd" and quarrelsome dispositions – adulterers, scolds, and incurable gossips – could be subjected, at the hands of their kinsmen or neighbors, to "rough music," the "charivari," or the "skimmington." Neighbors would bang pots and pans together to bring attention to disorderly persons, burn effigies of offending parties, force them to ride backwards on a donkey through the market square while being whipped with a riding crop, and otherwise parade them around town and make them the subjects of derision and ridicule. Women in particular might be subjected to the "ducking stool," in which they were ducked repeatedly into the local pond, or in some parts of the country, to the "scold's bridle," a piece of metal headgear that prevented its wearer from talking. These were all relatively harmless "shaming rituals" designed to restore order before more formal measures were deemed necessary.

These more formal measures could take the form of local members of the community arranging to bring malcontents in front of local "leet" courts, run variously by gentleman, yeomen, and clergymen who served as landlords, stewards, mayors, bailiffs, sheriffs, beadles, and deacons. Most of these men had no legal training but had considerable experience with local affairs and knew the standards of their community and the boundaries of behavior within which people should operate. These courts dealt with chronic disturbers of the peace, scolds, abusers, gamblers, drunks, blasphemers, fornicators, adulterers, vagrants, and other transgressors, meting out minor punishments such as small financial fines, a brief stint in the village stocks or gaol, or the requirement to be of good behavior, known as recognizances.

The practice of maintaining local norms, and of presenting individuals to the leets for punishment, also fell to the temporary, part-time, unpaid, and untrained constables, or headboroughs. These men were members of the community they served, selected from among their own kinsmen and neighbors, and sometimes undertook their responsibilities begrudgingly. As made clear by William Lambarde in *The Duties of Constables* (1583), while in office these men had wide-ranging authority to keep the peace, which could also take the form of immediate, summary punishment such as the stocks and pillory, comparatively harmless forms of punishment designed, like shaming rituals, to ridicule the offender and bring them back into the proper boundaries of behavior.

Family and Gender Authority

At its lowest, yet perhaps most important level, state, church, and community expectations regarding orderliness and strict boundaries of behavior resided in the family unit. Deemed the "microcosm of the state," it was believed and taught that the family was a commonwealth in miniature, headed by a man – as ruler of his household – who provided patriarchal physical, physiological, and financial protection, and firm but gentle discipline, to his wife and children in exchange for deference, obedience, and a happy home. Husbands, and to a degree wives as their partners, were also responsible for the conduct and discipline of their servants and apprentices, who were considered part of the family unit during their period of employment. The family was the breeding ground of moral instruction – which, owing to the increase in personal religious experience thanks to the Protestant Reformation, also involved enforcing the catechism and other church teachings – the patriarchal and deferential relationship, and community obligation. A well-governed home headed by a happily married couple translated into an orderly society, whereas household mismanagement and marital discord meant social disorder.

Marriage was deemed a "natural" state especially for women, who were recognized in conduct books and church teachings as physically and mentally inferior, subordinate to men, needful of guidance, less intelligent than men, and more easily tempted toward sinful behavior. Single women, known legally as *feme sole*, were thought to be less capable of governing their actions or operating among men, and were often treated with suspicion and intolerance, especially if they were seen to challenge male authority in public. Through marriage, women became *feme covert*, in which husband and wife merged as one person, with the man very much the senior partner, especially in the public sphere dominated by patriarchy. At least according to church teaching and conduct books (and as exemplified by Phillip Stubbes), both at home and in public, women were expected to be humble, dignified, virtuous, quiet, modest, and obedient, and evidence to the contrary could lead to community chastisement. The superiority of men as heads of household was also emphasized in the fact that servants who murdered their masters, or wives their husbands (as in the case of the Arden murder), were found guilty of "petty treason" and subjected to harsher punishment – being hanged, drawn, and quartered for men, or burned at the stake for women – than those who committed other forms of homicide (see **Voices of the Past**: **The Life and Death of Margaret Fernseed**).

Regardless of the perceived primacy of male authority in the home, both husbands and wives were commonly involved in making decisions for the good of the family unit, worked toward bringing harmony to the home by resolving conflicts, and strived for mutually acceptable and enjoyable sexual relations. Wives also had essential roles in keeping up the household, supervising servants, instructing and raising children, and sometimes transacting business on behalf of the family. Husbands relied on their wives as helpmeets who undertook many of the labors – cooking and cleaning; salting, pickling, and canning; sewing and laundering; et cetera – that they themselves often lacked the experience to perform. In fact, this type of spousal cooperation was strongly encouraged by the church, such as in clergyman William Gouge's *Of Domesticall Duties* (1622), which stressed the "mutual" relations of spouses who were "fellows and partners." If marriages sometimes fell into discord, which was inevitable, provided that such bouts were occasional or remained within the confines of the family home and did not scandalize the community nor jeopardize the natural order of things, neighbors remained tolerant.[2] Otherwise, the community was forced to get involved.

Of course, many women operated outside of official expectations. Those of rank held a higher social position than most male commoners and were treated with deference. These included Henry VIII's daughters, Mary and Elizabeth, who became regnant queens, and also many other ladies and gentlewomen whose fathers and husbands held status in society. These high-ranking women were treated, out of the respect for their position, ancestry, or marital title, with largely the same level of respect that their male counterparts enjoyed. Common adult women who were single – which, given that a majority of English society at any given time was female, was a normal condition – could enter into contracts, buy and sell land, engage in mercantile and other employment opportunities, sometimes including apprenticeships, and initiate legal proceedings. Provided that these women went about their business with an understanding of the patriarchal society in which they lived and worked, accepted their status as the "weaker vessel," did not actively seek to invert the proper order of things through quarrelsome or contentious behavior, and did not partake in vices – sexual or otherwise – that might earn censure, they were perfectly welcome as productive members and active agents in English society. Without challenging the clear fact that there was no gender equality in early modern England – nor many efforts to attain it – we should be careful not to exaggerate the degree to which women were or felt oppressed or lacked agency in this society.

Justices and Magistrates

Taken together, the authority exercised by patriarchs, neighbors, constables, husbands, and fathers was all associated with ensuring orderliness and obedience in local communities. These various measures had the advantage of allowing individual communities to express and maintain their internal norms, which were

---

2   Marriage will be discussed in more detail in Chapter Eleven.

often quite different throughout the country and in some cases deviated from the expectations of the centralized authorities representing the state and church. This distinction between the center and the periphery has been referred to by Keith Wrightson as "two concepts of order," which was based on the discretionary application of law at the local level for the primary purpose of restoring order, even if this meant disregarding the national rule of law.[3] This discretion allowed participants in the system – which, as we have seen, involved many members of the community – to believe the law worked for them rather than against them.

It was also necessary, at times, for the "weak" state to assert its authority, especially when the local community was either too lax or too zealous in its treatment of disorderly persons, or when certain people committed acts that required harsher punishment than members of the local communities were able to exercise. In such instances, officials working on behalf of the crown got involved and meted out justice in the name of the king or queen. The responsibility of administering royal justice fell, first and foremost, to local justices of the peace. Always members of the gentry, these men were named annually to the Commission of the Peace, a list that was compiled by the lord chancellor based on the advice of various ranking individuals in the realm, such as judges, privy councillors, bishops, lords lieutenant, and courtiers. Not all gentlemen were appointed; they needed to be able of both body and mind, with sound judgment and good reputation in their communities. They also needed to have sufficient wealth in order to perform their duties, because, like members of parliament and numerous other officeholders, they did not receive a salary for their services. Many justices of the peace served for decades, provided there was no reason for their names to be removed from the commission as a result of incompetence, their failure to conform to instructions from the central government, or their known disapproval of religious reforms or changes in monarchs.

Depending on its physical size and population, each county might have several dozen justices of the peace at a time. They were a visible and natural source of authority throughout the country, the major exception being in London and the large towns, whose franchises allowed them greater freedom to administer and oversee their own affairs. In these instances, the responsibilities of the rural justice of the peace fell to mayors, aldermen, beadles, overseers, and other officials.

Rural justices and their urban counterparts – collectively known as the magistracy – had numerous responsibilities, which were extensive, if somewhat ill-defined, though not unlimited. They were required to enforce royal

---

3   Keith Wrightson, "Two Concepts of Order: Justices, Constables and Jurymen in Seventeenth-Century England," in *An Ungovernable People: The English and Their Law in the Seventeenth and Eighteenth Centuries*, eds. John Brewer and John Styles (New Brunswick, NJ: Rutgers University Press, 1980).

proclamations and oversee the implementation of new legislation, set limits on wages, ensure weights and measures were properly calibrated (to prevent cheating), and regulate the movement and activities of vagrants. During times of difficulty, such as agricultural failure and other economic problems, they ensured that a sufficient supply of grain was available for fair prices, prevented attempts to manipulate the market of supply and demand, and assisted with the administration of poor relief. During times of plague they were responsible for ensuring that the inflicted were quarantined and the dead were buried, to limit the spread of the disease and to restore order. These and other duties were described in manuals produced by men such as William Lambarde and Michael Dalton, most notably in *The Country Justice* (1618). Above all, as their title implies, justices of the peace were responsible to keep the peace in their communities, and they possessed wide-ranging authority that allowed them to do so.

In addition to overseeing various regulatory offenses, which were usually accompanied by financial fines, justices were also key figures in the criminal justice system. When it came to crimes committed against individuals in their communities, they were often the initial point of contact. Victims or somebody on their behalf brought complaints to the attention of the justice of the peace, who detained the suspect in order to answer the charge. Often this was a simple case of arresting a specific individual against whom a complaint had been made, because in most cases crimes were of a highly personal and opportunistic nature and the accused was known to the community. At other times, aided by coroners,[4] sheriffs, bailiffs, constables, and members of the local community, justices of the peace went to great lengths to solve crimes committed by unknown persons, especially those of a serious nature, such as rape, arson, theft, and murder, all of which were technically capital felonies subject to a sentence of death upon conviction.

Once the accused was apprehended, justices of the peace examined all parties to determine the sufficiency of evidence and whether resolution through arbitration was possible. This likely happened frequently in the case of minor offenses, although there is little historical evidence of how often arbitration was used. It was at this point that the justice, as a member of the local community who understood its boundaries of acceptable behavior, could exercise discretion by choosing to overlook certain offenses or reduce their severity to lessen the sentence. The justice's discretion in these matters was grounded in the belief that his role was primarily to restore peace and order to the community, even if this meant a flexible interpretation of the law.

---

4   The coroner was a gentleman without medical training, who was appointed by the crown to investigate suspicious deaths in order to determine whether a homicide had occurred.

If it was determined that the case needed to go to trial, the justice of the peace, guided by instructional manuals, assembled the facts in a dossier, took confessions and witness depositions, drew up a formal indictment indicating the charges, took a recognizance to allow the accused his freedom under strict instructions to be of good behavior, or, if the offense was particularly serious or the accused a stranger to the community, ordered the accused into the custody of the town gaoler pending a trial. The gaoler was usually a private person who paid the local sheriff for the privilege of operating the gaol. He received a small county rate for each prisoner and charged inmates for luxuries such as beds, blankets, cheese, and meat. These expenses were borne by family members or by the inmates themselves, who collected money from passersby – wearing a "ball and chain" to prevent escape – outside the gaol. Inmates in gaol for more than a few weeks might succumb to gaol fever (typhus), owing to the inadequate diet, overcrowding, and unsanitary conditions.

In the case of lesser offenses, or misdemeanors, such as breaches of morality (bastardy, fornication, adultery, swearing, or refusal to attend church services) and disturbing the peace (defamation, drunkenness, vandalism, vagrancy, scolding, and general disorderliness), justices had the ability to act summarily (without a jury). In these instances, they acted similarly to the magistrates in leet courts, jurisdictions that, in rural areas, by the early seventeenth century had largely been replaced by individual justices of the peace sitting in Petty Sessions as needed. More serious misdemeanors, such as assault, quarreling, dueling, and other forms of violence were handled by justices of the peace sitting in groups of two or three during Quarter Sessions, which sat four times per year in key centers and took place in the presence juries of twelve men drawn from the community in which the crime occurred.[5] Their range of punishments included fines (adjusted according to the severity of the offense and means of the offender), banishment from the community (normally for strangers and vagrants), short periods of incarceration, and corporal punishment, such as whipping, ear cropping (the removal of the outer ear), and a stint in the local pillory or stocks.

Assizes and Executions

In the late sixteenth century, justices of the peace were formally deprived of the ability to try capital offenses, or felonies, although in practice they had rarely done so since before the Tudor age began. Felonies included serious crimes against the body or property of the king's subjects, including all forms of homicide, theft

---

5   Quarter Sessions magistrates were often members of the "quorum," a select group of justices of the peace who had more legal training or greater experience in criminal justice.

above 1 shilling, sexual assault, major economic crimes (such as forgery and coin clipping), riot, treason, and witchcraft. In allegations of felony, the charges were first heard by a grand jury – or a coroner's inquest in the case of suspicious death – comprising twelve men of yeoman rank, who determined whether there was sufficient evidence to proceed to trial. If it was determined that there was enough evidence, which was not a very high threshold, the case was presided over by a royal judge in the twice-annual Assizes.

Assize judges were either justices of the royal courts of King's Bench and Common Pleas or senior practitioners in those courts, known as sergeants-at-law, who were issued commissions to hear all felony cases in the counties. Twelve judges traveled in groups of two throughout the countryside in the early spring and late summer to approximately seventy-five towns. The arrival of such august royal officials reminded the community of the primacy of national over local interests and emphasized the ultimate power of the state to make life and death decisions about local malefactors. Those who refused to plead guilty or not guilty before the justices – and, in so doing, challenged the court's authority – were ordered to suffer *peine forte et dure*. This practice, described in Chapter Four, was used numerous times in the early modern period.

Trials were hasty affairs, commonly occurring within a matter of minutes, in which testimony was quickly gathered from victims, witnesses, and the accused, and perhaps also the justice of the peace, coroner, and constable. Although lawyers occasionally presented cases involving wealthy clients, they had very proscribed roles, and most trials did not include lawyers throughout the Tudor and Stuart period. Because judges could not technically command a certain verdict, juries had considerable leeway. In theory, they heard the evidence and pronounced their verdicts based on the elements needed to be proven for a particular charge, but there is plenty of evidence that, in practice, their decision was based on a variety of factors. This might include the character or demeanor of the accused or victim, the degree of violence present in the criminal act, and the extent to which the community was scandalized by the behavior of the accused.

The accused might be found not guilty, in which case he was free to go; guilty of a lesser offense, which was likely to reduce the severity of the sentence; or guilty of the charge in the indictment. Overall, about 60 per cent of those accused were convicted, which shows that juries took their responsibilities seriously and were neither too lenient nor too harsh. The percentage of those executed, however, was far lower. For all but the most serious of felonies (among which were murder, rape, arson, treason, and burglary), convicted criminals were able to claim "benefit of clergy," a medieval tradition that involved reading a biblical psalm, being branded on the thumb, and receiving a lesser sentence such as whipping. Other convicts might be given a reprieve from the bench pending a pardon from the king, which allowed judges to mitigate jury overzealousness, or could be placed into military service during times of war. Women who claimed they were pregnant might be spared through "benefit of belly," which had to be certified by a "jury of matrons" who examined the women for signs that they were with child.

Despite these frequent displays of mercy, which served as further proof that the law was designed to work for rather than against English subjects, about 25 per cent of those convicted of felonies were executed. To a modern eye, this probably seems like a high percentage. The English state and people often analogized society to a human body, in which the offending part needed to be removed to allow the remainder to heal and restore order. More practically, early modern English society did not have the centralized mechanisms required to place a dangerous criminal into long-term imprisonment, which meant that at this time death was seen as the only means to remove the offender from civil society. Most executions were performed by the county sheriff or town executioner in a public area, such as the town square, on either temporary or permanent gallows, in the presence of many members of the local community. It was believed that order could best be maintained and restored through this public viewing of executions, which were accompanied by "last dying speeches" that often reminded the audience to be law-abiding and orderly.

Executions were gruesome affairs. Men and women hanged by the neck would strangulate to death, an event that could take several minutes during which the audience, including loved ones, witnessed the condemned thrashing about and slowly expiring. Women convicted of treason – against their husbands or the crown – were burned at the stake, sometimes having first been strangulated into unconsciousness. Treasonous men, including many who took part in the riots discussed in earlier chapters, were hanged into senselessness, cut down and stretched out with ropes, emasculated, and eviscerated. While his genitals and intestines burned to ash in a fire, the condemned was finally beheaded, his body quartered, and the pieces displayed at the entrance gates to the towns (which were normally enclosed by walls) as a warning to others. This practice was known as drawing and quartering (see Figure 9.1). Men and women of noble status, such as Thomas More, Anne Boleyn, and Charles I, were beheaded, often at the Tower of London. In London, executions took place multiple times each year at Tyburn Tree, permanent gallows located in the present location of Marble Arch in the northeast corner of Hyde Park (see Figure 9.2).

Capital punishment and displays of mercy served as the ultimate form of authority exercised by the English government in the name of maintaining and restoring order. Indeed, these two centuries saw the peak period of criminal executions in all of English history. Executions in England began to decline significantly beginning about 1690. This was caused by the introduction of lawyers into criminal trials, greater political and religious stability that saw a decrease in incidents of riot and rebellion, and the new reliance on

Figure 9.1 *Head and limbs on pikes after drawing and quartering, from* The Godly End ... of John Stevens, *1632.*

Credit: Chronicle/Alamy Stock Photo.

Figure 9.2 *Execution at Tyburn Tree, from a contemporary woodcut in the time of Charles I.*

Credit: Classic Image/Alamy Stock Photo.

noncapital forms of punishment, such as the formal introduction of criminal transportation to the Americas in the early eighteenth century. Before this transition, however, state demands for order and public displays of death were inextricably linked in early modern England.

* * *

Discussion Question 9.4: Historians have shown that the sixteenth and seventeenth centuries were the peak period for felony executions in all of English history. Why do you think this was the case?

VOICES OF THE PAST
THE LIFE AND DEATH OF MARGARET FERNSEED

All people in early modern England were expected to operate within strict boundaries of behavior. Deference to authority, sexual propriety, and moral conduct were expected, especially of married women, whose behavior within the community and family needed to meet the highest standards of orderliness and virtue. Authors of pamphlet literature often wrote about women who operated outside of these expectations, partly as a reminder of proper behavior, and partly to shock and titillate their readers. The following tale of Margaret Fernseed is notable because, although there was little evidence that Fernseed murdered her husband, her disorderly lifestyle and reputation for being an outspoken woman and intemperate wife demanded that the court find her guilty, in order to make an example of her.

* * *

[W]e have before our eyes a most notable example in this wretched woman, of whom my present discourse entreateth, named Margaret Fernseed, a woman ... [who] kept a most abominable and vile brothel house, poisoning many young women with that sin wherewith her own body long before was filthily debauched. From this house at the Iron Gate she was married unto one Anthony Fernseed, a tailor dwelling in Duck Lane but keeping a shop upon Addle Hill near Carter Lane. This Anthony was amongst his neighbors reputed to be both sober and of very good conversation.

Now it happened that some few months ago, in the fields of Peckham near London, there was found a man slain having his throat cut, a

knife in his hand, gold rings upon his fingers, and forty shillings in money in his purse. His wounds of so long continuance that it was not only corrupted but there were also maggots, or such like filthy worms, engendered therein, which gave testimony to the beholders that he had not slain himself in that place, as well because the place was free from such a spectacle the day before, as also that such corruption could not proceed from a present slaughter. Again, what the person slain no man knew, both because his physiognomy [head shape] was altered in his death and because his acquaintance was little or none in those parts about Peckham.

In the end, searching his pockets and other parts of his apparel, ... certain discreet persons of Peckham, sent to London to Duck Lane and inquiring for the house of one Anthony Fernseed, delivered to his wife the disaster and mischance which had befallen her husband, which her hardened heart received not as a message of sorrow, neither did the grudging of an afflicted countenance gall her remembrance, but as if it had been the report of some ordinary or vulgar news. She embraced it with an irrespective neglect and carelessness.... Yet to observe a customary fashion or (as the proverb is) to carry a candle before the Devil, she prepares herself and her servant in all haste to go to Peckham to behold her husband....

So she and her boy came where the body was, where more for awe of the magistrate than any terror she felt she made many sour faces, but the dryness of her brain would suffer no moisture to descend into her eyes. Many questions were asked her, to which she answered with such constancy that no suspicion could be grounded against her. Then was her boy taken and examined, who delivered [revealed] the abomination of her life and that since her marriage with his master, she had lived in all disquietness, rage, and distemperature, often threatening his life and contriving plots for his destruction. That she had, ever since her marriage, in most public and notorious manner, maintained a young man with whom (in his view) she had often committed adultery. That the same young man, since his master's loss, was fled he knew not whither, and that his mistress had even then before the message of his master's death sold all his goods (as he supposed) to fly also after him whom she loved.

All these speeches were not only seconded but almost approved by some of her neighbors, which lived near unto her, insomuch that she was the second time taken into a more strict examination. Wherein, albeit she could not deny any of her general assertions, yet touching the death of her husband, she forswore and renounced the fact or practice thereof to be hers....

In the end, by authority of justice she was committed to the White Lion in Southwark. During the time of which imprisonment till her time of trial, thinking to outface truth with boldness and sin with impudence, she continued in all her examinations taken before several Justices in her former denials, and whereas the rod of imprisonment laid upon others is received as a gentle correction whereby to look into themselves, it was to her rather the bellows of indignation than a temperer to patience. Rather a kind of frenzy than a cooler of fury, and rather a provoker to evil than a persuader to goodness. For she was seldom found to be in charity with any of her fellow prisoners nor at any time in quiet with herself, rather a provoker than an appealer of dissensions, given to much swearing, scarce praying but continually scolding, so that she was as hateful to all them that dwelt with her in that her last home, the prison, as she

was to people of honest conversation (having deserved the name of a bawd [madam]) while she lived abroad.

In this uncivil order spending her hours, the time of trial coming on (when such offenders were to appear before the earthly Judge to give account of their lives past), amongst many others this Margaret Fernseed was one. At the Assizes last, according to the order of law, she was indicted and arraigned, the purpose of which indictment was to have practiced the murder of her late husband Anthony Fernseed.... To the indictment she pleaded not guilty, putting her cause to God and the country, which were a credible jury paneled, and had there made their personal appearance for that purpose. Then were these several witnesses produced against her, namely of the incontinentness of her life past, her attempt to poison her husband before this murder, as also to prepare broth for him and put powder in it, her slight regard of him in his life, and her careless sorrow for him after death. With other circumstances, as the flight of the fellow whom she had lived long in adultery withal, her present sale of her goods upon her husband's murder, as it may be justly thought, with purpose to fly after him. On which lawful evidence she was convicted and after judgment given her to be burned, and from thence she was conveyed back to the White Lion till the time appointed for her execution....

On Monday being the last of February, she had notice given her that in the afternoon she must suffer death, and a preacher commended unto her to instruct her for her soul's health, who labored much with her for the confession of the fact which she still obstinately denied, but made great show of repentance for her life past. So that about two o'clock in the afternoon she was stripped of her ordinary wearing apparel, and upon her own smock put a kirtle of canvas pitched clean through,[6] over

---

6   A kirtle is an outer garment, in this case one covered in tar to speed her death by burning.

which she did wear a white sheet, and so was by the keeper delivered to the sheriff, on each hand a woman leading her and the preacher going before her. Being come to the place of execution, both before and after her fastening to the stake, with godly exhortations he admonished her that now in that minute she would confess that fact for which she was now ready to suffer, which she denying, the reeds were planted about, unto which fire being given, she was presently dead.

Source: Anonymous, *The Arraignment and Burning of Margaret Fernseed* (London, 1608).

* * *

Discussion Question 9.5: In what ways did Margaret Fernseed upset the boundaries of behavior that were generally tolerated within early modern English society?

CHAPTER TEN

ELITE AND COMMON CULTURE

DEATH AND DISORDER:
THE SUTTON WITCHES

To explain misfortune in a superstitious society that lacked modern scientific knowledge, and to account for the strange or unwanted actions of those who operated outside of the orderly boundaries expected of their gender or rank, early modern communities often rallied together to accuse women of witchcraft. Indeed, among the ranks of disorderly women, none were more feared and reviled than those who entered into a pact with the Devil to cause death and destruction among their neighbors. Usually – though not always – their accusers were men whose family experienced tragedy, such as the loss of a wife, child, or livestock. As agricultural, economic, and demographic crises mounted in the late Elizabethan and early Stuart period, poor women in need of charity or widows who refused to remarry or sell their land found themselves especially vulnerable to accusation, prosecution, and execution. A harsh comment about male privilege or patriarchal church teachings or the utterance of a curse or swear in the presence of witnesses could also lead to this outcome.

It did not help matters that James I styled himself an expert in the discovery of the dark arts and

wrote the *Daemonologie* (1597), which highlighted the disorder that witches wreaked on society. This viewpoint conformed to earlier English legislation against witchcraft, passed in 1542 and 1563, and strongly informed the language of the frequently used Act against Conjuration, Witchcraft, and Dealing with Evil and Wicked Spirits of 1604. The latter act led to a witchcraft craze in the seventeenth century, especially under the prosecution of "Witchfinder-General" Matthew Hopkins during the height of persecutions in the mid-1640s.

In the standard narrative, witches forsook God and consorted with the Devil, who entered into a covenant written in the witches' own blood and suckled from them. This suckling was typically done by a "familiar," often a cat, on a "third nipple," a blemish that was commonly sought on the witch's body as proof of her consortium. Once the covenant had been consummated, the Devil arranged vengeance on the witch's behalf. This was essential in demonstrating *maleficium*, or using witchcraft for evil deeds, which was an element that needed to be proven at trial to secure a conviction. Another key means of determining whether a woman was a witch was to subject her to a "trial

Figure 10.1 *Testing the Sutton Witches, from* Witches Apprehended, *1613.*

Credit: Lebrecht Music & Arts/Alamy Stock Photo.

by water." This involved placing a rope around her waist or feet and thrusting her into the water. If she floated, she was guilty because it meant that God had rejected receiving the witch into the water, which was a symbol of baptism and a belief in Jesus Christ. If she sank, she was accepted by God and acquitted, in which case the rope was used to haul her out before she drowned. Other means of coercion, including more severe forms of torture, could be used to secure a confession.

These methods were employed when, in 1612, Mother Sutton and her daughter, Mary, found themselves accused of witchcraft (see Figure 10.1). A poor, widowed woman, Mother Sutton was given a job as the town hog-keeper as an act of charity. Although her charges often succumbed to miscarriages, "staggerings, frenzies, and other diseases," to the impoverishment of their owners, she was allowed to continue in these duties for twenty years.[1] Her daughter Mary was held to be a lewd woman, who had three bastard children, one of whom was her troublesome son, Henry. Neither

of these failings, in themselves, was sufficient to warrant an accusation of witchcraft until Mother Sutton became an enemy of a gentleman, Master Enger. One day, after a heated argument, Mother Sutton vocally vowed revenge against Enger. Soon after, his horses were found dead in his stable, with no explanation as to the cause of their deaths. Next, Enger's hogs, after eating meat served by Sutton, fell "mad and violently ill," and dozens of them ran over a dam and drowned themselves, to Enger's considerable financial loss. On another occasion, as one of Enger's servants – while he had been discussing the Suttons with a friend – was struck on the breast with a beetle, which caused him to fall into a temporary trance.

As he recovered at Enger's home, the servant claimed he saw Mary Sutton enter his room through a window. She sat at the end of his bed knitting, stared into his face, and eventually offered to go to bed with him so that his health could be restored. By "divine assistance," the servant was able to repulse Mary and upbraid her for her

---

1   This story is recounted in Anonymous, *Witches Apprehended, Examined, and Executed, for Notable Villainies by Them Committed* (London, 1613).

abominable life before she departed back through the window. When Master Enger confronted Mary about the incident, she denied it and refused to meet with the servant to hear his tale, whereupon Enger violently placed Mary on horseback and brought her to his house. Forced to be at the servant's bedside, Mary allegedly touched the sick man's neck with her finger and departed, causing him to become violently ill.

When Enger's seven-year-old son, who was well familiar with these events, saw Mother Sutton at the town mill, he flung stones at her and called her a witch. This prompted mother and daughter to call on their familiars, two spirits named Dick and Jude, which suckled from marks on their thighs while the women gave instructions for the torment of Enger's son. This torture soon resulted in his death: "For his tender and unripe age was so enfeebled and made weak by that devilish infliction of extremity as in five days, not able longer to endure them, death gave end to his perplexities." The boy's death was the last straw for Master Enger: he quickly gathered other men of the community, found Mary Sutton, beat her senseless with a cudgel, brought her to the dam, bound her thumbs and toes together, and threw her into the water, where she floated.

The women of the community then searched Mary's body for the Devil's mark, and discovered it on her left thigh. Mary and her mother were detained and bound for trial, where Enger and other members of the community testified to a long list of grievances against the Suttons. They were also betrayed by Mary's son, Henry, who exposed their plans to torment the boy and confessed to his mother's covenant with the Devil's familiars. Both mother and daughter were convicted of witchcraft and executed the following day, probably by being hanged at the gallows, as this was the common punishment for witches unless they were also found guilty of petty treason.

The Suttons fell perfectly into the stereotype of the vengeful witch. They were contentious and quarrelsome women, loose in tongues and morals, financial and social scourges on the community, and easy targets to explain misfortunes such as sickness and death, especially those of an elderly servant or an innocent child. Interestingly, it was not uncommon for women to confess to their consortium with the Devil and to the various cases of *maleficium* they were accused of committing, often without any coercion or torture. This was possibly because many confessed and convicted witches were not, in fact, executed, although their trials and tribulations served the key purpose of restoring them to the boundaries of behavior demanded by an orderly society. It might also have been because the popular belief system at this time supported the existence of witches and the idea that unexplainable events had supernatural causes.

* * *

Discussion Question 10.1: The peak of witchcraft persecutions in English history occurred between about 1560 and 1650. Based on evidence provided in earlier chapters, what reasons might account for this?

Elite Culture

The wealth, privilege, and title of aristocrats in early modern England – roughly defined as those of gentleman rank and above – meant that they often lived quite separate lives from commoners, who were those of artisanal and yeoman rank and below. We must, however, be careful when making such a clear distinction, as there were various factors that also determined a person's lifestyle and culture, including whether they lived in the countryside or the towns, gender, age, and personal circumstances. In addition, the income and material wealth of elites varied considerably during this period, with the fortunes of noble and gentry families rising and falling, based on the monarchs' pleasure and willingness to bestow or revoke honors; investment strategies and other unpredictable economic ventures, such as overseas trade, which could lead to enrichment or ruin; and when they lived during these complicated two centuries.

Established noble families held thousands of acres of land and earned a considerable income from rents and fees associated with their titles, offices, monopolies, and royal grants. Their annual income averaged about £3,000, though some earned several times that much and some considerably less. In addition to their annual incomes, many noble families possessed thousands of pounds in material wealth due to generations of inheritances. These few noble families, numbering forty to sixty between 1485 and 1690, usually owned two or more homes. One was a townhouse in London or another large city that was used when parliament was in session, when court protocol or their offices demanded their presence, or when business affairs so required. The other home was their county seat, or "country house." This was usually a large, multi-winged, multi-storied home with a central courtyard and several outbuildings.

The income of spiritual lords was less than that of their temporal counterparts, about £1,300 per year (the archbishops, however, typically made many times that amount), from tithes, services provided to parishioners, and rent collected from tenants who lived on church land. They lived in elaborate palaces that were owned by the church and were put at the bishops' disposal during their terms of episcopacy (usually for life), and they generally had less personal material wealth than the temporal nobility. The dozens of rooms in noble homes – whether country houses or bishops' palaces – included bed chambers (with four-poster beds), "stool" rooms (toilets), dining halls, entertainment parlors, chapels, beer and wine cellars, kitchens, and pantries and cold rooms.

Gentlemen (baronets, knights, esquires, and untitled gentry) and professionals (including physicians, lawyers, merchants, and wealthier clergymen, for example) possessed less land – ranging from a small plot in town to hundreds of acres in the country – and material wealth and had smaller, though still generous, incomes ranging from perhaps £150 to more than £1,000 per year from rents, fees, salaries, offices, or investments. Although this income was more modest than that of the average nobleman (yet greater than that of some poor lords), it was still enough to allow a gentleman to live in a townhouse or country house comprising two or three floors and many rooms.

Although their incomes could vary quite a bit, nobles and gentlemen had sufficient resources to employ a dozen or more (and in some cases a hundred or more) servants. These might include stewards, valets, tutors, cooks, maids, footmen, grooms, and kitchen boys, who provided for the needs of the lord and his family. Some of these were menial servants, living in a garret (attic) or a separate wing of the house or in outbuildings, while others were retainers, who arrived at the home each morning and left each evening. Supplementing their ranks were large numbers of groundskeepers and field laborers, who maintained the manor and common lands – known as demesne land – that was not rented to tenants.

Aristocratic residences were used as places of business, where affairs of the estate were managed, and also places of pleasure, such as during hunting season and holidays. Within these aristocratic homes, consistent with the wealth of their patron, artists, craftsmen, and architects were employed to build ornate fireplaces, furniture, and woodwork. Elite families filled their homes with tapestries, porcelain, books, and artwork from throughout Europe, all as visible signs of their owners' wealth and status within society. This was particularly important when the monarch and his or her courtiers arrived during the annual progress through the countryside, when the aristocrat was expected to offer exquisite food and entertainment that could cost thousands of pounds for a few days of activities. It was also not unusual for nobles and members of the gentry order to own a hunting cottage, which was usually more rustic and modest than their other residences, and to lend it to members of the court or other aristocrats on occasion.

The nobility and gentry were also able to dress the part. Clothing was immensely expensive, custom-fitted, and hand-tailored at this time, but the wealthiest people in society could purchase a wide range of apparel for different occasions. They could purchase silk, satin, and velvet cloth laced with gold and silver, lined with fur, and painstakingly embroidered. Men wore fine jackets, doublets, hose (to show off their legs), garters, gloves, robes, ruffs (elaborate collars), purses, swords, and hats. Women wore thick gowns, bodices (close-fitting jackets), sleeves, and skirts, which were pieced together with pins to allow their wardrobe to be mixed-and-matched, and accessorized with jewelry and lace. Many of the materials for these various pieces of apparel were purchased from merchants who brought them from Persia or other parts of Europe. According to the sumptuary laws, some of these items of clothing could only be worn by individuals of certain ranks or who earned at least £200 per year. This made aristocrats instantly visible in society and also ensured that those of lesser fortunes did not impoverish themselves and their families by dressing above their means.

Although aristocrats were often required to carry out various administrative and occasionally military duties associated with their ranks – sitting in parliament or as justices of the peace or lords lieutenant, for example – there was also ample time to partake of leisure activities. Depending on the time of year, during the day elites would engage in lawn bowling, shuttlecock, tennis, horse- and dog-racing, and hunting large game (deer), fowl (partridge, pheasant, and quail), and other animals (such as rabbits and foxes). The Tudor recovery of chivalric games, often organized into competitive tournaments, served as forms of entertainment and exercise. The events included jousting, wrestling, sword-fighting, and archery using the longbow, culminating in the naming of a tournament champion. Although most of these activities were once part of an aristocrat's preparation for military command, they had long since become defunct in battle, but were, nonetheless, considered necessary training for elite young men. In the evenings, aristocrats moved indoors for gambling, masques, music, reading, jesting, and playing board games, such as chess, draughts, and backgammon. Many of these outdoor and indoor activities were attuned to male interests, but elite women also became involved as supporters and participants and had their own forms of cultural expression as well, such as fine needlework, letter writing, and paying visits to friends and acquaintances.

The diet of elites also reflected their position in society. Wealthy people ate meat (venison, beef, pork, lamb, mutton, and poultry), seafood (especially during certain religious observances, or "fish days"), and fine-milled white bread and fresh cheese daily. They drank copious amounts of spirits, wine (or "sack"), and beer and often consumed fruit only in the form of sugary desserts such as pastries, puddings, and tarts. Elites also had the means to acquire and consume the various luxury products that increasingly became available as empire and trade expanded during the early modern period. Wine, olives, tobacco, sugar, coffee, chocolate, and spices from the Americas, Europe, Indonesia, and South Asia became regular dietary items. Often lacking in the elite diet were legumes and vegetables, in part because of the ready availability of other foodstuffs and also because of the perception that root vegetables – turnips, carrots, radishes, and gourds – were too base for elite palates because they grew too near the ground. As a result, elite diets were lacking in key vitamins and nutrients that often led to ailments such as gout, anaemia, rickets, bladder stones, blindness, gum disease, and rotten teeth.

Common Culture

Like aristocrats, the ranks of commoners were varied and factors such as income, location, gender, inheritance, and reputation also dictated their lifestyle. Toward the top of the social scale of commoners, artisans, yeoman, lesser members of the clergy, and some lower-earning professionals (such as teachers and shopkeepers) might earn £40 to £80 per year. The income of artisans came from the products they created from their trade, which began after many years of hands-on training. Yeomen farmed their land, growing crops such as wheat, barley, rye, and oats, or they raised livestock, which was either let out in the morning to graze in common fields and herded back into pens at night or, in the case of poultry, kept in coops on the farm. This livestock was sheared for wool (sheep), fattened for slaughter (cows, pigs, and chickens), or raised for their by-products, such as eggs and milk, which was turned into cheese and butter. In addition to their annual income, wealthy commoners might possess another £50 to £100 in chattel property, which they could pass on to their children as inheritances.

Although the income of artisans and yeoman was not substantial, it was sufficient to permit ownership of plaster- and wood-constructed homes – the famous "Tudor style" home was common among this rank – consisting of several rooms, two or three fireplaces, wooden floors, and some luxuries, such as multiple sets of good clothes, some books, cupboards, pots and pans, pewter cutlery, linens, wooden tables, chairs, and beds with straw mattresses. These wealthier commoners could also afford to employ several servants to help in the home and around the farm. Meat of a lesser quality than the elites ate (boiled feet, knuckles, hocks, jowls, and bacon) could be consumed on most days, which was supplemented with beer, wheat or rye bread, eggs, cheese, nuts and fruits from their orchards, and leafy greens and root vegetables grown on a parcel of land set aside for the household's personal use. Barring the onset of disease or famine during lean years, wealthy commoners lived a comfortable lifestyle and ate a well-balanced diet similar to that with which we are familiar today.

The situation was rather different for those lower on the social scale, who, according to Gregory King in his famous population study for the year 1688, composed some 60 to 70 per cent of society.[2] Cottagers, who rented homes and farmed small parcels of land, and laborers, who worked on somebody else's land, lived in small, thatched (straw- or sod-covered), plaster or wooden one- or two-room cottages with clay or dirt floors and a single fireplace dedicated to both heating and cooking. The entire family, including possibly a young female servant, slept on bundles of straw or hammocks around the fireplace, perhaps with curtains to protect the privacy of the master and mistress of the house. Farm animals (sheep or chickens, for example) sometimes also slept inside, for warmth. The sleeping arrangements were gathered up and set aside during the day to allow for full use of the common space for other activities. Soldiers and sailors, who also composed this group, often did not have fixed places of residence, and billeted at inns, barns, tented communities or with other families when they were not at sea or on campaign, which was also true of itinerant journeymen, peddlers, performers, and seasonal field workers.

With an annual income of perhaps £2 to £15, these commoners lived a subsistence lifestyle and possessed few things beyond a second set of poor-quality, often homemade and frequently mended clothes, a small wooden table, a couple

---

2 King estimated that in 1688 the English population was about 5,500,000 people, of whom about 3,500,000 (around 65 per cent) belonged to this poorer group. A century earlier, when agricultural crisis and plague loomed large, and before trade and empire triggered economic growth, it was closer to 80 per cent.

of benches, basic tools for cooking and cleaning, and perhaps a modest spinning wheel for piecework to help bring in extra money. Meat was a luxury few could afford, and "small beer," cheese, coarse bread prepared in communal ovens, foraged berries, and porridges, stews, and soups made from cereals or legumes produced in a tiny kitchen garden made up the bulk of their rather monotonous diet.[3] When meat was available, this was usually internal organs – liver, kidney, and other parts of the animal that butchers could not sell to wealthier customers – which were chopped or ground and stuffed into sausage skins, or baked or boiled into savory pies and puddings.

Commoners took part in entertainment that was sometimes more productive than that of wealthy elites. When they were not working in the fields, trades, or in service, they might participate in ploughing contests, which were competitive and enjoyable but also resulted in a farmer's field being made ready for planting. They took part in barn raisings and quilting bees, in which the men spent the day building a barn and the women produced a quilt, while their children played in nearby fields or rivers. The entire community then assembled for meals, with each family contributing. Families went to market and fairs together to transact business, meet with neighbors, watch executions and shaming rituals, see traveling troupes, and play games, such as intervillage football contests. In the evening, men (and sometimes women) went to alehouses, where they sang ballads and bawdy songs, gambled (on cards, dice, cockfighting, and similarly rough activities), and listened to popular books being read by the semiliterate. Commoners played board games at the pub or at home before the daylight was lost. Candles and oil were a luxury, so darkness usually signaled that it was time to retire for the night.

The common folk were also the primary participants during days of celebration, which were surprisingly numerous in early modern England. Religious holidays included Twelfth Night and Epiphany (January), Candlemas and Valentine's Day (February), Lady Day (March 25 – the new year), Easter, Michaelmas (September), All Saints' Day (November 1, with the day before being All Hallow's Eve), Christmas, and all Sundays. England also had several holidays relating to the agricultural cycle, including Saturnalia (January 1), May Day, Midsummer (June 21), and Harvest Day. Finally, there were several days of national memory, such as Coronation Day and the Royal Birthday (which changed for each monarch), St. George's Day (April 23, to celebrate England's patron saint), and days that

---

3   Water was not usually a beverage of choice, in part because it provided no calories and also because, owing to poor sanitary conditions, it was often contaminated and caused illness. Although milk was used to produce cheese and butter, it was not deemed a suitable drink for anyone except very young children, for whom it was used to soften bread. "Small beer" had a briefer brewing period than regular beer and was consequently lower in alcohol, making it suitable for children and also less expensive.

celebrated the defeat of the Spanish Armada (July 29), the Gunpowder Plot (November 5), and Charles II's escape from parliamentary soldiers in 1651 (Royal Oak Day, May 29). These were all days in which "bodily labor" was set aside and replaced with solemn worship or entertainment.

These days of celebration were among the few occasions when elite and common culture combined. Elites celebrated with commoners, especially during religious observances, but they were more conservative and provided the means of celebration, such as food and drink. During these occasions, commoners celebrated loudly and liberally through dancing, bell ringing, burning effigies, and enjoying whatever was given to them by the aristocrats. They could enjoy the spirits and wines, meat and fish, and puddings and pies that most were denied in their own homes. Especially on celebration days associated with pagan rituals (Saturnalia and May Day), elites often tolerated significant degrees of disorder, with the understanding that this provided a social safety valve, a way for the commoners to blow off steam and then return willingly and peacefully to a state of orderliness in which the great chain of being and the patriarchal-deferential relationship were restored until another occasion for revelry arrived.

At the very bottom of the scale were the sturdy beggars, who earned no income beyond that which they could get from begging, which might provide an evening meal and a corner of a barn to spend the night in, sometimes in exchange for a day's labor. Otherwise, they slept under bridges or in hastily erected tents and lean-tos at the river edge or in common fields, scavenged for rags for clothing and scraps of food, went perpetually undernourished, and lived the bleakest of existences in early modern England, officially unrecognized even by the poorest of laborers. Among this lowly group were occasional bands of thieves, who traveled the countryside, stole from the wealthy, and were much feared by propertied English people (see *Voices of the Past*: **The Wealthy Yeoman and the Tragical Midwife**).

* * *

Discussion Question 10.2: What problems are caused by the use of the terms "elite" and "common" (or "popular") to describe English culture at this time? Can you think of better terms?

Art and Literature

Following the reception of humanism in England in the early sixteenth century, and the significant increase in the use of the printing press after about 1560, England achieved a tremendous outpouring of artistic and literary works that remain important to the present day. In artwork, painting was the primary medium, which involved artists – mostly foreign-born men invited to England – being patronized by monarchs and nobles to produce depictions of important religious scenes, and also portraits of patrons and their families for posterity. Hans Holbein the Younger (1497–1543), for example, produced portraits of Henry VIII, Desiderius Erasmus, Thomas More and his daughter Margaret, in addition to numerous other aristocrats, diplomats, and scholars. Nicholas Hilliard (1547–1619), Isaac Oliver (1565–1617), Peter Paul Rubens (1577–1641) and Anthony van Dyck (1599–1641) produced many noble portraits, including well-known depictions of Elizabeth I and the members of the early Stuart royal family, both in full-scale and in miniature. These works were notable not only for their detail and realism, but also for their displays of mundane scenes and the natural world that reflected broader European approaches to Renaissance art. Naturally, the common orders rarely saw or had the opportunity to become part of this artistic culture.

Architecture also saw major advancements during this period and was likewise heavily influenced by the European Renaissance. Monarchs such as Henry VIII built or improved several key royal palaces, such as Hampton Court, which, first built by Cardinal Wolsey as a display of power, developed into a modern Renaissance palace. Although Henry's children were somewhat more parsimonious, James I employed the architect Inigo Jones (1573–1652) to expand Whitehall Palace with the addition of Banqueting House, which still stands, and to improve Greenwich's Queen's House. Wealthy aristocrats followed suit throughout the sixteenth and seventeenth centuries, which saw the erection of stone and brick edifices such as Burghley House, built by William Cecil, and other grand country houses. After the Great Fire of London in 1666, Christopher Wren (1632–1723) was employed by Charles II to rebuild the city, such that his influence is still evident in dozens of domed churches, including St. Paul's Cathedral. As mentioned earlier, the elite also employed artists, architects, and craftsmen to create ornate marble and wood artifacts within their homes as visible signs of their wealth.

Beginning in the Elizabethan era, England also saw the rise of the theater, which was performed by men in London's playhouses, the courtyards and parlor rooms of monarchs and aristocrats, and in town squares by traveling troupes. Christopher Marlowe's (1564–93) *Dr. Faustus* was wildly successful, as were the plays of Ben Jonson (1572–1637), Thomas Dekker (1572–1632), William Davenant (1606–68), and others. Chief among these playwrights, of course, was William Shakespeare (1564–1616), who operated in the company of the Lord Chamberlain's Men and whose works were performed in The Globe theater and other locales. Shakespeare wrote a total of thirty-seven plays, many still well known and performed today. They covered several genres, including histories, tragedies, and comedies, the latter often deeply allegorical and containing supernatural characters. The popularity of the theater, which struggled during times of radical reformation and plague, was owed to its large, multi-classed audience. Elites and commoners alike flocked to new productions, the former sitting on cushions around the covered outer edge within the theater and the latter standing as "groundlings" in the open space in front of the stage.

The theaters and parlor rooms of elites also showcased the various forms of musical expression and dance in early modern England. Traditional choir songs and *a cappella* madrigals were supplemented with music performed on lutes (small stringed instruments), viols (early violins), virginals, and organs to accompany dancers at balls, emphasize dramatic moments on stage, and offer entertainment before the show and between acts. This period saw the rise of numerous composers, such as Orlando Gibbons (1583–1625), keyboardist in the privy chamber of Charles I and organist at Westminster Abbey, and Thomas Campion (1567–1620), who wrote more than one hundred songs for the lute and madrigal. In elite homes, theatrical and musical expression often came in the form of masques, many produced by Inigo Jones, which involved masqueraded players, often the wealthy themselves, dancing and performing for their friends and guests. Indeed, the ability to play music, dance, and perform was considered a sign of noble status and proper breeding, and a perfectly suitable evening pastime for England's elite.

The plays of Shakespeare were first published by John Heminges and Henry Condell in 1623, thus placing them into the canon of literature as well as theater. Their publication came during England's print revolution, which saw the production of many other important works of politics, religion, and poetry. Some of this literature has already been discussed throughout this book, such as Thomas More's *Utopia*, John Foxe's *Acts and Monuments*, Edmund Spenser's *The Fairie Queene*, James I's *Trew Law of Free Monarchies*, the *King James Bible*, Thomas Hobbes's *Leviathan*, Charles I's *Eikon Basilike*, and John Locke's *Two Treatises on Government*. All of these were important works that continue to be read today.

To this list can also be added Desiderius Erasmus's *Praise of Folly*, Christopher Saxton's *Atlas of the Counties of England and Wales*, Richard Hakluyt's *Principal Navigations*, John Speed's *Theatre of the Empire of Great Britain*, Edward Coke's *Institutes of the Lawes of England*, John Milton's *Paradise Lost*, *The Proceedings of the Old Bailey* (which provided details about London crime), and the poetry of Shakespeare, Robert Herrick, John Donne, and Andrew Marvell, which often reflected the *carpe diem* theme discussed in the next chapter. These works were written by and for elite, educated audiences, who, as we have seen, could afford multi-volume, expensive copies to have leather bound, imprinted with their coat of arms, and added to their expanding libraries. In the late Elizabethan period, for example, John Dee's personal library was the largest in all of England, and Robert Cotton's library in the early Stuart age included a huge number of manuscripts. Both of their expansive collections still exist in major English archives and research libraries.

From the 1580s, popular literature was published for semiliterate and even illiterate audiences, who would have the work recited to them in pubs or town squares. Pamphlets on various subjects, almanacs of use to farmers, broadsides advertising national news, and ballads written to be performed to a familiar tune, all became common genres of literature during this period. This literature was typically sold by traveling peddlers to poor, rural audiences, and was consequently poorly printed, unbound, inexpensive, and disposable, likely turned into pie-plate liners, pipe starters, and "bum paper" soon after their consumption. Their themes were less overtly political or ideological than elite literature and focused on topics such as satire, astrology, witchcraft, crime, mocking wives, cuckolded husbands, ribaldry, and scatology. Straddling elite and popular literature were the various conduct books discussed in Chapter Nine. William Perkins's *An Exhortation Concerning Good Order and Obedience to Rulers and Magistrates* and Phillip Stubbes's *Crystal Glass for Christian Women*, for example, appealed to both elite and common audiences, because both were involved in maintaining the patriarchal and deferential order.

* * *

Discussion Question 10.3: Based on discussions in earlier chapters, what conditions existed in England that allowed or encouraged such a high degree of artistic and literary expression?

Popular Belief Systems

As we have seen in previous chapters, the people of early modern England were devoutly religious and believed in a literal interpretation of the Bible. They accepted on faith and were taught by the church that God and the Devil were providential beings who were directly involved in human affairs, that prayer could bring about tangible outcomes – health, prosperity, good harvests, and healthy children, for example – and that ordained churchmen had special capacities that enabled them to answer complex moral questions, a practice known as casuistry. The Devil, it was believed, acted to thwart God's laws and man's free will, often working through witches, such as the Suttons discussed earlier. Elites and commoners alike also believed that there was much that was unknown about the world and that mankind's ignorance was part of God's plan. This is why the popular belief system was commonly referred to as a branch of "natural philosophy" rather than science.

In the absence of more advanced scientific knowledge, the ability to explain misfortunes and the unknown usually involved resorting to explanations that leaned toward magic, the supernatural, and the common early modern quest for order and balance in all things. Especially in the sixteenth century, many accepted the notion of the "corresponding planes" of the macrocosm and the microcosm. Such planes included, for example, the superlunary and sublunary spheres (that which was above the moon – the cosmos – and that which was below the moon – Earth), Heaven and Earth, angels and man, the spiritual and the physical, and several others. In theory, the macrocosm was always more perfect, and thus the ability to understand and commune with the macrocosm could help to explain the microcosm and bring it to greater perfection.

The people who communed with the macrocosm were known as magi, or "cunning" men and women, who professed the ability to understand and manipulate the natural world. Cunning people were highly valued members of Tudor society, because they could offer answers when the contemporary limitations of science failed to do so. For a small sum of money, they could ward off evil, discover lost or stolen property, divine for water, predict the weather, conjure dead spirits, make aphrodisiacs, interpret portents (omens, signs, and dreams) to offer warnings or predictions, and promote health and healing. Regarding the latter, they used practices such as encouraging the sick to eat eggs boiled in their own urine, burning contaminated clothing, placing herbs or charms on doors or windowsills, reading palms (palmistry) and heads (physiognomy), giving blessings, and reciting chants and invocations (magic spells). Most of these methods were harmless, and positive outcomes were more likely related to giving the body time to heal, good detective work, or life experience, but their misapplication – such as the uttering of a curse or an unexpected outcome from a seemingly overt act of magic – could lead to accusations of witchcraft against cunning practitioners.

Although there were hundreds of magi in early modern England, perhaps the most famous of them was John Dee, Queen Elizabeth's court magician, who straddled the world of magic and emerging notions of science. Drawing on classical thinkers such as Aristotle, Plato, Ptolemy, and Pythagoras and using techniques such as geometry, astrology, alchemy, and theurgy,[4] Dee communed with the macrocosm to explain the microcosm. To do so, he relied on various tools, such as scrying stones (black mirrors and crystal balls) and mathematical tables and charts, methods that he learned from another famous magus (and conman), Edward Kelly. A vastly learned Renaissance polymath – we have already seen his contributions to English exploration – Dee used astrology, for example, to determine the best date for Elizabeth's coronation, in order to ensure a long and happy rule. He and Kelly also recorded numerous enigmatic conversations with

---

4   This is "divine magic," used by cunning people, as opposed to "black magic," used by witches and others who had evil intent.

angels, which provided guidance on understanding and perfecting man and the natural world.

As the Protestant Reformation wore on in the Tudor age, activities such as sorcery, enchanting, and invocations – particularly those not endorsed by the clergy – were explicitly forbidden by parliamentary legislation, signaling what Keith Thomas has referred to as the "decline of magic" and also the rise of witchcraft prosecutions. Nonetheless, as Dee's participation testifies, these forms of popular belief continued to be accepted, and not only among the poor and uneducated. Even in the post-Reformation world, when certain magical elements, such as the veneration of icons and transubstantiation, were dismissed by the English church as excessively superstitious, elites and commoners continued to accept as fact the existence of ghosts, fairies, demons, and witches. The ghost in Shakespeare's *Hamlet* and the fairies in *A Midsummer Night's Dream* were perfectly believable to contemporary audiences. This society also accepted the king's ability to heal scrofula, a form of tuberculosis, by his mere touch. Magistrates often brought suspected killers into the presence of their victims to see if the corpse would accuse its murderer through spontaneous bleeding, a practice known as cruentation. As these examples demonstrate, despite certain religious teachings and state interventions, many English people remained highly superstitious and accepted supernatural causation when faced with the unknown.

A related popular belief, also emerging from the recovery of classical ideas during the rise of humanism, was that the universe was interrelated and balanced (or organic), and that all matter consisted of five elements – earth, water, air, fire, and ether – in proper proportion according to its properties. This belief, supported by the church, upheld Ptolemy's geocentric universe, in which the Earth, consisting primarily of the heavy elements of earth and water, was in a fixed, central position in the universe around which all other celestial spheres – planets, the sun, and Heaven – revolved, in the perfect orderliness expected of their superlunary, macrocosmic position. Galen's medical theory of humoralism, in which the body consisted of four elements (blood, yellow bile, black bile, and phlegm), was also based on the idea of balance and order. Humors were supposed to exist in proper proportions within the liver, gallbladder, spleen, and lungs. Illness, disease, and temperament (sanguine, choleric, melancholic, and phlegmatic) were believed to be the result of an imbalance that could be cured through treatments such as sweating, purging, blood-letting, leeching, and the application of salves and poultices designed to draw toxins from the body. Ben Jonson's plays *Every Man in His Humour* (1598) and the lesser-known *Every Man out of His Humour* (1599) are based on the idea that the humoral theory determined an individual's temperament. It is, perhaps, little wonder that Tudor physicians were incapable of dealing effectively with outbreaks of plague, forcing people to turn instead to cunning men such as Dee. Despite numerous scientific advancements, these popular beliefs survived well into the seventeenth century.

Scientific Advancements

By the mid-Elizabethan period, elements of the scientific revolution began to be seen in England and offered, if not a completely new understanding of the world, some competing ideas. For example, Henry Billingsley (with the help of Dee), Thomas Digges, and Robert Recorde produced major works on geometry and mathematics. In *Prognostication Everlasting* (1576), Digges supported Nicolaus Copernicus's controversial – and, as of that time, unproven – theory of heliocentrism, the belief that the Earth revolved around the Sun, which was in a fixed position in the universe. In *The Jewell House* (1594), Hugh Plat argued that inquiry into nature must be grounded in practice and experience, an early articulation of scientific method. Another leading advocate of changes to the scientific method was Francis Bacon. In *Gesta Grayorum* (1594), Bacon proposed the building of a scientific institution founded on principles of rationality. He further developed this notion in his utopian adventure *New Atlantis* (published posthumously in 1627), which describes an institution – Saloman's House – dedicated to the scientific understanding of nature. Bacon also wrote *Novum organum scientiarum* ("New Instrument of Science," 1620), in which he criticized the older methods of syllogistic logic developed by Aristotle and advocated by neo-Platonists, and instead argued for the use of inductive reasoning, a form of empiricism grounded in observation and experimentation. This practice is now known as the "Baconian method."

Supported by Bacon's method, the seventeenth century also saw major advancements in astronomy, chemistry, medicine, and physics. Robert Hooke (1635–1703) and Edmund Halley (1656–1742) invented various techniques using a telescope and learned how to predict phenomena such as solar eclipses and the paths of comets. The commissioning of the Royal Observatory in 1675 provided additional support for these efforts. Robert Boyle (1627–91) proposed that there were numerous elements in nature, rather than the Aristotelian belief that there were only five, and used the scientific method to discover the laws of gas and pressure. Similarly, William Harvey (1578–1657) discovered the circulation of the blood and included numerous drawings in his *Exercitatio Anatomica* (1628) that came into direct conflict with Galen's humoral theory and initiated a wave of new medical literature and the beginnings of dissection of corpses. Harvey was also highly skeptical of the existence of witchcraft and his involvement in a 1634 trial resulted in the acquittal of four women and helped lead to the decline of witchcraft (notwithstanding a brief, powerful resurgence in the 1640s).

The most important early modern English advancements in the scientific revolution are to be found in the works of Isaac Newton (1643–1727) and John Locke (1632–1704). Newton conducted experiments and discovered the laws of motion and gravity, which were published in his *Principia Mathematica* (1687), giving rise to modern physics. One of the major implications of Newton's discoveries was that the universe worked according to fixed and discoverable laws, and, therefore, while God was responsible for creating the world and setting it in motion, it thereafter worked – like a perpetually wound watch – in predictable orderliness. This challenged the church's teachings about God's providence, the efficacy of prayer, and the literal interpretation of the Bible. Newton was also a central figure, and later president, of the Royal Society, a scientific institution established by Charles II in 1660 along the lines of Bacon's proposals. Boyle, Hooke, and other leading members of the scientific revolution were also members of the Society.

Locke, who as we have seen was also the author of the *Two Treatises on Government*, contributed to a different branch of inquiry and became a founder of modern social sciences. In particular, in *Essay Concerning Human Understanding* (1690) and *Thoughts Concerning Education* (1693), Locke speculated that humans were born with a *tabula rasa* – an empty mind – and did not possess innate knowledge. Instead, their knowledge was determined by their experiences, as exemplified especially by their education. As might be imagined in a society that believed aristocrats and gentleman were natural leaders of men because of their inborn capacity to govern, Locke's notion that all people were born equal in knowledge and that nurture, rather than nature, determined their abilities was met with resistance. This notion became, however, along with Newton's concept of the "watchmaker God," leading tenets of the eighteenth-century European Enlightenment.

Partly because most of the participants of the scientific revolution were members of a highly elite group of intellectuals centered at the universities and in learned societies, it took some time for their various lessons to be known and accepted by the popular masses. The point at which older ideas of natural philosophy gave way to newer ideas associated with the scientific revolution was about the middle of the seventeenth century, although some older notions – such as astrology – remained in use for long afterwards. This beginning of England's "age of enlightenment" corresponds closely, and not coincidentally, with the significant decline of witchcraft persecutions in England after 1650, although they continued in smaller, remote communities until the end of the century. By 1690, England had emerged as a global leader in scientific thought, and most earlier ideas associated with natural philosophy and supernatural causation had witnessed a substantial decline.

* * *

Discussion Question 10.4: Why do you think that popular belief in the supernatural could exist simultaneously with the rise of more advanced scientific knowledge?

VOICES OF THE PAST
THE WEALTHY YEOMAN AND THE TRAGICAL MIDWIFE

Although most people in England were poor and had little worth stealing, perhaps 20 per cent of families possessed enough wealth that they became targets for certain criminal elements within society. The following extract recounts that a hardworking husband and father, his loving wife, and their two children were assaulted by a band of thieves in their own home. After murdering the couple, the gang's leader – a "beastly" woman and "tragical midwife" – took the two children and (although the extract does not recount this part of the story) arranged for them to be murdered by an innkeeper and her son. With the active assistance of God, the girl survived. Even though her tongue had been cut out, she managed to avenge her brother's murder by bringing his killers to justice. The gang, however, remained at large, a reminder to early modern readers of the dangers that surrounded them.

* * *

Some four years since, near Devonshey Hundred in Essex, lived a yeoman, one Anthony James, who in repute of the world was counted rich, and by the report of his neighbors held credible and honest. This man in the desire of his youth matched himself to an honest country maid, whose virtuous disposition equaled his own thoughts, and whose diligent care was carefully to save what her husband brought home, as his labor did strive to procure it abroad. So that the providence of the one and the care of the other mixed such a mutual content between them that they lived like Abraham and Sara: he loving to her, she obedient to him.

In process of time this couple, growing wealthy by their labor, proved to be as happy by their issue for it pleased God to enrich them with two children, a boy and a girl, that the wishes of the father might be as well satisfied as the desire of the mother, and both contented in so comfortable a blessing. The mother being (as women use to say) stored first with a daughter, and called it by her own name Elizabeth James, so that when time brought the father as happy rejoicing of a son, he christened it by his own name, Anthony James. In the education and bringing up of these two children there was a pretty loving contention between the goodman and the wife, which of the two should prove most happy to the parent's delight, whose love indeed was alike to them both. So that time passing away in that comfortable strife between this loving couple, the daughter had attained to the age of eight years and the son to seven. In which passage, the mother having no other issue, was then with child with the third, and the better half of her time had carried so happy a burden.

About that season of the year a fair happened in Essex, to which the servants they then kept (some for pleasure, the rest about necessary business) were sent, so that the honest yeoman with his wife and children were only left at home, when mischief, like a bramble that takes hold on whatsoever it touches, caught this occasion and wrought in the minds of nine, I cannot call them men, but villains and another, not a woman, but a beast to make a prey of these harmless four and their increased possessions....

So these wretches, having fastened on this monstrous intent, made haste to the execution thereof, and so soon had attained to this wealthy yeoman's house, where finding little or no resistance, they first bound the man and the woman, and giving the two children to two of their associates to hold. The rest fell to ransack, where not contenting themselves with that store of riches they found, as gold, silver, plate, rings, and other wealth having made up their pack, they consulted with themselves for their further security to make spoil of the owners. It was not long in question ere this hellish jury had given up as damnable a verdict, for (suspicion always haunting a guilty mind) they determined with themselves they could not be safe from pursuit, from attachment, nay from shameful death which they worthily deserved, without the slaughter of the father and the mother, which they presently resolved upon, and then two of them stepping to the man, where he lay bound upon the ground, with their daggers stabbed him in the body. Who ere [before] his speech left him, lifting up his eyes, begged only this of them: "Take my riches. I cared for them to bring up my posterity, but now they are yours, I give them you freely. Then pity my wife, be merciful to my children."

These, his last words, seemed to beget some remorse (seldom seen) in the men which were murderers, which the more than monstrous woman perceiving (as in a rage threat) stepped to his wife, and calling to him with these words: "Talkest thou of pity," quoth she, "if thy eyes have yet left so much sight to be witness how I'll be pitiful? Behold how I'll perform thy petition." So drawing out her knife (O act too terrible to report, but the most damnablest that ever was heard of executed by a woman), she ripped her up the belly, making herself a tragical midwife, or truly a murderess that

brought an abortive babe to the world and murdered the mother.

The good woman having not leave to cry, and her husband having not the use of speech, they both lift up their hands, rolled their eyes one to another, and with that said, but silent, farewell ever. This tragical spectacle forced all the rest partakers in the robbery and actors in the murder to remorse, nay even to a repentance. That done, this horrible action had a beginning. But sin always seeking securely to shroud itself in, they began now to question of their safety, and (as villains are ever one afraid and in distrust of another) they conclude now to share their purchase and every knave to shift for himself. Some urged, "Let us first kill the children, as we have done their parents." Others, and the greater part, glutted with the present object and even ashamed of themselves and their sinful actions, not only denied, but confidently resolved they would be no further guilty in the blood of innocents. In brief, they agreed every party to have an equal portion of this ill purchased booty, which soon shared amongst them, and as it appeared, having more than they could tell what to do withal, they gave the remain to three of their consorts, of which the woman was one to convey away the children from thence, and bestow them in what place soever while they would give their parents burial.

Source: Anonymous, *The Most Cruell and Bloody Murther Committed by an Inkeepers Wife … and Her Sonne* (London, 1606).

* * *

Discussion Question 10.5: What does this tale, and the specific language used by the author, tell you about English society's obsessions with order and fear of disorder?

CHAPTER ELEVEN

FROM CRADLE TO GRAVE: THE STAGES OF LIFE

DEATH AND DISORDER: MONSTROUS BIRTHS AND MURDEROUS MOTHERS

As might be imagined in a society with frequent bouts of starvation and disease, limited sanitation, minimal understanding of women's reproductive systems, and carefully constructed social norms surrounding pregnancy and legitimacy, the death of infants and toddlers was a common phenomenon. It has been estimated that nearly 30 per cent of children died of disease, illness, disability, neglect, or accident before the age of fifteen and that roughly 15 per cent of babies died during the birth process or within the first year of life. This is not to mention the number of pregnancies that resulted in miscarriage and did not even come to term, which was a far higher percentage. A woman might have been pregnant six to eight times over a period of twenty years, with only two or three children surviving into adolescence.

The frequency of death during childbirth gave rise to a genre of pamphlet literature that described, often in vivid and horrid detail, a wide variety of "monstrous births," such as the delivery of conjoined twins and babies born with missing limbs, caused by genetic abnormalities, malnutrition, and other ailments suffered by the mother or the fetus while in utero. This literature depicting the death of children was used to show the agency of the Devil in the birth process or God's displeasure against certain mothers, communities, and society in general.

Another all-too-common, and highly disorderly, cause of infant death in early modern England was infanticide, or the deliberate act of a mother murdering her child. This commonly involved a single, young woman, often a servant, who had become pregnant as a result of a secret – and often coerced – assignation with the master of the house or one of his sons or male servants. To hide the shame of their nonmarital sexual relations and remain a good prospect for future marriage, women sometimes took extreme measures to terminate their pregnancies, either by using illegal abortifacients or by committing violence upon themselves in the hopes of bringing about a miscarriage.

Others disguised their pregnancies, which was not difficult to do given the style of clothing at the time, and retired to a secret location once the signs of labor revealed themselves, to give birth without anybody's knowledge. After the birth, these "murderous mothers" would kill their babies, through means such as strangulation, blunt force trauma, or drowning, or simply by denying them the necessities of life during the critical first few hours. They would then dispose of the remains in a place they hoped would not lead to discovery, such as an outhouse. Being amateurs in the ways of murder, however, many of these mothers made mistakes that led to their arrest. One of the most famous cases of infanticide was described as yet another monstrous birth: one pamphleteer claimed that, in 1569, twenty-seven-year-old Agnes Bowker gave birth to a cat. In all likelihood, Bowker, possibly with the active assistance of her midwife, murdered the child and substituted a cat for the deceased baby in an attempt to protect herself from prosecution.

Infanticide became such a serious issue in early modern England that the state passed the Act to Prevent the Murdering of Bastard Children, commonly known as the Infanticide Act, in 1624:

> Whereas many lewd women that have been delivered of bastard children, to avoid their shame and to escape punishment, do secretly bury, or conceal the death, of their children, and after if the child be found the said women do allege that the said child was born dead.... For the preventing therefore of this great mischief, be it enacted ... that if any woman ... be delivered of any issue of her body male or female, which being born alive ... and that she endeavour privately either by drowning or secret burying thereof, or any other way, whether it were born alive or not ... conceal the death thereof ... in every such case the mother so offending shall suffer death as in the case of murther.

By this, the mere act of a woman concealing her pregnancy and the death of her child led automatically to the presumption of guilt for homicide. In the absence of witness testimony to the contrary, the courts assumed that the child was born alive and that the mother had murdered it, unless she could otherwise prove that she had made preparations for the child, in the form of gathering linen, clothing, and other baby paraphernalia.

This law gave little consideration to the possibility that the woman might have suffered from postpartum depression or madness – then known as *non compos mentis*, "of unsound mind" – which sometimes led to charges of infanticide against women who were outside of the typical "lewd" or "seduced" woman stereotype. One incident of 1686, for example, involved a happily married woman named Mary Philmore, who took her nine-week-old boy from the arms of his sleeping father and drowned him in a bucket of water. Despite obvious signs of a diminished mental state, Philmore was executed, "a reward due for so unnatural and barbarous a crime, ... to be an example to all such bloody assassins."[1] Although Philmore's baby was not a bastard, nor was its birth secretive, the mere act of a mother murdering her own child was deemed highly disorderly, and only her public death could help to restore order.

* * *

Discussion Question 11.1: Why do you think infanticide was distinguished from regular murder and what does this tell you about women and society in early modern England?

---

1   Anonymous, *A True and Perfect Relation, of a Most Horrid and Bloody Murder Committed by One Philmore's Wife* (London, 1686).

The Stages of Life

In early modern England, the stages of life were expected to be experienced in as orderly a manner as all other aspects of society. Some of these stages were described by William Shakespeare in *As You Like It* (c. 1599):

> All the world's a stage,
> And all the men and women merely players;
> They have their exits and their entrances,
> And one man in his time plays many parts,
> His acts being seven ages. At first, the infant,
> Mewling and puking in the nurse's arms.
> Then the whining schoolboy, with his satchel
> And shining morning face, creeping like snail
> Unwillingly to school. And then the lover,
> Sighing like furnace, with a woeful ballad
> Made to his mistress' eyebrow. Then a soldier,
> Full of strange oaths and bearded like the [leo]pard,
> Jealous in honour, sudden and quick in quarrel,
> Seeking the bubble reputation
> Even in the cannon's mouth. And then the justice,
> In fair round belly with good capon[2] lined,
> With eyes severe and beard of formal cut,
> Full of wise saws and modern instances;
> And so he plays his part. The sixth age shifts
> Into the lean and slippered pantaloon,[3]
> With spectacles on nose and pouch on side;
> His youthful hose, well saved, a world too wide
> For his shrunk shank, and his big manly voice,
> Turning again toward childish treble, pipes
> And whistles in his sound. Last scene of all,
> That ends this strange eventful history,
> Is second childishness and mere oblivion,
> Sans teeth, sans eyes, sans taste, sans everything.

Shakespeare's "seven ages" – infant, schoolboy, lover, soldier, justice, old man, and dying man – speak primarily to a member of the aristocratic order, who had the

---

2 A capon is a castrated rooster considered a delicacy among the elite orders and sometimes depicted as a bribe to justices to improve legal outcomes.

3 A pantaloon is a stock character from the *commedia dell'arte*, a form of theater in early modern Europe. He is an older, wealthy, sometimes widowed, and usually foolish man who has retired from professional life.

greatest likelihood of achieving each of these seven stages and living to become an old man before dying a natural death. As we have become aware throughout this book, not everybody managed to live to a ripe old age.

As with most aspects of this society, the stages of life that an English person might experience were dictated by a large number of factors. These included whether he or she was from a common or elite background, as wealth and rank often resulted in significantly different lives and lifestyles. The stages of life were also based on whether one lived in the rural countryside, as most of society did, or in the urban towns and cities. Occupation, vocation, and education – whether one was a farmer, miner, artisan, professional, or courtier, for example – also dictated how one progressed through life. Finally, men and women had very different roles in this society, and life stages were also dictated to a substantial degree by their gender and their status as married or unmarried adults.

Birth and Infancy

English society divided the first major stage of life, from birth to adulthood, into three key phases, each lasting about seven years. These were infancy (birth to six years old), childhood (or *pueritia*, seven to thirteen), and adolescence (or *pubertas*, fourteen to twenty). Labor and birth were nearly always acts carried out in all-female environments. Once the signs of labor were present, pregnant women were surrounded by those with experience in childbirth, perhaps a grandmother, mother, aunt, married sister, or neighbor. These "gossips" would be joined – and instructed – by a midwife, a woman who had gained experience in the birth process during a two- to three-year apprenticeship under the supervision of a more senior practitioner. Midwives could also be called in for a late-term miscarriage to perform the manual extraction of the fetus. Most births went smoothly, with a typical, head-first delivery, followed by the cutting of the umbilical cord and the delivery of an intact placenta. If a breech position complicated the birth, the midwife was trained to turn the fetus by manipulating the abdomen, and she also had the necessary skills to position the expectant mother's torso to enable the passage of the baby's shoulders and hips. More complicated deliveries that required the use of medical instruments (hooks, forceps, and scalpels), involved calling in a licensed male surgeon,[4] who sometimes caused more harm than good.

---

4   At this time, surgeons were the lower rank of the medical profession. Most were educated through an apprenticeship at a training hospital and often did not possess a university degree. They were referred to as "master," not "doctor," which was reserved for the higher rank, physicians, who ran hospitals and oversaw the work of surgeons. Many surgeons are still referred to as "mister" or "miss" today in the United Kingdom, despite their elevation in status.

During the process of labor and birth, there were numerous situations in which death might occur. From the time of delivery to a few weeks afterwards, the mother might succumb to puerperal sepsis, an infection caused by unclean instruments, careless midwives or surgeons, or the failure to remove the entire placenta. Approximately one in twenty women, including Henry VIII's third wife, Jane Seymour, died in this manner. If the mother died during the delivery, the baby could be physically removed from the uterus, with the strong possibility of causing fatal harm to the child. The traumas of childbirth could also lead to the death of the baby, which could be born still because of suffocation or other complications during the labor and birthing process. If the baby survived the delivery, it might die within minutes, hours, days, or months from a wide variety of potential difficulties, including malformation of the organs, premature arrival, careless delivery, or inadequate postnatal care.

Babies were nursed as long as possible, by mothers in the case of common children and by wet nurses for elite children. Wet nurses were women who had recently been pregnant and were thus able to breastfeed. They were former household servants or tenants who took the child to their own homes and raised them for a period of months or even years, thereby freeing up elite women to carry out the duties associated with their status in society. Breastfeeding was a practical and inexpensive way to provide nutrition for growing infants and was also considered to have a contraceptive effect in the belief that nursing women could not get pregnant.

Children at this stage had few expectations placed upon them. Parents were more concerned to get their children through this delicate stage of life alive and free from lifelong ailments than with instructing them on the finer points of English society. Infants could play with toys, which were purchased for elite children and made for commoners by their parents or kinfolk, and had the opportunity to play children's games with friends and neighbors. They were taught basic manners and politeness, deference to authority, how to address and behave toward their parents, extended family, and other members of society, and the rudiments of Anglican worship. Otherwise, in most cases, children were allowed to be children. In this early stage of life, both boys and girls wore smocks or gowns, such that it is often difficult to determine the gender of young children in much early modern portraiture. This manner of dress was preferred because of the practicalities associated with toilet training. It was also a social construct, as the "breeching" of boys in the next stage of childhood was something of a coming-of-age ritual.

Childhood

In the childhood phase, children began to be dressed as miniature versions of their parents, with boys moving into shirts, waistcoats, breeches, and hose, and girls wearing dresses over their smocks, which became an undergarment, all consistent with the wealth and status of their parents. The expectations for children also rose considerably during this stage. They were required to be obedient and respectful to adults, and especially to men. According to William Gouge in *Of Domesticall Duties* (1622), children were required to love, fear, respect, and obey their parents, stand and remain silent in their presence unless given leave to do otherwise, and refer to them as "father" and "mother." Negative qualities – Gouge lists pride, loquacity, stoutness, indiscretion, stubbornness, rudeness, wantonness, ambition, "erroneous opinion," and "disdainful stateliness" – were to be met with correction. Although parents undoubtedly loved their children, at least according to the standards of the time, they did not overly dote upon them and accepted the need, reinforced by the church, for strict child-rearing. Children needed to be disciplined, typically using strong (though not cruel) physical punishment. There is plenty of evidence that many children were wanted, loved, and cherished by their parents, but it is also clear that some children – stepchildren, orphans, the illegitimate, and the unwanted – were treated with cruelty, neglect, and abuse.

It was also during this phase of childhood that a child's education truly began. Boys began mirroring their father's activities, joining him in the field or in the shop and undertaking tasks that would provide some basic skills and an understanding of male responsibilities. This might involve planting, reaping, herding cattle, fishing, and hunting small game for food, consistent with the abilities of the child and the needs of the family. Likewise, girls would mirror their mothers, taking part in the many activities associated with keeping up an early modern household. This might include preparing food for winter storage, cooking and cleaning, watching after younger children, and undertaking "cottage industry" tasks, such as spinning and sewing. Elite children would also mirror their parents, though often in ways that were different than their less wealthy counterparts. Elite boys, especially if they were first-born sons and heirs to their fathers, were more likely to get involved in estate management, while elite girls would begin training in needlepoint (embroidery), household management, courtly etiquette, and how to live as ladies and gentlewomen. Per their social status, and the fewer expectations of undertaking work, elite children might also partake in youthful forms of entertainment, such as learning to shoot the longbow or taking part in the annual hunt.

This was also the phase in which formal education typically began. Common boys and some girls might be sent to the local parish school, to be taught reading, writing, and arithmetic by clergymen. The curriculum typically involved reading and writing out religious texts or primers prepared for children. Protestant humanists hoped that, at the very least, a child would be educated sufficiently to read the Bible and the *Book of Common Prayer*. But, in reality, how long one stayed in school depended on a number of factors. The children of laborers or lesser farmers, should they be lucky enough to attend the parish classroom at all, were usually removed after gaining very rudimentary skills limited perhaps to the ability to write their own name. Their labor was simply too valuable to waste time with an education that would, for most, not be a useful part of their everyday lives. Children of artisans and yeomen might remain in school longer, possibly for several years, perhaps moving into grammar schools with more advanced curricula taught by university-educated teachers. Typically, boys remained in the classroom longer than girls, explaining why roughly three times as many boys – about 30 per cent – than girls were literate in the early modern period.[5]

The education of elite children was more complete. For a period of years, both sons and daughters would be educated by private tutors who taught – and sometimes lived – in the family home. Their curriculum went beyond basic reading, writing, and arithmetic, moving into subjects associated with the reception of humanism into England in the early sixteenth century: history, classics, ethics, grammar, languages, literature, theology, and politics, drawing on the works of Greek and Roman classical thinkers such as Aristotle and Cicero, and contemporaries such as Thomas More, Desiderius Erasmus, and Roger Ascham, tutor to Princess Elizabeth and the author of *The Scholemaster* (1570). Around the age of ten, elite boys would sometimes be sent to boarding schools, where they would continue their studies while living apart from their parents. A Tudor expansion of educational "endowments," which were designed to provide opportunities to common boys who showed intellectual promise allowed some non-elite boys to attend these "public" schools and rise to high social and governmental positions. Thomas Wolsey and Thomas Cromwell are both excellent examples.

Adolescence and Early Adulthood

Beginning at about age fourteen, children moved into the final phase of their youth. Most common boys (and some girls), sometimes with the exception of those who would inherit their father's land, left their childhood home and entered apprenticeships, while girls (and some boys) entered service. As discussed in Chapter Nine, the Act of Artificers to an extent regulated apprenticeships. Some apprenticeships could be purchased by yeomen families, to place their sons into positions with prominent merchants or master artisans, while others were less desirable and easier to enter. Parents' decisions in this matter were very important, as it was generally expected that once an adolescent entered an apprenticeship, he or she would continue in this trade their whole life. In many cases, children

---

5   Historians usually determine literacy rates based on the ability to write one's name, as it was common at the time for children to be taught reading first, then writing, whereas today both are taught simultaneously.

were expected to follow in their father's trade, which meant apprenticing children to colleagues in the same artisanal guild.

The list of possible apprenticeships was as long and varied as the list of trades in early modern England: ironmongers and farriers (tools and horseshoes); bowyers and fletchers (bows and arrows); gold and silversmiths (jewelry and gilding); glaziers and potters (glass and ceramics); glovers, saddlers, and cobblers (leather goods and shoes); chandlers (candles); armorers (armor, guns, ammunition); weavers, dyers, tanners, and skinners (cloth, tapestries, and furs); carpenters and shipwrights; vintners, brewers, and tapsters (wine and beer makers and merchants); bakers, butchers, and fishmongers; drapers, tailors, seamstresses, milliners, wigmakers (clothes, hats, wigs, and collars); apothecaries (herbs and powders); book producers; and many, many more. Some boys were also apprenticed to farmers and husbandmen to learn the skills of agricultural production and the raising of livestock, important especially for those who would, like their fathers, become field workers.

The period of apprenticeship and service was about seven years (though contracts typically went from year to year), during which the youths often lived in the same household as their master and became subject to his discipline and instruction. In exchange for their labor, youths received room and board, with possibly a token amount of money and a single suit of clothes – new or used – each year. It was expected that the youth would, under these circumstances and in separation from more lenient parents, learn how to become an adult and develop skills that would provide for a good life. The alternative was that girls would lack the skills to become good marriage prospects and that boys would become lazy and defiant and enter a world of delinquency and criminality (see *Voices of the Past*: **The Penitent Death of Thomas Savage**). Often, girls were sent to families within the same village, or one very close by, where they undertook various household chores, including watching younger children, which would provide them with the skills necessary to become wives and mothers one day. More than 50 per cent of early modern households – including many below yeomen status – had domestic servants, a large percentage of whom were adolescent girls, so it was not difficult to find a position. Some of the youths placed into apprenticeships and service were orphans and wards forced to do so by the Elizabethan poor laws.

Again, the situation was different for elites. Girls typically remained at home and continued to develop the skills consistent with their lifestyles. Some were able, under these circumstances, to continue in a formal or semi-formal tutoring relationship, developing additional skills that would make them better conversationalists, hostesses, and marriage prospects. One beneficiary of these conditions was Sir Thomas More's daughter, Margaret, who was lauded as being perhaps the most learned women in sixteenth-century England. Elite boys had several options, based to a certain extent on whether they were inheritors of estates. In such cases, at around fourteen, heirs might attend one of the two English universities – Oxford or Cambridge – but would typically not complete a course of studies, because they would not be required to practice as professionals. After one or two years, these youths might then undertake a tour of Europe to develop knowledge of different cultures and prepare themselves for their lives as lords and gentlemen, and perhaps as diplomats and civil servants. Younger sons of elites, who would need a career to support themselves, often completed their degree and then entered one of four professions: law, the church, medicine, or the military, each of which offered the possibility of advancement through the ranks that was accompanied with greater wealth and status. Some elite children might seek their fortune – and opportunities for land ownership – in other ways, such as traveling across the Atlantic and settling in America or the Caribbean, or becoming a merchant with the Levant or East India Company.

Between the ages of twenty-one and twenty-four, elite young men typically completed their university studies (including post-degree programs) and began their careers, while common men finished their seven-year period of apprenticeship, in which case they began their lives as journeymen, which also lasted about seven years. Although the date of legal maturity was fluid rather than fixed during this period, it is around this age that men, especially, gained a level of independence that might be termed adulthood. Professionals and merchants began building their careers, while journeymen, exercising some geographical mobility in search of work, plied their skills in exchange for money and sometimes board, until they developed artisanal mastery that would enable them to apply for admission into their craft guild, open up their own shop, begin to take apprentices of their own, and develop a level of financial independence that enabled them to start thinking about marriage and family. If there was a war going on, these were the men who might volunteer or be commanded to fight as soldiers. Common young women were likely to remain in service, while elite women remained in the family home, in both cases until marriage.

Sex and Sexuality

As we saw in Chapter Nine, according to church and state doctrine, one purpose of marriage was to preserve the patriarchal structure and orderliness of English society and place women into a position of deference that recognized their inferior position and their need to remain under male authority. But there were other reasons for marriage that better reflected reality and human physiological and psychological needs. Men and women sought romance, love, companionship, and sexual relations, the latter of which could only, in theory, be accomplished within the confines of legally contracted marriage.

This belief was based partly on the practical concern for the birth of children outside of marriage, which this society took very seriously and which imposed a heavy burden on single women or, if new mothers abandoned their children at a church, hospital, or orphanage (such children were commonly known at the time as "foundlings"), on society. As discussed earlier, young, single, sexually active women were the demographic most likely to commit infanticide. In addition, the church's official position on sex, even if this was not shared by the majority, was that it, like women's subjugation to men, was part of women's punishment for original sin. That is, it was retribution for Eve's encouraging of Adam to eat from the Tree of Knowledge in the Garden of Eden, which resulted in their expulsion from paradise and a life of physical hardship, which included sexual reproduction. Under this strict interpretation, sex was deemed to be a punishment for sin and was to occur only for the purpose of procreation, which required marriage.

The official expectation that sex only occur during marriage did not, of course, reflect the reality of the situation. Adolescents entered puberty at about the age of thirteen, and it is difficult to imagine that early modern English men and women refrained from acting out on basic human instincts for a dozen years before marriage. Many, of course, resorted to masturbation, an act known at the time as "self-pollution," which was considered a sin but was not prosecuted by the courts. Others engaged in illicit acts of fornication. Once again, the incidence of premarital sexual congress differed according to one's status in society. Elite young men had various opportunities to gain sexual experience, through prostitutes, private assignations during their time in Europe, and dalliances with servant girls brought into the home by their fathers, the latter of which were sometimes consensual but often coercive and always power-imbalanced.

Elite men were also the most likely to procure the services of prostitutes, for the simple reason that the poor could rarely afford the opportunity. Prostitution was technically illegal and many "lewd" women were gathered up and placed into the bridewells; nonetheless, brothels or "bawdy" houses were common especially in the cities by about 1550. Both women and men (as brothel-keepers and procurers of would-be prostitutes and their clients) were involved in the economics of brothelry. Prostitutes were also relatively common in male-heavy realms, as "camp-followers" during military campaigns and in mining and fishing villages where women were in short supply. In these milieu, prostitution was sometimes tolerated as a necessary evil to protect innocent women from assault.

It was also common for elite men – whether or not they were married – to maintain mistresses or otherwise seek out female companionship through consensual affairs. Although this was technically illegal, and was sometimes punished by fines, it was generally overlooked provided that the relations did not result in pregnancy. Even then, provided the man maintained the child, there were likely no consequences. As we have seen, Charles II had fourteen illegitimate children with at least seven mistresses, which was little more than a source of court gossip. Women were willing partners, too, although if they were married this was prosecuted as adultery, a gender double-standard that was not, as discussed, unusual at this time. While contraceptives existed – normally as "sheaths" to prevent wealthy young men from contracting sexually transmitted diseases while "sowing their wild oats" in Europe – they were not widely used. The occasional use of pessaries (a form of diaphragm), post-coital douches, and *coitus interruptus* were also used as means to prevent pregnancy, with varying degrees of effectiveness. These methods were technically illegal, especially for married couples whose principal task was to produce children, but were tolerated if they prevented the birth of bastard children.

If these assignations resulted in pregnancy, the matter was different because of the stigma associated with bastard children in this society. Often, parents and magistrates would resolve the issue by insisting that the couple marry as soon as possible, so that the baby was born into a married home. In many cases, the couple was already contractually engaged to be married and had begun sexual intercourse early, which meant that the situation was resolved during the normal course of events. In other cases, women, sometimes induced by men, took greater steps to protect their reputation. As discussed earlier, this included the use of abortifacients, which were mixtures of herbs ingested orally to induce miscarriage, or infanticide, the deliberate killing of newborns. These steps were taken either because the man was married or otherwise unable or unwilling to marry, and also because women believed to be sexually promiscuous were not considered good marrying prospects. The idea of being ineligible for marriage because of a single act of indiscretion was simply too much for some women (and their parents) to bear, leading to more aggressive and sometimes life-endangering decisions.

Several forms of sex were considered perversions, in part because they were explicitly forbidden in the Bible. Among the most serious of these was homosexual behavior, especially among males. In addition to biblical injunctions against this behavior, this society set strict rules about gender expression; men were supposed to be strong and masculine and thus effeminacy or androgyny, which homosexuality was believed to demonstrate, were perceived to be weaknesses that damaged the social fabric. Sodomy and buggery – the two crimes under which men who engaged in homosexual acts were prosecuted – were felonies and, in theory, men found guilty of these acts were liable to execution upon conviction. In practice, however, most discovered homosexuals were imprisoned or whipped unless there were extenuating circumstances, such as forceable buggery, which sometimes occurred in master-apprentice-servant relationships. Homosexuals, therefore, had to be very discreet in their activities, which sometimes involved frequenting secretive "molly houses." Sodomy also included sexual acts that could not result in procreation, including oral and anal penetration, which could be charged against both men and women. Bestiality was also a sexual "act against nature," often recounted in popular literature, that could lead to execution. This usually involved adolescent boys buggering mares, cows, goats, or sheep, acts that were officially proscribed in the "Buggery Act" of 1534.

Finally, nonconsensual sexual intercourse was not taken lightly in this society and was prosecuted as the felony charge of rape.[6] In these instances, the standard of proof was strongly in favor of men. The crime needed to be witnessed or at least reported immediately, the victim needed to call out for help and undertake active resistance, and penetration and emission were necessary for a conviction. At a time of limited reproductive knowledge among physicians, some commentators also argued that pregnancy could only occur from a desired sexual coupling, which placed pregnant victims at a significant disadvantage. In part, these legal standards existed because of Matthew Hale's dictum that rape, while "detestable" and "heinous," was "an accusation easily to be made." Hale was both concerned about the possibility of malicious prosecution for rape, undertaken by women in hopes of a forced marriage or financial settlement, and also the fact that it was a non-clergyable crime (as dictated by an act of 1576), which meant that anyone convicted would be hanged, thus warranting in Hale's opinion greater scrutiny than clergyable felonies. Sexual relations between adults and youths under the age of twelve, technically known as pederasty, were never considered legal in this society and did not involve such high standards of proof, as it was understood that children did not have the capacity to give consent.

* * *

Discussion Question 11.2: Given the constraints on sexual expression and exploration at this time, especially those articulated by the church, what surprises you about early modern England's attitudes toward sex?

Marriage

Perhaps surprisingly to modern readers who are familiar with Shakespeare's *Romeo and Juliet*, who wed as teenagers, first marriages occurred relatively late in life in the early modern period. In theory, marriage could be legally contracted at the age of seven and consummated at the age of fourteen for boys and twelve for girls. Henry VII's son Prince Arthur wed by proxy when he was eleven years old and allegedly consummated the marriage at a "public bedding" at the age of fifteen, a few months before his death. In practice, however, such early marriages were rare. In order to marry and start his own household, a man needed to be in a position of financial independence, which meant finishing a course of university studies and achieving success in a career or completing

---

6   The major exception being when a wife was forced by her husband, in which case it was believed that no crime was committed.

the work required to achieve the status of master artisan – each of which could easily take a dozen years – or waiting for his inheritance in the case of common heirs. Thus, the average age for a first marriage was about twenty-seven years for men and twenty-four years for women. The median age for women was primarily because most men, as today, preferred to marry a woman close to their own age. Elite male heirs and elite women tended to marry a bit younger (but not much) because they did not have the same obligations to achieve an independent lifestyle.

It has been estimated that up to 20 per cent of the English population never married. Some men simply could not achieve the requisite level of independence, because they had failed to secure or maintain an apprenticeship or career, were destined to a life of service, or were among the ranks of the sturdy beggars. Some were in professions – such as sailors, merchants, and soldiers – that made marriage impractical or undesirable. Other men preferred to remain as bachelors, especially if they could otherwise satisfy their sexual desires or if they were homosexual and did not see the need to maintain the semblance of "normalcy." Some women, too, did not marry, despite society's belief that a patriarchal marriage was a natural state for women. No woman could technically be forced to marry against her wishes (although parents could be extremely persuasive), so some chose to exercise their own agency by refusing to do so. Other women, such as mothers who had borne bastard children, those known to be sexually active or promiscuous, those who were maintained as elite men's mistresses, or those who could not bring a dowry into the union, were not considered good prospects for marriage. In addition, as the result of war and other factors, there were always more women than men in early modern England, thereby limiting the number of eligible bachelors.

Historians have vigorously debated whether couples married for economic or emotional reasons and have generally arrived at the conclusion that both factors were considered, although this depended to an extent on the circumstances in which the marriage occurred. Elite marriages were often arranged by parents or matchmakers, based on criteria such as rank, wealth, and status. In making these arrangements, parents considered the advantages of the match, with the expectation that both families would somehow benefit. The marriage of a rich merchant's daughter to the son of a poor earl, for example, brought restored wealth to the earl's family – since it was the bride's family that provided the dowry – and title to the merchant's. In addition, nobles usually wanted to marry into other noble families, for economic and dynastic reasons. However, the extent to which elite marriages were arranged has been exaggerated. Elite sons and daughters who were not heirs or heiresses had considerable freedom to choose, because the matches were less likely to be beneficial. Moreover, while parents would express their opinions and exert pressure, sons and daughters could veto clearly unsuitable matches. Parents could also effectively veto matches desired by their children by withholding dowries or other property that would normally transfer upon marriage. In the end, however, if two consenting adults elected to marry and there were no legal encumbrances (such as an earlier promise of marriage to another), parents had no legal remedy to prevent the marriage from taking place.

Among commoners, arranged marriages occurred far less often. Few commoners owned property and none had title, which meant that there were no particular advantages to an arranged marriage. Couples had the opportunity to meet in church and at community events, in homes where they worked as apprentices and servants, and sometimes during family gatherings, as it was not unusual at this time for second cousins to wed. Naturally, parents provided their opinions, and few sons or daughters would marry if their parents strongly objected to a union, but in most cases commoners were allowed to select their own spouses. They used numerous criteria in making this selection: parity in age, shared religious or personal beliefs, physical and emotional attraction, personal reputation and characteristics, a man's prospects for financial success, a woman's skills at household management, and the likelihood of the partner being a good parent and lifelong companion. Many of these are the same reasons people choose partners today. Despite, as we have seen, the social expectation of husbands and fathers to maintain authority over the household as part of the important patriarchal-deferential relationship, there is considerable evidence to support the conclusion that most marriages were entered into voluntarily and that couples had, or soon developed, deep affection for one another.

After a usually brief courting period, marriages proceeded quickly. The engagement was a formal, legally binding contract that obliged the couple to marry unless there were impediments, such as a pre-existing engagement, a living spouse, or if the couple was too close in affinity (for example, half-siblings or first cousins). These issues were resolved when the marriage banns – announcements of the impending marriage – were read in church, providing anybody with knowledge of an impediment to the marriage to come forward. Some fiancés also took part in a "bundling" ceremony, which involved the man and women sleeping together in the same bed, to determine their ability to be intimate toward one another, though without engaging in sexual intercourse. Nonetheless, there is evidence that many couples began sexual relations after their engagement, and that despite the attitudes of the church and certain Puritan elements within society, this was considered acceptable provided that the marriage took place before the birth of the child. After a church wedding, the couple consummated their marriage – sometimes, as in the case of Prince Arthur and Catherine of Aragon, in the presence of witnesses for elite marriages that would result in titled heirs – therefore completing the legal requirements for an indissoluble marriage.

It was assumed at this time that marriage could only be terminated by the death of a spouse, which was all the more reason that parents and their children sought desirable partners. Divorce was virtually impossible and an annulment could only occur if there was a proven defect in the legal validity of the marriage for reasons already mentioned. The only option for an unsatisfactory marriage was for spouses to live apart from one another, but this arrangement did not permit remarriage or, at least officially, the ability to find a new sex partner. Separation was usually the result of significant marital discord, with husbands citing their wives' scolding, adultery, infertility,[7] or refusal of sexual congress, and wives their husband's sexual proclivities, drunkenness, and violence as reasons for domestic conflict. As mentioned, however, many married couples came to love and respect one another. Numerous letters, diaries, and wills – often using familiar words such as "sweetheart," "darling," and "dear" – attest to the affectionate nature of early modern marriages, despite the claims of some historians, most notably Lawrence Stone, that marriage was mostly an economically driven enterprise lacking in modern notions of love, romance, or affection.[8]

Marriage was an important milestone for people in early modern England, because of the common belief that it was only through marriage that a man truly became an adult, capable of participating in other aspects of public affairs, such as, in the case of elites, running for public office. Most first marriages lasted, on average, twenty years before the death of a spouse, though some lasted far fewer as the result of childbirth complications and other fatalities. Remarriage, sometimes quite quickly, was not unusual, especially if the women had not yet entered menopause, which typically occurred around the age of forty-five, and was therefore still capable of childbearing. Second (or third) marriages provided men with continuity of household management and childrearing, women with economic support, and both partners with companionship and legitimate opportunities for sexual fulfillment. Remarriage was also valuable because many widows possessed property (real and chattel) inherited from their husbands, which made them attractive prospects. In addition, as discussed in the last chapter, widowhood was not always a desirable state for women because of the stigma attached to a woman who did not have a man in a position of authority over her.

Old Age

Old age was considered to have begun at about the age of forty-five. This likely seems young from a modern perspective, but makes sense considering that the average age at death was around sixty and, as we have seen throughout this book, a great many people did not come even close to living that long. It has been

---

7   The biology of fertility was still something of a mystery to early modern physicians, such that the blame for the inability to conceive or produce living children – or in the case of Henry VIII, male children – was usually placed on the woman.

8   Lawrence Stone, *The Family, Sex and Marriage in England, 1500–1800* (London: Penguin, 1979).

estimated that only about 8 per cent of the population was over sixty, compared to nearly half of the population being under the age of twenty-five. This is not to say that there were no septuagenarians or octogenarians in this society. Queen Elizabeth's principal secretary, William Cecil, lived to seventy-seven, and her court magician, John Dee, died at the age of eighty-one. Some contemporaries claimed to be nonagenarians and centenarians, and there are gravestones to attest to this, although in the absence of better evidence historians have become suspicious of claims that were accepted uncritically at the time.

Women tended to enter the category of old age earlier than men. This was because menopause and their inability to bear children signaled a major life change, because women were more likely to be widowed (to use the contemporary term, "relict") in their forties, and because women were usually a few years younger than their husbands, and married couples were generally thought to enter old age together. Attitudes toward old women varied considerably depending on their situation. Elite women, mature wives, or financially independent widows were treated with the respect accorded their rank and their many years of life experience, and also their probable, multiple escapes from death over a lifetime of childbearing. Respected older women were encouraged to sit in pews closer to the front of the church (at a time when women typically sat toward the back, away from their husbands and sons), gained legal authority over their deceased husband's business affairs if they were widows, and were consulted by village authorities and neighbors about childbirth, poor relief, and homegrown medicinal remedies.

For poor widows and lifelong spinsters, however, the situation was different. These women were at the mercy of the village and the parish, which were required to provide work (sometimes in bleak workhouses), charity (in almshouses), and other support, often for extended periods of time, straining the limited resources of the community. It will be recalled from the last chapter that Mother Sutton spent many years as the town's hogkeeper, a position she was given as an act of charity, until she was eventually accused of witchcraft and executed. It is no coincidence that a large percentage of those accused of witchcraft were poor, single or widowed women, as their execution relieved the community of their care. The best-case scenario for a common woman was to produce enough children that she would be taken care of in her elder years and that she could continue to be of service to her extended family as a caregiver. "Stranger" women (and men) – those who lived among the sturdy beggars and had not grown up in the community – could not even expect basic charity; perhaps fortunately, for numerous reasons, few of these undesirables would have entered old age in the first place.

When men entered old age, how they were treated depended on a number of factors as well. The harsh physical labor associated with farming, husbandry, mining, soldiering, artisanship, service, and other types of employment undertaken by many common men required them to step aside when the opportunity presented itself. In some cases, of course, it never did, and many men worked until they fell dead in the field or workshop from exhaustion, stroke, or heart attack. There was no social welfare system to provide a retirement plan, and charitable alms were rarely directed to men, who were expected to take care of themselves. Other men were more fortunate, in that they had living male heirs ready and willing to take on their father's duties, which allowed the elderly to live with their children and grandchildren, or take on a smaller cottage on the acreage, and live a more sedentary lifestyle. Under these circumstances, the father (literally or figuratively) gave up his position at the head of the dinner table to his son, who became the new head of the household. Sometimes, despite the legal and moral obligations of their children, fathers and mothers – and aunts, uncles, and grandparents – became a burden and were subject to abuse as they became increasingly dependent and decrepit.

Elite old men found themselves in better circumstances. By percentage, they represented a tiny portion of society and were thus revered for their maturity, judgment, wisdom, and self-mastery. Certainly, among their numbers were the "slippered pantaloons" derided by Shakespeare, but others had key roles in society. Many were wise sages and teachers, dispensing advice and justice as local aldermen and magistrates. In an age of limited record-keeping, and when the English common law was grounded in custom and immemorality,[9] their long memories were valued when it came to property disputes, common rights, and the ways in which things had always been done. English crown appointees – privy councillors, bishops, judges, and university officials, for example – often took up their positions in their fifties, creating what Keith Thomas has referred to as a "gerontocracy." It would have been unusual for a man to attain high political or judicial office younger than age forty-five and perfectly common for a royal judge to be appointed well into his sixties. For a man – or a woman, for that matter – to be regarded as "ancient" was a high compliment.

✳ ✳ ✳

Discussion Question 11.3: Why were the various phases of life – from birth, through childhood, adolescence, marriage, and old age – so prescribed? Given the complexities of English society, to what extent do you think that this model was an ideal rather than reality?

---

9   That is, if a practice had existed longer than anybody could remember, it was law.

Death

As we have seen throughout this book, death could come calling at any time in early modern England. Crowd diseases such as bubonic plague, smallpox, tuberculosis, cholera, and many others were rampant especially in London. Illnesses such as dysentery, malaria, and influenza were common. War and rebellion claimed hundreds of thousands of lives. Childbed death was common for both babies and mothers. Murder, infanticide, and witchcraft, plus numerous other felonies leading to capital punishment, made the sixteenth and seventeenth centuries the peak period of criminal executions in all of English history. Given the prevalence of death, parents expected to lose their children and children their parents, husbands their wives and wives their husbands, in resigned acceptance that death was an inevitable consequence of life.

There were plenty of other opportunities for death to come calling, too. Even by early modern European standards, hygiene and sanitation in England, especially in the cities, was deplorable. Fresh water was contaminated because of its proximity to outhouses and human waste. Urine and excrement were thrust out of windows into the street or into the same rivers used to wash clothing and clean dishes. After butchers slaughtered animals and fishmongers cleaned fish, the carcasses were tossed into the same street where horses and cattle deposited their waste. During times of plague, corpses were stacked in large, hollow graves that were only covered when they were full. The great putrid stench of the cities was masked by nosegays and perfumes, and decaying meat was salted and spiced to disguise the taste of rotting flesh. Undergarments were rarely cleaned, and bathing was discouraged by physicians, for fear that the practice provided an avenue for bodily imbalance. In the cities, fire could consume numerous homes – which were built of wood and attached together for entire blocks – and cause horrible deaths. Combined with frequent bouts of starvation and malnutrition, diets insufficient in key vitamins and nutrients, physical exhaustion from back-breaking labor, and rudimentary medical expertise that was usually limited to purging bodily fluids and excruciating amputation in the unclean theaters of barber-surgeons, it is perhaps little wonder that death was such a common feature of this society. A simple laceration, stomach ailment, or infection could result in death within days, especially for the majority who could not afford medical assistance when the situation worsened.

The specter of death in early modern England was so prevalent that it became a central theme in artwork and literature. One common theme in artwork was the *danse macabre*, a reminder of the frailty of life and the eventuality of death. Hans Holbein's painting *The Ambassadors* (1533), for example, depicts a large, human skull at the bottom center of the image, which can only be seen in true form by looking at the image sideways from the right. Numerous other pieces of art depict individuals holding skulls or the presence of skeletons surrounded by images associated with time, such as cut flowers and hourglasses. Other forms of art, such as woodcut images often appearing on title pages or as book illustrations, depict humans and skeletons together, or skeletons joyously dancing on the graves of corpses, commonly depicting people from different classes in society – from kings to children to laborers – to show the universality of death. Again, Holbein is an excellent English representative of these forms but hardly their only practitioner.

Another common, and somewhat more positive, theme was that of *carpe diem*, used in seventeenth-century poetry. Robert Herrick's poem "To the Virgins" (1648) is a good example:

> Gather ye rosebuds while ye may,
> Old Time is still a-flying;
> And the same flower that smiles today
> Tomorrow will be dying....
> That age is best which is the first,
> When youth and blood are warmer;
> But being spent, the worse, and worst
> Time still succeed the former.

This theme about the passage of time, the fleeting nature of life, and enjoinders to live life to its fullest is also prominent in Spenser's *The Faerie Queene*, Shakespeare's *Sonnets*, and his "all the world's a stage" speech that opened this chapter. The sentiment is more commonly expressed in the modern-day phrase "you only live once."

The narrative of death was controlled primarily by the Church of England. Owing to the doctrine of predestination, in which one's salvation was long predetermined, the church taught that upon the death of the body, either an angel brought the soul to Heaven or a minion of the Devil carried it to Hell. Although opinions differed, Heaven was thought to be a place of everlasting happiness and joy, where saved souls enjoyed perfect health and communed with God in perpetual worship, as compared to the corporeal challenges on Earth that never made life truly fulfilling. In Hell, the damned suffered the agonies of separation from God's love and the mobilization of the senses to discern extreme heat and cold, the stench of fire and brimstone, and the howling of tormented souls for all eternity. There was no agreement on how many souls were saved as opposed to condemned, but it was generally thought that outward signs of grace – wealth, honesty, morality, faith, and charity, for example – and proper Christian burial in consecrated ground constituted the best chance of making it to Heaven.

This is why the most severe of punishments – to be hanged, drawn, and quartered, or burned at the stake, followed by burial in unconsecrated ground – were so feared in this society. In theory, even criminals and those executed for their crimes would have the opportunity to attain salvation, but the dismemberment of the body and the lack of a Christian burial, which usually occurred for traitors, heretics, and suicides, was believed to lead automatically to eternal damnation.[10] For those who had lived a good life, however, death was thought to be an occasion of felicity, because they felt reasonably assured of admission into Heaven.

To an extent, this assurance also depended on whether a person died a "good death." The best death was one in which a person passed peacefully, preferably during sleep, when the soul was at its calmest state, or when one was surrounded by a loving family. Oppositely, a "bad death," one that involved agonizing sickness or, worse, violence against the body (murder, execution, or sudden trauma, for example) was more feared, because death occurred at a time when the soul was in distress. This is yet another example of the quest for order and fear of disorder in this society.

When elites died, especially those who held high rank or office, elaborate funerals were planned, and the deceased were memorialized through tombs and monuments erected at great expense. Many of England's leading figures, including monarchs and their consorts, great statesmen, and key intellectuals (such as Isaac Newton), were laid to rest in St. George's Chapel in Windsor or in Westminster Abbey.[11] Senior churchmen, noblemen, and gentlemen were frequently buried in chapels in the university and cathedral cities, while others were interred in small chapels or consecrated vaults on their own lands. Commoners' funerals were less elaborate but provided an opportunity for the community to join together in mourning. Wakes, which in the pre-Reformation period were solemn events involving vigil and prayer, gave way, after the Reformation, to feasts celebrating the life of the deceased, bringing healing to the community, and enabling the living to move on with their lives. Cemeteries were located at the center of the town or village, adjoining the parish church. They served as places where loved ones could visit the deceased and as opportunities to reflect upon one's own eventual demise and salvation.

The dead could also achieve posthumous memory through bequeathals in wills, such as giving money to the community for a specific purpose, and keepsakes such as pieces of silver, books, coins, rings, gloves, swords, and clothing. For some, a legacy could be guaranteed through the continuing existence of diaries and commonplace books, portraiture, and literary output. For many in the early modern period, this led to virtual immortality, for we have not yet forgotten Coke, Hobbes, Holbein, Locke, Shakespeare, Spenser, or Samuel Pepys – whose famous diary chronicling the Restoration period was first published in the early

---

10 Suicides were sometimes buried with a stake through the heart, to pin the soul to the body and prevent it from remaining behind as a ghost, because it was unclear whether a soul would be claimed from those who took their own life.

11 All of the Tudor and Stuart monarchs are buried in one of these two locations.

nineteenth century – not to mention hundreds of others who produced art and literature during this remarkable period of productivity.

Of course, many men, women, and children, mostly from among the ranks of the poor, including beggars, died without so much as a gravestone to mark their existence. For many, their entire time on Earth was reduced to a few meager lines in a parish register marking their dates of baptism, marriage, and death. This was especially true during frequent plague epidemics, when thousands were shoveled into mass graves and their bodies were covered in lye, where they quickly decomposed: "Sans teeth, sans eyes, sans taste, sans everything."

* * *

Discussion Question 11.4: In what ways did the frequency of death from causes other than old age, and the uncertainty of living a good, long life, instill a "culture of death" in early modern England?

VOICES OF THE PAST
THE PENITENT DEATH OF THOMAS SAVAGE

Many boys were apprenticed as young teenagers to gain skills that would allow them to become artisans, which in turn would provide them with an independent living leading to marriage and family. Some youths, however, challenged these prescribed roles, which led to a pattern of backsliding. This decline began with minor transgressions, such as drinking and gambling, and led eventually to the commission of crimes, including murder, that resulted in the execution of the offender (see Figure 11.1). Tales of this nature, such as the following story of Thomas Savage, were frequently reported in popular pamphlets, to remind readers of the wages of sin and the importance of an orderly progress through life.

* * *

Thomas Savage, born of honest parents, in the parish of St. Giles in the Fields, was put apprentice to a vintner at Ratcliff, where he lived about one year and three quarters. In which time, he appeared to all that knew him to be a monster in sin, giving himself up to all sensual pleasures, and never so much as delighted to hear one sermon, but if he went into the Church at one door, but would soon go out at another, and accounted 'em fools that could spare so much time to hear the ministers of God's Word. He spent the Sabbath usually at an alehouse, or at least a base house, with that strumpet, H. Blay, … and used to bring her bottles of wine, which satisfied not her base desire. [She] told him, if he intended to be welcome, he must bring money with him. He said he had none, but what was his master's, and he had never wronged him of twopence

in his life. But she enticed him to bring it privately….

He going home about one o'clock, his master standing at the street door, did not dare to go in that way, but climbed over a backdoor, and comes into the room where his fellow servants were at dinner.

"Oh," says the maid, "you have now been at this lewd house, you will never leave till you are ruined."

He was much concerned at her words and while he sat at dinner the Devil and passion entered so strongly into him that he resolved to kill her. So when his master with his family was gone to church, leaving none at home but him and the maid, he steps to the bar, and reaches a hammer…. [On] a sudden he threw the hammer with great force at the maid's head, so that she fell down shrieking out. Then he took the hammer … and striketh her many blows with all the force he could, rejoicing that he had finished the murder. This done, he goes to his master's chamber, breaking open a cupboard, and taking a bag of money under his clothes, goes out at a backdoor to this base house again. The strumpet, seeing what he had done, would feign have had the money, but he refusing, gave her half a crown [a coin worth two shillings and six pence], and so departed.

That night he wandered toward Greenwich, … where he lay, acquainting his landlord that he was bound for Gravesend. But in the night he arose and knew not what to do. Conscience so terrified him that he could take no rest. In the morning he took his leave, but the landlady perceiving he had a sum of money, said to her husband, "I wish [hope] this youth came by this money honestly."

Figure 11.1 *The execution of Thomas Savage, from* The Wicked Life and Penitent Death, *1680.*

Upon which he was sent for back and he told them such a plausible tale, that he was an apprentice to a wine-cooper in London Bridge and was carrying it to this master in Gravesend, and if they pleased he would leave the money with them and they might send to his mistress and be further satisfied…. [T]hey took him back to the aforesaid house at Greenwich, where meeting with his master and some other acquaintants, he was immediately conveyed to a justice at Ratcliff, who committed him close prisoner in Newgate, where several eminent divines came to discourse him.

Whereof one said, "Are you the young man that committed the murder on your fellow servant at Ratcliff?"

Then he replied, "I did."

"Then what do you think of your dismal state and of your precious soul? You have not only brought yourself to public shame and punishment, but without God's infinite mercy, have brought your soul to eternal misery and torment. Were you not afflicted when you have considered what you had done and heartily sorry for committing so horrid a crime?"

Then he answered, smiting upon his breast, and tears trickling down his cheeks, "Yes, I was troubled to my very soul, that I had shed the blood of she who never thought me no ill. And so for ought I know, made her as miserable as myself, in that I gave her no warning, so much as once to call upon God, but sent her out of the world in the midst of her sins. Oh, how will I be able to appear before God, when she shall be present to accuse me of my crime, and say 'Lord, this villain bereaved me of my life, not affording me the least space of time to prepare for eternity.'"

… Then they asked him his age. He told them sixteen years. "Then you are but youthful and blooming and yet indeed an old sinner. Oh turn, turn from thy sins, that the Lord may be gracious to thee." With this advice they left him for that time.

Soon after they visited him again, and asked him, how his soul stood affected towards God? And whether or no he had repented him of his sins?

He answered, "I daily endeavored to do, but I find my heart so hardened that if there be a heart of iron, I have one, it is not fit to be called a heart. When I consider how many pray with me and are afflicted for my condition, and yet when they are done, I myself cannot be sufficiently troubled for my deplorable state."

The night before the Sessions [Assizes], they asked, if they thought it not terrible to appear before this present bar of justice? Said he, "When I consider the bar of men, and comparing to the justice seat of God, it is not to be feared. Oh, when I think of appearing before the great tribunal, there instead of saying 'Take him to a gaoler,' I may expect that dreadful sentence, 'Depart from me into everlasting torments.' Oh, this makes my very hair to stand on end, my heart to ache, and my soul to tremble."

Thus he continued lamenting his dismal condition, often in fervent prayer to God, that he would be graciously pleased to pardon him, so that before his death, he had a great deal of comfort in his soul, and could freely leave the world, not fearing the terrors of death, through the hope of having a being with God in glory, after these clouds of sorrow should be passed over. Thus, the nearer he grew to his end, the more comfortable hopes there appeared in him.

His Speech at the Place of Execution.

"Here am I come to suffer a shameful death, which I indeed most justly deserve. For I have shed the blood of an innocent creature, who never gave me the least provocation. I have not only murdered her body, but if God had no more mercy of her poor soul, than I had of her body, she is undone to all eternity. So that I deserve not only death from men, but damnation from God. I desire all that behold me, to take warning by me. The first sin I began with was Sabbath-breaking, whereby I got acquaintance with bad company, and so frequented alehouses at the time of divine service, and from the alehouse to the bawdy house, where I came acquainted with this vile strumpet, who enticed me to rob my master, and commit this murder.

"Young men, I would have you look steadfastly upon me and consider how one sin draws on another. First, Sabbath-breaking brought me to ill company, where I practiced not only drunkenness, but likewise whoredom, and was soon drawn away to wrong my master, for the accomplishment of which, murdered my fellow servant, and have brought myself to be a public shame to all that behold me.

"Oh, make me your example, and learn to amend your lives, before it be too late, for sin will not only bring your bodies to the grave, but your souls to Hell. Oh, walk in the ways of God, and He will be your guard and guide to support you from temptations. Now I am going to take my leave of the world, humbly entreat you all to pray with me to God, that he will have mercy upon my poor soul, and that I may be able to go through the bitter pangs of death, and not fall from him, and that my soul may find acceptance with him, through Jesus Christ our Lord. Amen." …

After he rose from prayers, and his cap was over his eyes, he used these expressions: "Lord Jesus receive my spirit, Lord one smile, good Lord, one word of comfort, for Christ's sake. Though death make a separation between my soul and body, let nothing separate between thee and my soul. Good Lord hear me; good Father of mercy hear me. Oh Lord Jesus receive my soul."

So he was turned off the ladder. These melting expressions drew many tears from the beholders' eyes, to see so much penitence from him, who was but sixteen years of age.

After he had hung the usual time, the sheriff commanded him to be cut down and his body received by some of his friends, who carried it to a neighboring house. Where, being laid upon a table, he was discerned to stir and breathe, so that they immediately put him into a warm bed which recovered him so, that he opened his eyes, and moved his body and hands, but could not attain his speech. The news was soon abroad, so that officers came and conveyed him to the former place of execution, and hung him up again until he was quite dead, and never came to himself again.

Source: Anonymous, *The Wicked Life and Penitent Death of Thomas Savage* (London, 1680).

* * *

Discussion Question 11.5: To what extent do you think this biography of Thomas Savage was an accurate description of events? What parts of the narrative make you question its veracity?

CONCLUSION: DEATH AND DISORDER, CHANGE AND CONTINUITY

We have seen throughout this book that death loomed large in early modern England. It was the result of numerous causes, including murder, execution, assassination, riot, rebellion, disease, illness, war, and perceived supernatural causes. Death was also closely related to disorder. Public execution was a tool used by the state against those who caused disorder, under the belief that this form of punishment would restore order to society. Because of this belief, many rioters, rebels, traitors, and felons met this fate, at a rate much higher than any other time in English history. At other times, death had the effect of causing disorder, especially when mortality peaked during times of war, plague, and dearth, all of which occurred in early modern England. In a society obsessed with order, death and disorder went hand in hand.

Despite the overarching narrative of death and disorder in this society, it has also been seen that England managed to bring about major changes in religion, politics, global relations, and intellectual thought. Even as plagues ravaged the cities, wars and rebellions disrupted the countryside, and public executions drew large crowds to town squares throughout the nation, Anglicanism emerged as a permanent national religion, the sovereignty of parliament and limitations on royal prerogatives were recognized, the British Empire witnessed its auspicious beginnings, and great literary and scientific achievements made England a key historical agent during major European events of the seventeenth and eighteenth centuries. These changes endured long after the early modern period and their legacies continue to impact many societies today: Australia, Bermuda, Canada, India, New Zealand, the United States, and many other "former settler" societies have inherited England's legal, parliamentary, religious, and social systems. Some of these nations continue to recognize the British crown as their head of state or belong to the modern consortium of more than fifty Commonwealth countries and dependencies.

Despite these enduring changes, England in other respects remained much the same during these two centuries. By the end of the seventeenth century, England was still (and remains) a monarchy, albeit a less powerful one, Catholicism still existed in certain pockets of the nation, parliament was dominated by wealthy land magnates, relatively few men (and no women) were entitled to vote, and notions of class and gender were largely unaltered. The vast majority of the population was still among the laboring poor, most people continued to reside in the English countryside in small rural villages, order and authority remained a priority of the state and church, most people could not read and write, and many continued to rely on older belief systems. Most of these aspects of English society would not witness significant change for at least another century, when industrialization, urbanization, the lessons from the European Enlightenment, lengthy wars in Continental Europe, substantial population increase, and a much larger and more sustainable empire demanded change over continuity. Even then, modernizing features such as universal suffrage and class, gender, and religious equality were still a long way off.

Both change and continuity, then, characterized the history of early modern England, as indeed they did of all early modern European societies. And through all that changed and all that remained the same, people died and death was ever present. Death was and is a universal constant that impacts all people regardless of class, gender, religion, or any other factor. Therefore, understanding how and why a society brought about and dealt with the death of its citizens and subjects tells us a great deal about how those of the past lived. This is, after all, the historian's principal task to discover.

FURTHER RESOURCES

The historical scholarship on Tudor and Stuart England is immense and only a select list of further resources can be provided here. This time period is also well represented in academic articles that appear in a wide range of journals, such as *English Historical Review*, the *Journal of British Studies*, and *Past and Present*, in addition to many others that focus on various social and intellectual themes. These articles can be accessed by searching the *Historical Abstracts* database, which is available through most postsecondary libraries.

General

Brigden, Susan. *New Worlds, Lost Worlds: The Rule of the Tudors, 1485–1603*. New York: Penguin, 2002.

Bucholz, Robert, and Newton Key. *Early Modern England, 1485–1714: A Narrative History*. 3rd ed. Chichester, UK: Wiley-Blackwell, 2019.

Collinson, Patrick. *The Sixteenth Century, 1485–1603*. Short Oxford History of the British Isles Series. Oxford: Oxford University Press, 2002.

Coward, Barry. *The Stuart Age: England, 1603–1714*. 2nd ed. London: Longman, 1994.

Doran, Susan, and Norman Jones, eds. *The Elizabethan World*. London: Routledge, 2011.

Guy, John. *Tudor England*. Oxford: Oxford University Press, 1990.

Kishlansky, Mark. *A Monarchy Transformed: Britain, 1603–1714*. London: Allen Lane, 1996.

Miller, John. *Early Modern Britain, 1450–1750*. Cambridge: Cambridge University Press, 2017.

Roberts, Clayton, David Roberts, and Douglas Bisson. *A History of England, Vol 1: Prehistory to 1714*. 6th ed. New York: Routledge, 2014.

Smith, Lacey Baldwin. *This Realm of England, 1399–1688*. 7th ed. Lexington, KY: D.C. Heath and Company, 1996.

Williams, Penry. *The Tudor Regime*. Oxford: Oxford University Press, 1979.

Wormald, Jenny. *The Seventeenth Century*. Short Oxford History of the British Isles Series. Oxford: Oxford University Press, 2008.

Family, Gender, and Authority

Amussen, Susan Dwyer. *An Ordered Society: Gender and Class in Early Modern England*. Oxford: Blackwell, 1988.

Beier, A.L. *Masterless Men: The Vagrancy Problem in England, 1560–1640*. London: Methuen, 1985.

Ben-Amos, Ilana. *Adolescence and Youth in Early Modern England*. New Haven, CT: Yale University Press, 1994.

Berry, Helen, and Elizabeth Foyster, eds. *The Family in Early Modern England*. Cambridge: Cambridge University Press, 2007.

Crawford, Patricia. *Blood, Bodies and Families in Early Modern England*. London: Pearson, 2004.

Crawford, Patricia. *Parents of Poor Children in England, 1500–1800*. Oxford: Oxford University Press, 2010.

Dolan, Frances E. *Marriage and Violence: The Early Modern Legacy*. Philadelphia: University of Pennsylvania Press, 2008.

Fletcher, Anthony. *Gender, Sex and Subordination in England, 1500–1800*. New Haven, CT: Yale University Press, 1995.

Foyster, Elizabeth A. *Manhood in Early Modern England*. London: Routledge, 1999.

Gowing, Laura. *Domestic Dangers: Women, Words, and Sex in Early Modern London*. Oxford: Oxford University Press, 1999.

Gowing, Laura. *Gender Relations in Early Modern England*. New York: Routledge, 2012.

Griffiths, Paul. *Youth and Authority: Formative Experiences in England, 1560–1640*. Oxford: Clarendon, 1996.

Griffiths, Paul, Adam Fox, and Steve Hindle. *The Experience of Authority in Early Modern England*. New York: Palgrave Macmillan, 1996.

Houlbrooke, Ralph. *Death, Religion, and the Family in England, 1480–1750*. Oxford: Oxford University Press, 1998.

Houlbrooke, Ralph. *The English Family 1450–1700*. London: Longman, 1984.

Peters, Christine. *Women in Early Modern England, 1450–1640*. Basingstoke, UK: Palgrave Macmillan, 2004.

Shephard, Alexandra. *Accounting for Oneself: Worth, Status, and the Social Order in Early Modern England*. Oxford: Oxford University Press, 2018.

Stone, Lawrence. *The Family, Sex and Marriage in England, 1500–1800*. London: Penguin, 1979.

Thomas, Keith. "Age and Authority in Early Modern England." *Proceedings of the British Academy* 62 (1977): 205–48.

Wall, Alison. *Power and Protest in England, 1525–1640*. London: Arnold, 2000.

Culture and Thought

Cressy, David. *Bonfires and Bells: National Memory and the Protestant Calendar in Elizabethan and Stuart England*. London: Sutton, 1980.

Cressy, David. *Literacy and the Social Order: Reading and Writing in Tudor and Stuart England*. Cambridge: Cambridge University Press, 1980.

Harkness, Deborah. *The Jewel House: Elizabethan London and the Scientific Revolution*. New Haven, CT: Yale University Press, 2007.

Helgerson, Richard. *Forms of Nationhood: The Elizabethan Writing of England*. Chicago: University of Chicago Press, 1992.

Hindle, Steve. *The State and Social Change in Early Modern England, 1550–1640*. New York: Palgrave Macmillan, 2002.

Reay, Barry. *Popular Cultures in England, 1550–1750*. New York: Addison Wesley, 1998.

Shagan, Ethan. *The Rule of Moderation: Violence, Religion and the Politics of Restraint in Early Modern England*. Cambridge: Cambridge University Press, 2011.

Sharpe, J.A. *Early Modern England: A Social History, 1550–1760*. 2nd ed. London: Arnold, 1997.

Spufford, Margaret. *Contrasting Communities: English Villagers in the Sixteenth and Seventeenth Centuries*. Cambridge: Cambridge University Press, 1974.

Spufford, Margaret. *Small Books and Pleasant Histories: Popular Fiction and Its Readership in Seventeenth-Century England*. Cambridge: Cambridge University Press, 1985.

Stone, Lawrence. *The Crisis of the Aristocracy, 1558–1641*. Oxford: Oxford University Press, 1992.

Tillyard, E.M.W. *The Elizabethan World Picture: A Study in the Idea of Order in the Age of Shakespeare, Donne, and Milton*. New York: Vintage, 1959.

Underdown, David. *Fire from Heaven: Life in an English Town in the Seventeenth Century*. New Haven, CT: Yale University Press, 1994.

Wrightson, Keith. *Earthly Necessities: Economic Lives in Early Modern Britain*. New Haven, CT: Yale University Press, 2000.

Wrightson, Keith. *English Society, 1580–1680*. New Brunswick, NJ: Rutgers University Press, 1982.

Wrigley, E.A., and R.S. Schofield. *The Population History of England, 1541–1871*. Cambridge: Cambridge University Press, 1989.

Death and Disorder

Cressy, David. *Birth, Marriage and Death: Ritual, Religion, and the Life Cycle in Tudor and Stuart England*. Oxford: Oxford University Press, 1997.

Dolan, Frances E. *Dangerous Familiars: Representations of Domestic Crime in England, 1550–1700*. Ithaca, NY: Cornell University Press, 1994.

Fletcher, Anthony, and John Stevenson, eds. *Order and Disorder in Early Modern England*. Cambridge: Cambridge University Press, 1987.

Gaskill, Malcolm. *Crime and Mentalities in Early Modern England*. Cambridge: Cambridge University Press, 2000.

Gittings, Clare. *Death, Burial and the Individual in Early Modern England*. London: Croom Helm, 1984.

Gordon, Bruce, and Peter Marshall, eds. *The Place of the Dead: Death and Remembrance in Late Medieval and Earl Modern Europe*. Cambridge: Cambridge University Press, 2000.

Harding, Vanessa. *The Dead and the Living in Paris and London, 1500–1670*. Cambridge: Cambridge University Press, 2001.

Houlbrooke, Ralph. *Death, Religion, and the Family in England, 1480–1750*. Oxford: Oxford University Press, 2011.

Jupp, Peter C., and Clare Gittings, eds. *Death in England: An Illustrated History*. New Brunswick, NJ: Rutgers University Press, 2000.

Marshall, Peter. *Beliefs and the Dead in Reformation England*. Oxford: Oxford University Press, 2002.

Sharpe, J.A. *Crime in Early Modern England, 1550–1750*. 2nd ed. London: Longman, 1999.

Sharpe, J.A. *Instruments of Darkness: Witchcraft in Early Modern England*. University Park: University of Pennsylvania Press, 1997.

Tarlow, Sarah. *Ritual, Belief and the Dead in Early Modern Britain and Ireland*. Cambridge: Cambridge University Press, 2013.

Thomas, Keith. *The Ends of Life: Roads to Fulfilment in Early Modern England*. Oxford: Oxford University Press, 2009.

Politics, War, and the State

Ackroyd, Peter. *The Life of Sir Thomas More*. New York: Anchor, 1998.

Braddick, Michael. *God's Fury, England's Fire: A New History of the English Civil Wars*. London: Penguin, 2009.

Braddick, Michael. *State Formation in Early Modern England, c. 1550–1700*. Cambridge: Cambridge University Press, 2000.

Burgess, Glenn. *British Political Thought, 1500–1660*. New York: Palgrave Macmillan, 2009.

Burgess, Glenn. *The Politics of the Ancient Constitution: An Introduction to English Political Thought, 1603–1642*. University Park: University of Pennsylvania Press, 1992.

Cogswell, Thomas. *The Blessed Revolution: English Politics and the Coming of War, 1621–1624*. Cambridge: Cambridge University Press, 2005.

Cogswell, Thomas. *James I: The Phoenix King*. London: Penguin, 2018.

Cressy, David. *Dangerous Talk: Scandalous, Seditious, and Treasonable Speech in Pre-Modern England*. Oxford: Oxford University Press, 2010.

Cunningham, Sean. *Henry VII*. London: Routledge, 2007.

Cust, Richard, and Ann Hughes. *The English Civil War*. London: Hodder Arnold, 1997.

Dean, David. *Law-Making and Society in Late Elizabethan England: The Parliament of England, 1584–1604*. Cambridge: Cambridge University Press, 2002.

Ellis, Steven G. *Tudor Frontiers and Noble Power: The Making of the British State*. Oxford: Oxford University Press, 1995.

Elton, Geoffrey R. *The Tudor Revolution in Government: Administrative Changes in the Reign of Henry VIII*. Cambridge: Cambridge University Press, 1967.

Fletcher, Anthony. *Reform in the Provinces: The Government of Stuart England*. New Haven, CT: Yale University Press, 1986.

Fletcher, Anthony, and Diarmaid MacColloch. *Tudor Rebellions*. 6th ed. New York: Routledge, 2016.

Harris, Tim. *Restoration: Charles II and His Kingdoms*. London: Penguin, 2005.

Harris, Tim. *Revolution: The Great Crisis of the British Monarchy, 1685–1720*. London: Allen Lane, 2006.

Hill, Christopher. *The World Turned Upside Down: Radical Ideas During the English Revolution*. London: Penguin, 1972.

MacColloch, Diarmaid. *Thomas Cranmer: A Life*. Rev. ed. New Haven, CT: Yale University Press, 2017.

Matusiak, John. *Wolsey: The Life of King Henry VIII's Cardinal*. Stroud, UK: History Press, 2016.

Pincus, Steve. *1688: The First Modern Revolution*. New Haven, CT: Yale University Press, 2009.

Pocock, J.G.A. *The Ancient Constitution and the Feudal Law: A Study of English Historical Thought in the Seventeenth Century (A Reissue with a Retrospect)*. Cambridge: Cambridge University Press, 1987.

Sharpe, Kevin. *The Personal Rule of Charles I*. New Haven, CT: Yale University Press, 1996.

Slack, Paul. *Poverty and Policy in Tudor and Stuart England*. London: Longman, 1988.

Underdown, David. *Revel, Riot and Rebellion: Popular Politics and Culture in England, 1603–1660*. Oxford: Oxford University Press, 1987.

Weir, Alison. *The Wars of the Roses*. New York: Ballatine, 1995.

Religion and Reformation

Bernard, G.W. *The King's Reformation: Henry VIII and the Remaking of the English Church.* New Haven, CT: Yale University Press, 2005.

Dickens, A.G. *The English Reformation.* 2nd ed. Philadelphia: University of Pennsylvania Press, 1992.

Duffy, Eamon. *The Stripping of the Altars: Traditional Religion in England, 1400–1580.* 2nd ed. New Haven, CT: Yale University Press, 2005.

Elton, G.R. *Reform and Reformation: England, 1509–1558.* Cambridge, MA: Harvard University Press, 1977.

Haigh, Christopher. *English Reformations: Religion, Politics, and Society under the Tudors.* Oxford: Oxford University Press, 1993.

MacCulloch, Diarmaid. *The Later Reformation in England, 1547–1603.* 2nd ed. New York: Palgrave Macmillan, 2001.

Marshall, Peter. *Reformation England, 1480–1642.* London: Hodder Arnold, 2003.

Scarisbrick, J.J. *The Reformation and the English People.* Oxford: Oxford University Press, 1985.

Shagan, Ethan. *Popular Politics and the English Reformation.* Cambridge: Cambridge University Press, 2002.

Thomas, Keith. *Religion and the Decline of Magic.* London: Penguin, 1971.

Watt, Tessa. *Cheap Print and Popular Piety, 1550–1640.* Cambridge: Cambridge University Press, 1991.

Empire and the Wider World

Andrews, Kenneth. *Trade, Plunder, and Settlement: Maritime Enterprise and the Genesis of the British Empire, 1480–1630.* Cambridge: Cambridge University Press, 1984.

Armitage, David, and Michael Braddick, eds. *The British Atlantic World, 1500–1800.* 2nd ed. New York: Palgrave Macmillan, 2009.

Canny, Nicholas, ed. *The Origins of Empire: British Overseas Enterprise to the Close of the Seventeenth Century.* Oxford: Oxford University Press, 1998.

Elliott, J.H. *Empires of the Atlantic World: Britain and Spain in America, 1492–1830.* New Haven, CT: Yale University Press, 2006.

Games, Alison. *The Web of Empire: English Cosmopolitans in an Age of Expansion, 1560–1660.* Oxford: Oxford University Press, 2008.

Kupperman, Karen Ordahl. *The Jamestown Project.* Cambridge, MA: Belknap Press of Harvard University Press, 2007.

MacMillan, Ken. *Sovereignty and Possession in the English New World: The Legal Foundations of Empire, 1576–1640.* Cambridge: Cambridge University Press, 2006.

Mancall, Peter C. *Hakluyt's Promise: An Elizabethan's Obsession for an English America*. New Haven, CT: Yale University Press, 2007.

Mancke, Elizabeth, and Carole Shammas, eds. *The Creation of the British Atlantic World*. Baltimore: Johns Hopkins University Press, 2005.

Oberg, Michael Leroy. *The Head in Edward Nugent's Hand: Roanoke's Forgotten Indians*. Philadelphia: University of Pennsylvania Press, 2008.

Pincus, Steve. *Protestantism and Patriotism: Ideologies and the Making of English Foreign Policy, 1650–1688*. Cambridge: Cambridge University Press, 2002.

Richardson, Glenn, and Susan Doran, eds. *Tudor England and Its Neighbours*. London: Palgrave Macmillan, 2005.

Online Primary Sources

The following online resources offer a wide variety of accessible English historical documents. Use each site's advanced search engine, where available, to find sources for the early modern period.

British History Online, https://www.british-history.ac.uk/.

Cambridge Digital Library, Cambridge University, http://cudl.lib.cam.ac.uk/.

Centre for Reformation and Early Modern Studies, https://www.birmingham.ac.uk/research/activity/crems/resources/index.aspx.

Constitutional Documents of the Puritan Revolution, 1625–1660, http://www.constitution.org/eng/conpur.htm.

Digital Bodleian, University of Oxford, https://digital.bodleian.ox.ac.uk/.

Digitized Manuscripts, British Library, https://www.bl.uk/manuscripts.

Early English Books Online (EEBO), https://eebo.chadwyck.com/home (by institutional subscription).

Early Modern Resources, http://earlymodernweb.org/resources/category/primary-sources/.

EuroDocs, Harold B. Lee Library, Brigham Young University, https://eudocs.lib.byu.edu/index.php/Britain_1486-1688.

Internet Modern History Sourcebook, Fordham University, https://sourcebooks.fordham.edu/mod/modsbook.asp.

Newgate Calendar, https://www.exclassics.com/newgate/ngintro.htm.

Online Collections, National Archives of the United Kingdom, http://www.nationalarchives.gov.uk/help-with-your-research/research-guides/?research-category=online.

Proceedings of the Old Bailey, https://www.oldbaileyonline.org/.

Records of Early English Drama Online, https://ereed.library.utoronto.ca.

State Papers Online, https://www.gale.com/intl/primary-sources/state-papers-online.

INDEX

Numbers in italics refer to illustrations.